Sophocles

KARL REINHARDT

Sophocles

Translated by Hazel Harvey and David Harvey
With an introduction by Hugh Lloyd-Jones

BASIL BLACKWELL · OXFORD

This edition is published by arrangement with Vittorio Klostermann, Frankfurt am Main

British Library Cataloguing in Publication Data

Reinhardt, Karl
  Sophocles.
  1. Sophocles – Criticism and interpretation.
  I. Harvey, Hazel II. Harvey, David, b. 1937
  882'.01   PA4417

  ISBN 0–631–18480–5

Phototypeset in V.I.P. Bembo by
Western Printing Services Ltd, Bristol
Printed in Great Britain by
J. W. Arrowsmith Ltd., Bristol

Dedicated to Kurt Riezler

CONTENTS

FOREWORD

This book is not intended as yet another competitor for a place among all the latest accounts of the three ancient tragic poets. Nor is it intended as an act of homage to Sophocles on the part of a popularizer of the humanities. It is an attempt to examine his work by means of comparisons, in order to rescue it from certain prevalent methods of interpretation which succeed only in obscuring it.

The views of other scholars are criticized in a number of notes for those who wish to see to what extent my views coincide with those of others and to what extent they diverge from them. The translations from the Greek are intended as no more than rough guides to aid interpretation.*.

January and July 1933   Reinhardt

*[But see Translators' Note.]

Apart from a few alterations and corrections the text of the second edition remains unchanged from that of the first. The notes, however, have undergone more extensive changes, and now take into account, as far as possible, work which has appeared since the first edition. An index has been added, containing both proper names and the main themes, so that these may be traced through the eight sections which constitute the unity of this book.

October 1941   Reinhardt

The third edition reinstates what was suppressed in the second: the dedication and note 1 on p. 269. Otherwise there are only a few minor changes in the translations and notes. An important addition to the secondary literature is C. M. Bowra's *Sophoclean Tragedy* (Oxford 1944).

June 1947   Reinhardt

TRANSLATORS' NOTE

'Jede Übersetzung ist, verglichen mit dem Original, Verlust im ganzen . . .'

Karl Reinhardt, Preface to his translation
of the *Antigone*

Reinhardt's style is not easy, even for German readers. We have not sought to disguise this fact in our English version.

In the original edition, when quoting Sophocles, Reinhardt offered his own verse translations. In the present edition, these have been replaced, in the case of quotations from the seven surviving tragedies, by translations by various hands from *The Complete Greek Tragedies* edited by David Grene and Richard Lattimore (Chicago 1954, 1957); we are most grateful to the University of Chicago for permission to make use of these. The translators however are responsible for the versions of the fragments.

Figures in the left-hand margin indicate the pagination of the German text.

Additions to Reinhardt's text are enclosed within square brackets. Those by Lloyd-Jones are distinguished by the initials H. Ll.-J.; the rest are by the translators.

We would like to thank Professor Bernard Knox, who first suggested that we should translate this book; Frau Reinhardt, whose intervention made it possible; Jim Feather of Blackwell for constant and friendly encouragement; Robin Mathewson, for his assistance in reading the proofs and for a number of helpful suggestions; and, above all, Professor Hugh Lloyd-Jones, who went carefully over our first draft and made numerous improvements. We alone are responsible for any errors or infelicities that remain.

H.M.H.

F.D.H.

1977

ABBREVIATIONS

(i) Ancient authors and works:

Acharn.: Acharnians

Aesch.: Aeschylus

Agam.: Agamemnon

Alc.: Alcestis

Ant.: Antigone

Ar. *Rhet.*: Aristotle, *Rhetoric*

Choeph.: Choephori

El.: Electra

Eur.: Euripides

fr. and frr.: fragment(s)

Heracl.: Heraclidae

Oed. Col.: Oedipus at Colonus

Oed. Tyr.: Oedipus Tyrannus

Or.: Oration

Phil.: Philoctetes

Suppl.: Suppliant Women

Thesm.: Thesmophoriazusae

Thuc.: Thucydides

Trach.: Trachiniae

(ii) Commentaries, collections of fragments, and other modern works:

Bruhn: *Sophokles* erklärt von F. W. Schneidewin & A. Nauck, besorgt von E. Bruhn, 3 vols., Berlin 1904–12

Diehl: E. Diehl, *Anthologia lyrica graeca*, third edition, 3 vols., Leipzig 1949–52

Diels-Kranz[6]: H. Diels & W. Kranz, *Die Fragmente der Vorsokratiker*, sixth (or subsequent) edition, 3 vols., Berlin 1951–2

Friedländer: P. Friedländer, 'Die griechische Tragödie und das Tragische', part II, *Die Antike* i (1925), 295–318 [reprinted in P. Friedländer, *Studien zur antiken Literatur und Kunst*, Berlin 1969, 133–53]

Howald: E. Howald, *Die griechische Tragödie*, Munich 1930

Jebb: Sir R. C. Jebb, *Sophocles: the plays*, 7 vols., Cambridge 1883–1900

Kaibel: G. Kaibel, *Sophokles: Elektra*, Leipzig 1896

Mette: H. J. Mette, *Die Fragmente der Tragödien des Aischylos*, Berlin 1959

Nauck[2]: A. Nauck, *Tragicorum graecorum fragmenta*, second edition, Leipzig 1889

P. Oxy.: *The Oxyrhynchus papyri*, ed. B. P. Grenfell, A. S. Hunt & others, London 1898–

Page: D. L. Page, *Select papyri III: literary papyri*, Loeb Classical Library, London & Cambridge Mass. 1941

Pearson: A. C. Pearson, *The fragments of Sophocles*, 3 vols., Cambridge 1917

Pohlenz: M. Pohlenz, *Die griechische Tragödie*, 2 vols., Leipzig 1930 [second edition Göttingen 1954]. The second volume (notes) is referred to as Pohlenz, *Erläuterungen*.

Radermacher: *Sophokles* erklärt von F. W. Schneidewin & A. Nauck, besorgt von L. Radermacher, 4 vols., Berlin 1909–14

Tycho von Wilamowitz: Tycho von Wilamowitz-Moellendorff, *Die dramatische Technik des Sophokles*, Berlin 1917

Webster: T. B. L. Webster, *An introduction to Sophocles*, London 1936 [second edition London 1969]

Wilamowitz, *Griechische Tragödien*: U. von Wilamowitz-Moellendorff, *Griechische Tragödien übersetzt*, 4 vols., Berlin 1899–1923

INTRODUCTION TO THE ENGLISH EDITION

by Hugh Lloyd-Jones

In our time classical scholars often tell each other that they should cease to concentrate too much on technical scholarship and do more for the literary interpretation of the classics. That is easier said than done; although Housman doubtless exaggerated when he claimed that the faculty of literary criticism was the rarest gift,[1] it is certainly not common, and it has been denied to many learned men. When a learned man does appear who is liberally endowed with that rare gift, he surely deserves to be read not only by those who can read him in his own language, but by others also.

Karl Reinhardt[2] occupied a unique place among the classical scholars of the particularly gifted generation to which he belonged. He was born on 14 February 1886, the son of highly cultivated parents; his father was head of the chief secondary school in Frankfurt, and later helped to found the famous school called Salem, whose former headmaster, the late Kurt Hahn, founded Gordonstoun. The Reinhardts were both keenly interested in the literature and art of their own time, as well as of the past; Paul Deussen, the early friend of Nietzsche, was among the interesting visitors who were often in their house. Karl Reinhardt might have become an imaginative writer, a historian of art or a distinguished actor, and in his writing and his teaching he revealed the qualities that might have helped him to succeed at any one of these professions. He began his student career at Bonn and later moved to Munich; but in 1904 his father accepted an appointment in the Ministry of Education in Berlin, and Reinhardt moved to the university of the imperial capital. There he was fascinated by the inspiring teaching of Ulrich von Wilamowitz-Moellendorff, the last man to attempt to attain excellence in virtually every branch of Greek learning.[3] Reinhardt had already come to share Nietzsche's discontent with the dryness and materialism into which the dominance of historicism had led German scholarship, and his fastidious taste must have revolted from the start against the element of philistinism revealed by Wilamowitz' approach to literature. But he was captivated by the rare personal charm of Wilamowitz, was carried away by his daemonic energy and conceived a deep admiration for his profound learning. In his own person, Reinhardt contrived to combine the profound scholarship of a worthy pupil of Wilamowitz with the enlightened realism of a follower of Nietzsche and the refined feeling for poetry of a gifted contemporary of George and of Hofmannsthal.

In 1910 Reinhardt obtained his doctorate with a thesis on the allegorical interpretation of Homer current in antiquity,[4] and in 1914 habilitated with a study of the first three books of Strabo, in which that writer expounds the theoretical basis of his Geography. The choice of these useful but somewhat dry subjects is an index of his determination to acquire technical competence in his profession; yet though he never published the work on Strabo, it must have helped to lead him to Posidonius. After teaching for a while in Bonn and Marburg he became full Professor in Hamburg in 1919, but in 1923 he returned to occupy a chair at his birthplace, Frankfurt. In 1933, the year of Hitler's coming to power, Reinhardt offered his resignation. When pressed to remain, he decided with considerable misgivings that he should stay and try to keep the university alive through the period of crisis. In 1942, when the university of Frankfurt had almost ceased to function, he accepted a call to Leipzig; in 1946, when he and his wife were threatened with starvation, he returned to Frankfurt, where he remained even after his retirement until his death on 9 January 1958. He himself has sketched his early career, and also his experiences under the National Socialist regime, in two brief but highly interesting memoirs.[5]

In 1916 Reinhardt published a book about Parmenides[6] which, although many of its contentions are not now generally accepted, was a striking and original contribution to the understanding of pre-Socratic philosophy. He followed this with three successive studies of Posidonius[7] (135–51 B.C.), except Plotinus, the last great philosopher of the ancient world, who constructed an eclectic version of the Stoic philosophy more humane and tolerant than that of its earlier exponents and also did epoch-making work in history, geography and anthropology. The work of Posidonius has to be reconstructed from scattered testimonies and fragments, which were not adequately collected until 1972, fourteen years after Reinhardt's death.[8] His method of treatment is often open to question. In his first volume, in particular, he can hardly be said to offer sufficient evidence in support of his contentions, and his confidence that his grasp of the inner form of the philosopher's system has enabled him to re-establish it in detail has not been shared by all his critics. Not all the evidence which might be considered relevant has been taken account of, as the user of the learned encyclopaedia article on Posidonius,[9] to which Reinhardt felt it his duty to devote three of his precious last years, will thanks to him find it easier to see. Yet the three books not only represent a vast advance upon all previous efforts, but are written with a flair and sympathy rare in the historical study of philosophy.

The first half of Reinhardt's career had been devoted mainly to philosophy; the second was to be given mainly to poetry. The book on Sophocles appeared in 1933,[10] when its author was forty-seven years old. In 1949 he followed it with a short but most perceptive and imaginative book about Aeschylus,[11] whose spectacular stage effects Reinhardt held to be closely bound up with his theology. In 1961, three years after his death, his former pupil, Uvo Hölscher, brought out his study of the *Iliad*.[12] Its unitarian point of view is not shared by all, and its disregard for Parry's work on oral poetry has excited some disapproval in the Anglo-Saxon world; but it is written with its author's keen intelligence and fine feeling for poetry, and cannot safely be neglected.

Throughout his career Reinhardt produced important articles as well as books; these are collected in two volumes, published in 1960, one devoted to philosophy and history and the other to Greek and German poetry.[13] Reinhardt's studies of the adventures of the Odyssey, of Heraclitus, Herodotus, Thucydides, Euripides and Aristophanes are of great importance; and his work on modern writers, especially Goethe, Hölderlin and Nietzsche, seems hardly less distinguished.

It is easy for the reader of these works to believe those who heard Reinhardt speak when they say that as teacher and lecturer he exercised a unique fascination. By speech and gesture he was able to convey, more adequately than by the written word, his awareness

of the impossibility of returning cut-and-dried answers to many of
the acutest problems and his sensitivity to the innumerable
ambiguities of literature and of life itself. His method, as he says
himself with reference to his *Sophocles*, was a comparative method;
but it was far from the comparative method of those who are
content to categorize a work in terms of its author's supposed
psychology or supposed literary ancestry, or to enumerate the *topoi*
under which each element of it is supposed to fall without explaining how these are modified by the nature and purpose of the writer
or the requirements of the context.

*   *   *

During the later part of the nineteenth and the early part of the
twentieth century, Greek tragedy was too often interpreted as
though its aims and methods were identical with those of modern
drama. In particular it was assumed, as it was also in the case of
Shakespeare and his contemporaries, that the portrayal of character
was one of the main elements, if not the main element, in the tragic
art. Most critical discussions of tragedy during this period abound
with minute psychological analysis, most of it unprofitable. The
great scholar Wilamowitz was no exception to the prevailing tendency, as many examples given by Reinhardt in his *Sophocles* help to
show. Reinhardt in his essay on Euripides[14] quotes a particularly
revealing instance from the great man's edition of the *Hippolytus*
which Wilamowitz published in the year of the première of *Hedda
Gabler*. 'She is no ordinary woman', Wilamowitz writes of Phaedra,
'. . . She is every bit the society lady, knows and performs her duties;
she has a husband and children, relations and a social position, and is
well able to accord to all these the consideration that she owes them.
But she has no inner relationship to husband or children, let alone to
anything else. Her life lacks the blessing of work, and she is too
intelligent to find satisfaction in idleness and in empty society. . . .
So she is ripe for passion. Suddenly she encounters in her stepson a
being who fascinates her, simply because she cannot understand
him. . . . She for her part dreams of a life free from the shackles of
convention, a life of freedom and of feeling such as she has never
known. To pick flowers with him beside the brook, to hunt and
ride by his side; that would give content to her existence. That is
what her feelings tell her. Her understanding does not fail to give
her counsel. She knows that she must not and will not go astray. . . .

It is not sin that she is afraid of; far from it, she knows that she cannot help being in love. What she is afraid of is disgrace. Acting her part was her whole life. She was the irreproachable wife, because it was proper to be so; because it would be proper, she wants to die; impossible that she, Phaedra, the daughter of Minos, the Queen of Athens, should create a scandal. . . .' This Ibsenite Euripides has little to do with the reality, like the Shavian Euripides of Gilbert Murray that was so popular in England.

The first sharp reaction against this kind of interpretation came with the posthumous publication in 1917 of the doctoral thesis of Tycho von Wilamowitz-Moellendorff, son of Wilamowitz and grandson of Mommsen, who had died fighting on the Russian front in October 1914. This was a study of the dramatic technique of Sophocles which is still of great value.[15] Tycho Wilamowitz agreed with Aristotle that the characters in a tragedy were there for the plot, not the plot for the characters. He denied that exact character-ization was the principal aim of the tragedians, and was able to point to countless cases where the holders of this view had tried to deal with a problem posed by Sophocles' text by means of a psychologi-cal explanation which was wholly untenable. Taking no account, he complained, of the conditions of performance or the likely effect upon an audience, such critics tried to explain the actions of the characters as though they were real people. So far, he argued, from aiming always at convincing characterization, Sophocles did not even trouble to make his characters consistent. Just as a factual detail, like the content of an oracular pronouncement, could take one shape at one moment and another later, according to the dramatist's convenience, so a character could behave now in one way and now in another wholly different fashion, if that suited his creator.

Tycho's work threw much light on the dramatic methods of the poet, and eliminated for good much unconvincing psychological speculation about the motives of his characters. Scholars were as slow to grasp the importance of his book as they always are when they are confronted with real originality; but from about the early thirties its effect became visible, and now many of his tenets have become generally accepted.

In some ways Tycho went too far. Many of the departures from probability or consistency, or at least from modern notions of those concepts, which he notes, simply go to prove the truth of what he himself argues, that Sophoclean technique is far removed from that of nineteenth-century naturalism. Further, there is a sense in which Sophocles is interested in character, or at least in what the Greeks call *ēthos*. He does not care about personal idiosyncrasie˹ or psychological niceties; but he cares greatly about the main qualities of his chief characters as human beings, and about the emotions which in virtue of those qualities they reveal. The famous Sophoclean scholar Sir Richard Jebb once met George Eliot, who told him that she had carefully studied Sophocles, whom she read in the original, and had been influenced by his work. When Jebb asked how Sophocles had influenced her, George Eliot replied, 'In the delineation of the great primitive emotions.'[16] It is these, and not psychological complexities, that are the main objects of the poet's study; and the emotions felt by different persons tend not to be the same.

Reinhardt's book, which appeared as early as 1933, accepted and developed what was best in Tycho's work and provided an ideal corrective to what was wanting. Reinhardt chose to treat of 'Sophoclean situations, or . . . of the Sophoclean relation between man and god and between man and man, and to show how they develop, scene by scene, play by play, stage by stage in the poet's career. . . .' Using Tycho's results and applying his own kind of close analysis, Reinhardt with his mature taste and his unusually fine feeling for poetry was able to throw light on the poet's methods of depicting those emotions which Sophoclean situations evoke from the persons who are involved in them.

An important part of Reinhardt's purpose was to throw light on the difficult problem of the chronology of the seven complete plays of Sophocles that have survived. In this aim he achieved considerable success; but it was only part of his purpose, it was not the most important part, and the success which he attained in it was not complete. Let us consider his theory of Sophoclean chronology before coming to the more general aspects of his treatment.

The only surviving plays whose date is directly attested by external evidence are the *Philoctetes* (409 B.C.) and the *Oedipus at Colonus*, produced in 401, three years after the author's death, at the age perhaps of eighty-nine. In view of the very limited amount of material on which statistics can be based, the evidence of style and metre must be used with great caution. It is true that, in the case of Euripides, Zielinski was able to establish that the indications of one particular criterion of date, the increase in the number of resolutions of long elements in the iambic trimeter, yielded inferences as to date that roughly corresponded with the chronological facts known to us from external sources. But we have nineteen complete plays of Euripides, eight of them dated by external evidence. Excessive confidence in our ability to date Sophoclean plays from the evidence yielded by their style and metre is, or ought to be, discouraged by our experience in the case of Aeschylus, of whom we have seven complete plays, five of them dated by external evidence. For the first half of this century it was almost universally believed that one of the remaining two, *The Suppliant Women*, must be a very early work, composed perhaps as early as 500 B.C.; in 1952 a hypothesis preserved on papyrus showed that the play was produced not before the sixties of the fifth century. Statistics seem to indicate that the *Prometheus Bound* shows in an accentuated form tendencies visible in the *Oresteia* (458 B.C.), and that has encouraged some scholars to conclude that it must have been written during the two years of life remaining to the poet after the production of that trilogy. Considering the limited amount of material available and the dangers of assuming a linear development in the stylistic tendencies in question, this inference seems to me exceedingly unsafe, even if we take it for granted that the *Prometheus Bound* is by Aeschylus. In guessing at the dates of the five plays of Sophocles not dated by external evidence, we have even more reason to be cautious.

Reinhardt recognized that the indications of style and metre could not safely be relied on here, and approached the problem by a wholly different method. He believed that a gradual artistic development could be detected by means of his own method of studying, scene by scene, Sophoclean situations. At the start, he argues, each character simply gives utterance to his own fixed point of view, never allowing it to be modified in the light of the positions adopted by the other persons present. Dialogue involving three persons does not occur before the *Oedipus Tyrannus*; in the latest plays, it is handled with increasing skill, and each actor is affected by the standpoint of the other persons present on the stage. Reinhardt believed that his close analysis of the plays, scene by scene, actually revealed the stages by which this development took place.

It must, I think, be admitted that he has somewhat overestimated the degree of exactitude in dating which this method can be expected to attain. So far as chronology is concerned, his greatest achievement has been to make it highly probable that the *Trachiniae* is one of the earlier extant plays and that the *Electra* is one of the later. Most scholars would agree with him in placing the *Ajax* early, but he has hardly made it certain that it is the earliest extant play, or that it is as early as the fifties; Paul Mazon thought the *Trachiniae* earlier, and it may be argued that it shows a less mature technique. Reinhardt's criteria certainly seem to indicate that the *Antigone* stands between these two supposedly early plays and the *Oedipus Tyrannus*. He does well to warn us that the anecdote that Sophocles was elected general in the expedition against Samos because people had admired his *Antigone* offers most inadequate grounds for thinking that that play must have been produced in 441; for all we know, the play might be earlier or later, even if we are right about its chronological relation to the other works. Again, the first *Oedipus* certainly seems to show a technical advance on the *Antigone*; no one has argued this more convincingly than Reinhardt. But we cannot be certain that the *Oedipus* was produced during the thirties; evidence for an earlier or a later date would hardly come as a surprise. Reinhardt seems to have shown that the *Electra* shows an affinity with the two late plays whose date is known. He thinks it somewhat earlier than the *Electra* of Euripides, which from the middle of the nineteenth century till 1955 was generally thought to be firmly placed in 413 B.C. But in the latter year G. Zuntz[17] pointed out that the argument on which this date rested was really very feeble. The Dioscuri, about to leave the stage, say that they are off to the Sicilian Sea to protect mariners; and that was taken by many generations of scholars to show that the play must have been produced in 413, just as the great Athenian expedition against Sicily was about to sail. But the Sicilian Sea was notoriously dangerous for sailors, and washed the coast of that Peloponnese which had been the home of the Dioscuri; as an argument for dating the play the passage is as good as useless. Zuntz pointed out that the criteria which in general serve as a useful guide for dating the plays of Euripides would indicate for the *Electra* a date about 422. If this is approximately right, and if

Reinhardt was correct in thinking the Sophoclean *Electra* to be earlier than the Euripidean, the *Electra* of Sophocles will have been produced during the twenties, perhaps about fifteen years before the *Philoctetes*. Despite the similarities between the two plays which Reinhardt pointed out, we know of no reason why this should not be so. None the less, his method seems likelier to yield results, in the absence of external evidence, than any calculation based upon the style and metre of a very limited quantity of material.

But though Reinhardt's contribution to the establishment of the plays' chronology is important, it is less important than his contribution to their understanding. He takes us through each play, or rather through the dialogue portions of each play, delineating the emotional impact of each scene and the means adopted to achieve it with great delicacy and sensitivity. Most classical scholars are more interested in facts than in emotions, and prefer what is tangible and concrete to its opposite; they therefore give most of their attention to the constitution of the text, the explanation of the verbal meaning, and the religious beliefs and attitudes supposed to be implicit in the plays. Reinhardt is concerned chiefly with the emotional effect of each succeeding episode, and unlike most scholars he was singularly well qualified to describe it. It must be remembered that he offers not a full-length study of the poet, but an examination of Sophoclean situations, and of the relation between man and god and between man and man so far as they are revealed in the speeches, the episodes and the movement of the drama. He seems to have thought it unnecessary to examine the lyric portions of the plays with anything like the care which he devoted to the dialogue scenes, and in this it seems to me that he was mistaken. The lyrics form an integral part of the plays, and the total effect cannot be grasped without taking account of them; in particular, the relation between man and god is illuminated by the lyrics. Gerhard Müller in an interesting article[18] has lately argued that the Sophoclean chorus has simply the status of an actor, and does not serve, as an Aeschylean chorus may, as the mouthpiece of the poet. Kranz in his great book *Stasimon*, 1933, wrote (p. 171) that the chorus is at once a character in a tragedy, an instrument that can be used to accompany, to divide up, and to deepen the significance of the drama, and an organ of the poet's individual self. If Müller is right in denying the chorus the third of these functions, is he also right in denying it the second? Reinhardt throws no light upon this problem. But his positive achievement is very great, and it cannot be summarized. What he has written must be read carefully and as a whole in order to be fully understood.

*   *   *

Reinhardt did much to set the stage for the debate over the part played by the gods in Sophoclean drama that has occupied so much space in the extensive literature devoted to Sophocles during the last thirty years. He sees the relation between man and god in Nietzschean terms. According to Nietzsche, it is through his defiance of the universe and the ruling powers that the hero meets his end, and in the moment of annihilation confirms for ever his heroic status. The man who practises 'safe thinking'— *sōphrosynē*—will remember the limitations imposed upon him by his mortality; the hero will ignore them, and so provoke the gods to destroy him and so attest his heroism.[19]

Nietzsche's conception of the hero enables Reinhardt to do justice to aspects of Sophocles that had been most inadequately explained by the attempts of nineteenth-century scholars to discover the workings of divine justice in his plays. We are in certain cases given information that might enable us to account in Aeschylean terms for the actions of the gods. Yet in other cases we are given no such information; and even when we are given it, it makes little difference to the drama. In the *Ajax*, we are told which god punishes Ajax and why; yet how unimportant this is in the total sum of the impressions we are left with! In the *Trachiniae*, the mentions of Zeus in relation to Heracles in the early part of the play may cause the spectator familiar with the genre to wonder what Zeus may now intend, and when Lichas describes Heracles' dealings with the family of Eurytus, such a spectator may guess that Heracles may expect trouble; at the end of the play, the chorus pronounces that all that has happened is Zeus. Yet the fulfilment of Zeus' justice is never insisted on, only barely hinted at, richly though Aeschylus might have developed such a theme. In the *Antigone* Tiresias makes it plain how Creon has angered the gods, because the plot happens to demand it. Yet the gods do not intervene to save Antigone, who has vindicated their rights at the cost of her own life. There is indeed sufficient mention of the curse upon the Labdacids to encourage the spectators to believe the chorus when they claim that the curse has been effective; yet the matter has little importance in the drama. Attempts to show Oedipus or Jocasta to be personally guilty have failed completely. If a spectator of the *Oedipus Tyrannus* asks why Oedipus is destroyed, he may remember the curse upon the Labdacids; yet in the play the curse has no importance. In the *Electra* there is no disputing the guilt of Clytemnestra and Aegisthus, and the curse upon the house of Atreus supplies one of the play's themes. The final scene, which is not adequately explained in recent treatments, any more than it is in Reinhardt's own, seems to suggest that the working of the curse continues. Yet the curse upon the family and the guilt of the murderers are always kept subordinate; the stress is upon the nature of Electra and its violent extremes of love and hatred. In the *Philoctetes* the gods require the hero to sacrifice his individual feelings so as to further the accomplishment of their grand design. In the second play about Oedipus, we are told little about the reasons which have led the gods to ruin Oedipus and little about those which have led them to rehabilitate him.

Reinhardt notes all this, and remarks that we find in Aeschylus a very different attitude towards divine justice. Like a pupil of Wilamowitz and an heir of nineteenth-century historicism, he tries to explain the difference in terms of an historical development. The will of the gods in Sophocles, he says, 'is no longer an ever-present force which hovers over a character and makes itself felt in his deeds and in his life. On the contrary, it confronts him one day as something alien, incomprehensible. . . .' Yet Reinhardt himself clearly shows how the action of a Sophoclean play is rapidly swept onwards to its appointed conclusion by the force of what he calls the daimon. In speaking of the daimon, the word 'fate' is inappropriate; in Sophocles, the daimon is a god-directed force, and the gods control the action quite as firmly as they do in Homer or in Aeschylus. Because Sophocles does not encourage us to ask the question Aeschylus would have asked, how the gods have arrived at their decision, Reinhardt does not ask it either. But if we do ask it, we see that although in most cases the direct evidence is incomplete, in every instance the question would admit of being answered in purely Aeschylean terms. Sophocles as an artist is by no means as interested as Aeschylus in questions of divine justice, of guilt and of responsibility. But that does not mean that his religion was different, or that he was trying to express a different point of view. The difference is not ideological but artistic; it can scarcely be altogether unconnected with the passing of the fashion for writing trilogies on continuous themes, although this by itself cannot account for the poet's individual preference.

Sophocles, like Aeschylus, remained content with the traditional religion of early Greece. Both believed in the justice of the gods;[20] and for both that justice meant not only that Zeus punished men or their descendants for their offences but that the gods maintained the order of the universe. The purposes of the gods involved the fates of innumerable men and cities and took into account chains of crime and punishment that reached back to the beginnings of human history, and were too complicated for any mortal to understand. Even when the gods deigned to impart knowledge through the medium of oracles and prophets, human intelligence seldom sufficed to interpret them correctly.

This religion recognized that great heroes were exposed, as ordinary men were not, to the danger of provoking the anger of the gods. That anger could be avoided by the practice of what Reinhardt called Sophoclean humility, by recognizing the limitations of human capacity; but such humility came more easily to ordinary persons, like Ismene or Chrysothemis, the Odysseus of the *Ajax* or the Creon of the *Oedipus Tyrannus*, than to great heroes. In a grave crisis an Ajax or an Oedipus can give more effective protection than an Odysseus or a Creon; yet the hero is more prone to offend a god by seeming to refuse him honour than is an ordinary person. In the moment of the hero's catastrophe, when he is abandoned by the gods, the poet and his audience will not withdraw their sympathy; the modern scholar who wrote with reference to the Aeschylean Cassandra that 'it is difficult to sympathize with a mortal who has betrayed a god' was grotesquely dragging into Greek religion an attitude derived by Christianity from its Oriental element.

Greek *dikē* is not identical with modern justice, and the Greek poets were acutely conscious of the terrible aspect of the gods. An extreme example comes from a papyrus fragment certainly from Sophocles' *Niobe*, published in 1971;[21] Apollo is pointing out to his sister Artemis that one surviving daughter of Niobe is cowering behind a great jar. 'Shoot a swift arrow at her', he cries, 'before she manages to hide!'; this is the ruthless Apollo of the Cassandra scene of the *Agamemnon* or the pediment at Olympia. At the same time the reader of Sophocles, most of all the reader of the two late plays, can hardly overcome the impression that the poet feels towards his own remote and awe-inspiring gods a strange piety and a strange affection. The second play about Oedipus displays as clearly as any document that we possess the simple sentiments which an early Greek felt towards his own locality and its divinities, a sentiment like those of the peasants who chanted, 'Rain, rain, dear Zeus'; it shows also in its most austere and complex form the reverent respect for the awful and inscrutable superhuman that marked the ancient religion at its sublimest level. In all the beauty and splendour of the world the early Greeks saw the working of the gods; they had to live with them, and could under certain conditions even be their friends; for the piety mingled with awe with which they regarded them was not conditional upon the gods' treating mankind or individual men with any special kindness.

Hugh Lloyd-Jones

NOTES to INTRODUCTION to the ENGLISH EDITION

1. At the beginning of his Leslie Stephen Lecture on 'The Name and Nature of Poetry', reprinted in A. E. Housman, *Selected Prose*, ed. John Carter, 1961, 168 ff.

2. Speeches about Reinhardt delivered at a memorial ceremony on 3 June 1958 by Helmut Viereck, Matthias Gelzer and Uvo Hölscher were printed in the pamphlet *Gedenkreden auf Karl Reinhardt*, Frankfurt, 1958. The second chapter of Uvo Hölscher's pamphlet *Die Chance des Unbehagens,* 1965 (31 ff.) contains an excellent account of Reinhardt. See also the obituary notice by Rudolf Pfeiffer in the *Jahrbuch der Bayerischen Akademie*, 1959, 147 ff. and the *Nachwort* appended by Carl Becker to the collection of Reinhardt's essays called *Tradition und Geist*, 1960 (431 ff.). See n. 13 below.

3. Reinhardt's account of him will be found in the volume of his essays called *Vermächtnis der Antike*, 2nd ed., 1966, 361 ff. I have attempted to give a brief account of Wilamowitz to English readers in the introduction to an English version of his *History of Classical Scholarship*, soon to be published by Gerald Duckworth.

4. *De Graecorum theologia*, Diss. Frankfurt, 1910.
5. 'Akademisches aus zwei Epochen', *Die Neue Rundschau* 66, 1955, 1 ff. = *Vermächtnis der Antike*, 380 ff.
6. *Parmenides und die Geschichte der griechischen Philosophie*, 1916; 2nd ed., 1959.
7. *Poseidonios*, 1921; *Kosmos und Sympathie*, 1926; *Poseidonios über Ursprung und Entartung*, 1928 (in *Orient und Antike* vi, reprinted in *Vermächtnis der Antike*, 402 ff.).
8. See L. Edelstein and I. G. Kidd, *Posidonius* i, *The Fragments*, 1972: the commentary is in preparation.
9. 'Poseidonios von Apameia', in Pauly–Wissowa–Kroll, *Real-Enzyklopädie*, xxii, 561 ff. (also obtainable separately).
10. 2nd ed., 1941; 3rd ed., 1947.
11. *Aischylos als Regisseur und Theologe*.
12. *Die Ilias und ihr Dichter*.
13. *Vermächtnis der Antike: Gesammelte Essays zur Philosophie und Geschichtsschreibung*, 2nd ed., 1966; *Tradition und Geist: Gesammelte Essays zur Dichtung*, 1960.
14. *Tradition und Geist*, 236.
15. Tycho von Wilamowitz-Moellendorff, *Die dramatische Kunst des Sophokles*, 1917; reprinted 1969. An essay of mine entitled 'Tycho von Wilamowitz-Moellendorff on the Dramatic Technique of Sophocles' and intended as an introduction to a reprint of this work will be found in the *Classical Quarterly*, xxii, 1972, 214 ff.
16. See Caroline Jebb, *Life and Letters of Sir Richard Claverhouse Jebb*, 1907, 156; cf. Gordon Haight, *George Eliot*, 1970, 173.
17. G. Zuntz, *The Political Plays of Euripides*, 1955, 64 ff.; cf. my review of A. Vogler, *Vergleichende Studien zur sophokleischen und euripideischen Elektra*, 1967, in the *Classical Review*, xix, 1969, 36 ff.
18. In *Sophokles* (Wege der Forschung xcv) ed. H. Diller, 1967, 212 ff.
19. See my article 'Nietzsche and the Study of the Ancient World' in *Studies in Nietzsche and the Classical Tradition*, ed. James C. O'Flaherty, 1975.
20. In the fifth chapter of *The Justice of Zeus*, 1971, I tried to show in what sense Sophocles believed in divine justice. I did not intend to suggest that the theme of divine justice had special importance in his works.
21. This fragment, together with the other remains of Sophocles' *Niobe*, is admirably edited and explained by W. S. Barrett in Richard Carden, *The Papyrus Fragments of Sophocles*, Berlin, 1974, 171 ff.
22. See *The Justice of Zeus* (quoted in n. 20 above), 33, with 173, n. 34.

INTRODUCTION

Sophocles has been a great name ever since the period of classicism in Germany, but his influence has been slight and uncertain. One can hardly say that the world of scholarship did much to make him accessible. Times were more favourable for his rivals in the art of drama. Just as the era of the foundation of the German Empire, with its hunger for power, its material pleasures and its cult of personalities, knew how to assimilate the art of the Hellenistic age, so too it assimilated its forerunner, Euripides, and could give him a contemporary look. Aeschylus profited from the awakening appreciation of the archaic both in literature and in art. Sophocles remained the great name, but existed, as it were, in a vacuum between the other two; and despite all efforts to attach a label to him—whether it was Sophocles the classical, the harmonious, the εὔκολος, whether it was Sophocles the master of stage technique, or whether it was Sophocles the orthodox, priestly believer in oracles who proclaimed the omnipotence of the gods and worthlessness of man—as soon as there was any attempt to interpret the texts which have survived, there was always a heavy emphasis on their negative qualities. There was an awareness of where, in comparison with his superiority elsewhere, he fell short—for example, that he did not care about the logic of the action or unity of character; and this awareness was not matched by any advance in comprehension of the validity of his formal rules or the symbolic value of his use of myth. And more recent attempts to overcome this contradiction have either remained mere good intentions or have run into difficulties.[1]

In this book you will find that discussion is confined to Sophoclean *situations*, or, if you prefer another expression, the relationship in Sophocles between man and god and between man and man; and this relationship is studied, moreover, as it develops scene by scene, play by play, period by period. For since it is only gradually that the

relationship between man and man emerges out of the relationship
between man and god as something distinct from it, it makes
practically no difference in the early period whether I speak of the
tragic situation or of the Human and the Divine. For other poets one
may choose a different point of departure—for example, experience, the inner life of the poet, or his principal ideas, or the play of
his characters as they mirror the world and bear their own outward
or inner fates. Thus with Shakespeare one may arrange the world of
his characters according to the order of their relationships, rank and
degree as if they were in a 'universal theatre' before the judgment
throne of genius; there the character stands, facing his peers and the
world, with nothing between or above them. If one tried the same
approach with Sophocles one would soon find that everything had
slipped through one's fingers. Not because there is no tragedy of
character in Sophocles (though this has been argued), but because it
takes a secondary place: it is overshadowed by something more
important: the portrayal of universal human types—not, as was
imagined during the period of classicism, of 'typical' figures, but of
mortality, outlined and defined against the background of the
divine by the contours of its mortal quality.

Sophocles' deities offer no comfort to man, and when they lead
his fate to a point where he recognizes what he is, it is his discovery
that he is abandoned and alone that makes him realize his human
condition. It is only at breaking-point that his being attains a quality
of purity and seems to move from dissonance to a state of harmony
with the divine order. That is why Sophocles' tragic characters are
lone, uprooted, exiled creatures: μονούμενοι, ἄφιλοι, φρενὸς οἰοβῶ-
ται, and so forth.[2] But the violent uprooting would not be so painful
if the roots were not so deep.

In the plays of Aeschylus there is no trace of this deep-rootedness,
or of its opposite, this particular kind of nakedness and defenceless-
ness. Man, demi-god or hero, wherever he stood, did not stand
alone; he always remained part of the divine and human order.
Nothing happened to him without some divinity secretly per-
meating and possessing him. This divine possession might take
either a friendly or an unfriendly form, whether the god were Apollo,
an Erinys, Hera, Aphrodite or Zeus; the god does not take over the
burden of a man's own guilt, or rob him of his virtue, it is true, but
the god does secretly co-operate, even to the extent of sharing the

guilt or the credit. However Aeschylean man acted or felt—
whether nobly or basely, submissively or defiantly—he never took
a single step into a separate existence of his own in which he was
conscious of himself as a being distinct from others. In Aeschylus
even Prometheus still holds one trump card: his relationship with
Zeus remains, even if they have quarrelled. The Aeschylean hero
might fall victim to the clash between gods and men, he might be
overthrown, hunted, driven and tortured in the most horrible way,
but he could never lose at one stroke his connection with what
surrounded him, his sense of belonging, and so he could never stand
alone, excluded, abandoned and betrayed like Sophoclean man. For
in Aeschylus there is as yet no purely mortal sphere that is distinct
from the divine whole. Aeschylus belongs to the end of the late
archaic period, but he evokes much older forces which still loomed
dimly over his age in the realm of ritual, law and custom more than
in that of poetry and fully-formed concepts; he is more interested in
bringing out the contradiction between these forces, their richness,
their distribution, overthrow or rebellion, than in the riddle of the
boundary between man and god; and if we want a motto for him,
the old saying 'Everything is full of divine forces', πάντα δαιμόνων
πλήρη, is more appropriate than its successor 'Know thyself'.

It is true that the will of the gods also prevails in the tragedies of
Sophocles; but it is no longer an ever-present force which hovers
over a character and makes itself felt in his deeds and his life. On the
contrary, it confronts him one day as something alien, incomprehensible, a breath from a non-human world, from which he can
only be rescued by Sophoclean humility; and this is not any kind of
Christian or other-worldly humility but more like what we call
pessimism: the humility of 'coming to one's senses'. If a man wants
to find the right path, he can only do so by recognizing his own
limits—by a continually renewed, painful exploration, as it were, of
his outer self, which, like an unprotected, vulnerable skin, separates
a mortal from the surrounding atmosphere in which the gods
operate. And yet this humility, this 'coming to one's senses', would
not receive such high praise if the genuinely great mortal were not
so reckless, so arrogant, so averse to moderation, so preoccupied
with his own virtue, so endangered and so proud. In one sense, all
Sophocles' tragic characters are outsiders. What is valid for them is
not to be measured by the usual standards; their central interest is

not the centre of the events in which they are involved. One of the tensions which differentiate Sophoclean situations from those in Aeschylus, and indeed from almost all others, arises from the fact that the true meaning of the speeches no longer coincides with the meaning of the situation in which they are spoken, so that the one clashes with the other like a dissonant voice in a polyphonic work; and this is one of the most important causes of what we admire as the 'effect' of his art. For from this clash a peculiarly Sophoclean interplay of harmonies, sequences and transitions is developed, an interplay which, as his work advances over the years, becomes richer and more complex. Finally, it becomes more intimate and produces an effect of greater restraint despite the growing profundity of its inner content.

Thus a comparison between the dramatic art of Sophocles and that of Aeschylus is like a comparison between two musical styles. In Aeschylus what stays most firmly fixed in the memory, apart from passages in the nature of, for example, a cantata, a hymn, or a threnody, are certain pregnant phrases in certain circumstances determined by the gods, phrases of premonition, of fear, sorrow, defiance. . . . But the fact that they have a pregnant meaning reveals, with an infinite yet always harmonious force, the inseparability of the divine and the mortal. When Aeschylus' Achilles receives back the dead body of the friend whom he had sent into battle at his own request, and then remembers the 'Libyan *ainos*' (fr. 139 Nauck = fr. 231 Mette):

Achilles
            This is what the eagle said,
  when he saw the feathering of the arrow which pierced him through:
  'It is not to another that we have fallen prey,
  but to our own wings'

13   the meaning of the whole *Iliad* is there *in parvo*, in the discordant unity and concurrence of man's limited will and divine power. When Agamemnon, treading the purple tapestries which Clytemnestra orders to be spread in front of his chariot, says (*Agam.* 946–7):

  And as I crush these garments stained from the rich sea
  let no god's eyes of hatred strike me from afar,

his speech, unlike that of Oedipus, is not determined by deceitful appearances: sound and fate, significance and the secret force of the moment form a unity, to such a degree that, as in the *ainos* which I have just quoted, the words become almost too light, almost too bare an expression in comparison with their latent force. Similarly, when Aeschylus' Clytemnestra tells a lie, she lies not only as befits her kind, her 'character', not only as befits the requirements of the dangerous, decisive moment, but as though Zeus had given the daimon of lies itself the power of control over this moment; her lie is in harmony with the cosmos of all the powers of fate—she does not lie in a manner at all 'out of true' or crooked; she labours under no illusions; no balance is disturbed. The discord and tension between person and person has been raised in this scene of deceit to a higher unity and concurrence of human action and divine power. Even Io in the *Prometheus* does not speak a single word in her madness which does not reveal unambiguously the sense behind the senselessness with which Zeus at the same time both chose his victim and persecuted her.

Euripides has just as many shifts, tensions and discords between levels of meaning as Aeschylus; but with him, in contrast to Aeschylus, they are to be found in the psychological, or even the spiritual realm—either as an internal conflict between the powers or forces of the soul, in the course of horrifyingly elevated or pathetic misdeeds, sacrifices or sufferings, or in the relationship of an overflowing spirit, a noble soul that is excited and inflamed, to the power of circumstances, or to the resistance of the cold, scornful or indifferent world that surrounds it. Thus in his plays the tragedy of passion turns from mental conflict to a tragedy of protest. For 'justice' usually sides with one spiritual force, and base 'utility' with the other, and the more the one melts and fuses in the glow of the soul, the more firmly the other becomes embedded in the way of the world. So that finally even the contrast between 'just' and 'useful', together with its variants, twists and turns, its glittering personifications and its array of rhetoric, reveals itself as only another form of the same tension. If one adds, first, the colourful contrasts of the play of intrigue, the outward surprises, the antitheses between cunning intention and the deceptive power of circumstances, between social rank and undignified incongruities of relationship; then the mythical trappings and the contemporary problems; and finally the conflicts between the gruesome and the tender, between inward appearance and outward action, hallucination and reality, between the masked and the revealed, between frailty and youthful deceit, and the whole range of this kind of psychological contrast, one gets, not everything, but at least some notion of everything that goes into a dramatic situation in Euripides. We can understand why the Hellenistic age could surrender itself so readily to this kind of tragedy; we can understand why Euripides was already called the 'most tragic' of the poets by Aristotle. For it was with Euripides that a new kind of tragedy came into being, a kind of tragedy which no longer had its roots in cult and belief, in the ties of blood or in awe of primeval powers. Euripidean tragedy was transferable, adaptable, imitable; it was accessible to later ages: the Roman could remain a Roman while he read it; so too with the child of the sixteenth and seventeenth centuries. Shakespeare is not a descendant of the two earlier poets; they do not influence his content or his form, and they are neither his spiritual nor his literary ancestors—but he does resemble the third—in kind, I mean, not in greatness. Seneca, who carried on the tradition of pathos for the following centuries,[3] follows no single writer as much as Euripides, and on the one occasion that the Roman does take a tragedy of Sophocles as his model, he turns it unwittingly into a Euripidean kind of play, even before he begins to translate it and intensify the Roman idea of pathos and the Roman idea of fate. Thus until the eighteenth century and the classical period of German literature the plays of Euripides cast a spell as a result of which other works, even earlier ones, were assimilated to them and seen in the light of their style; and this spell could be broken only when a full understanding of the origins of civilization was attained. It is only since then that we have had a clear view of Sophoclean tragedy as a product of Athens and as a product of humanity.

Sophocles began by writing religious plays in the style of Aeschylus. His *Triptolemus*, with which he won his first victory at the age of twenty-eight (468), proclaimed the power of the gods of Eleusis, as the *Oresteia* proclaimed the power of the gods of Delphi and Athens, and the *Prometheus* the rule of Zeus. Some lines from the speech with which Demeter sends the hero out into the world to proclaim her bounty have been preserved because they were quoted by a later author. They are full of mythical geography and sound Aeschylean to a degree unparalleled by anything in the surviving tragedies. We also have the poet's own testimony about his inner development, which is so strange that it must be genuine (Plutarch *Moralia* 79b): he said he had first rid himself of Aeschylean bombast, then of the harsh and artificial elements of his own style, in order, thirdly, to turn to the form of speech which would be 'the most ethical and the best' (using the word *ēthos* in the sense of 'character'). Even though this certainly refers to an early period from which no work has survived, it is still possible to recognize in the extant plays a *development* in the direction indicated by these words.

But in this region everything still lies in confusion. We still have scarcely any way of telling whether a given work is early or late, embryonic or fully developed. The only certain dates are: year of birth 496, *strategia* 441, performance of the *Philoctetes* 409, death 405, and performance of the *Oedipus at Colonus* 401. We date the *Antigone* from the year of his *strategia*, in accordance with the anecdote that tells us that its success helped the poet in the election. One can only hope that this association of the highest office with the finest drama goes back to a contemporary source. Otherwise there is so much uncertainty that the *Trachiniae*, for example, has been set in the forties, the thirties, the twenties, and, most frequently, in the penultimate decade of the century. It is as if we did not know whether Goethe's *Iphigenie* were written in 1780 or 1820, and it makes just as much difference.

In this instance, the establishment of a relative chronology becomes both means and end. For even if the order in itself is of concern only to scholars, it becomes more important as soon as we realize that style, language and scene-construction begin to change as time passes. Or if, vice versa, we start with the form, our only hope of avoiding arbitrariness is if the differences that we believe we have perceived can be corroborated by the sequence. To anticipate my conclusions: the seven dramas of our collection fall into two sharply distinguished groups according to their language and the structure of their scenes: one group in which the centre of interest is still entirely the dramatic first person, and the other in which the centre of interest is increasingly the second person singular or plural; in other words, one of monologue form and concerned with fate, and the other, by contrast, of dialogue form and overlapping; the former composed of pathos-filled, inflexible and unchanging elements, the other of shifting, changing elements, both in the details and in general. By 'monologue form' I do not mean soliloquy or speaking to oneself in solitude, but rather the nature of the scene, the language and the dramatic action by which a person's fate is announced to the audience, either through his own mouth or that of another, without his reaching through as a person to another outside himself, or joining with another in any lasting relationship.[4] Between the two groups there are two transitional works: they might well be called the poet's middle period, since they display his strongest powers; they are the plays translated by Hölderlin [the *Antigone* and the *Oedipus Tyrannus*].

17   The objection may be raised that it is hardly permissible to draw such conclusions about style and dating from a selection of only seven dramas out of a total of more than a hundred satyr-plays and tragedies. But the surviving selection is not an arbitrary one: it reflects the judgment of antiquity, and we may be sure that it neither omits the greatest nor immortalizes the insignificant.

I

AJAX

The *Ajax* is a drama which plunges right into the middle of the catastrophe, or its consequences; it does not begin with what had preceded that catastrophe. The subject of the tragedy is not Ajax's quarrel with Odysseus and the Atridae, or how, cheated of the arms of Achilles, Ajax resolves on vengeance, or how he is seized by madness—all of which might well have provided highly dramatic themes. On the contrary, the drama begins on an unprepared *fortissimo*: during the prologue the mad Ajax is summoned out of his tent; at this point there is a break; and what follows is virtually a new, contrasting beginning. Then comes, as the first part of the tragedy, the melancholia and death of a man fully conscious of what he is doing, and, as the second part, the dispute about his burial. We have here a kind of catastrophe-drama which shows from the very beginning how a human being has to *come to terms* with his fate, which has already been *decided*.[1] This type of structure and content is by no means common in Attic drama; of all the tragedies that survive, the *Ajax* is the only one of this kind. The *Ajax* is also unique among Sophocles' tragedies in that it opens with the entrance of a visible deity who points to the victim of its wrath. In front of the tent of Ajax, Odysseus hears the voice of his patron goddess, Athena, visible in her divine splendour only to the audience and to the demented Ajax; she summons her victim out of the tent, encourages him in his confusion, pretending to support him, but at the same time really betraying him to his enemy; and not content with this cruel behaviour, she goes on to drive home a moral (118 ff.):

Athena
Do you see, Odysseus, how great the gods' power is?
Who was more full of foresight than this man,
Or abler, do you think, to act with judgment?

Odysseus
   None that I know of. Yet I pity
   His wretchedness, though he is my enemy,
19   For the terrible yoke of blindness that is on him.
   I think of him, yet also of myself;
   For I see the true state of all of us that live—
   We are dim shapes, no more, and weightless shadow.

Athena
   Look well at this, and speak no towering word
   Yourself against the gods, nor walk too grandly
   Because your hand is weightier than another's,
   Or your great wealth deeper founded. One short day
   Inclines the balance of all human things
   To sink or rise again. Know that the gods
   Love men of steady sense and hate the proud.

The speech of the avenging deity, and the fact that the drama begins *after* the catastrophe, are both unparalleled and have therefore struck critics as odd. Those who were not content to account for this in terms of aesthetic considerations put the blame for what they considered a faulty structure on an alleged primitiveness on the part of a poet 'not yet quite sure of himself'. They tried to lessen the *fabula docet* effect, the didacticism which offends our sensibilities, by regarding it as addressed to the audience only, and by separating it from the action; as if Sophocles were making use of the goddess to mention something in passing. . . .[2] But in fact these two difficulties, the nature of the deity, and the opening of the play at the point of the catastrophe, are closely bound together. And the lesson to be drawn from the words of the goddess, however strange it may seem that she apparently stands outside the realm of morality, gives her intervention an unmistakable meaning: this is Man before God!

But where is the origin of this to be found? The Ajax theme had already been treated in epic, in the *Little Iliad* or in the *Aethiopis*; and although it is no longer known what rôle Athena played in these works, it was certainly not the rôle she plays in Sophocles. In the *Iliad* Athena deceives Hector in his flight, in order to deliver him into Achilles' hands. But Sophocles' Athena goes much further than Homer's: she continues to play her tricks on the man after he has been betrayed. And it is this element of pointing, demonstrating, making an example of a man, which is as far removed from epic as anything can be, especially with the additional didactic element. But if it comes from neither epic nor saga, where does it come from? Is it an innovation by Sophocles? But in that case why do we have nothing else like it? And if it is Sophoclean, is it early or late? Is it developed or primitive?

These questions can now be answered, thanks to a text which has only recently been discovered. The unique elements in the *Ajax* are not to be explained by any lack of skill or any wilfulness on the part of the poet; they are due to the influence of an earlier work and reveal a style which is still bound by archaic conventions. In the light of this discovery we can now estimate for the first time how much Sophocles 'learnt from Aeschylus', as the *Vita* puts it. It is the first certain proof that the *Ajax* is an early play. It must be the earliest of all the surviving plays, certainly much earlier than the *Antigone*, which is generally considered to be the earliest.[3]

The discovery to which we are indebted for this is a piece of papyrus containing fragments of Aeschylus' *Niobe*. From the twenty-two lines—for that is all that survives, and the beginning and end of each line are lost—we may infer an unexpected amount of information concerning the history of tragedy. Like the *Ajax*, the *Niobe* was a tragedy of shattering destruction, opening—*after* the judgment of the deity, *after* the *hybris* of the heroine—with the sufferings of a character persecuted by a divine being: a drama of dumb anger, of dull pain, of the need to come to terms with the terrifying power of fate; a representation of passive pathos, with just as little 'action' as the *Ajax*. When Ajax has become conscious of what he has done, he sits absorbed in his own thoughts, brooding on his fate, without uttering a word; he reveals himself in his misery and breaks his silence in answer to the cry of his family in order to bid farewell to his little son, only to plunge immediately all the more violently into silence within his tent. That is exactly how Niobe sat in dumb misery 'without a word during half the drama', veiled, at the tomb of her children. Just as Athena points her finger at the mad hero, we learn from the new papyrus that Leto, the immortal mother, revealing herself in all her power, pointed at the mortal mother: for just as Ajax had boasted before Athena of his heroic deeds, Niobe had boasted before Leto of the number of her children. And the moral conclusion which the goddess in Aeschylus

21 adds is astonishingly similar to the didactic passage which is put
into the mouth of Athena in the *Ajax*:[4]

Leto

> Now you can see the marriage's conclusion.
> This is the third day that she has sat by this tomb,
> the living mother wailing over her dead children,
> lamenting the wretched fortune of their beauty.
> A mortal brought to ruin is nothing but a shadow.
> Mighty Tantalus will soon come here
> intent on bringing her back home again. . . .
> To you—since you are not unsympathetic—I will
> explain: a god implants a fault in mortals
> when he intends to ruin their house utterly.
> Even so, a mortal must not speak presumptuously
> but guard the fortune that the gods have sent him.
> Yet in great prosperity men never think that they
> may stumble and spill the full cup they're holding.
> And so, exultant in their beauty, she . . .*

The same stylistic elements—the visibility of the goddess,
gnomic interpretation, the victims' consciousness of their fate—are
peculiar to both tragedies; even before the discovery of the papyrus
a fragment [fr. 159 Nauck² = fr. 278 D Mette] was known which
read:

Tantalus

> My destiny, which reached up to the heavens
> now plunges down to earth and says to me:
> 'Learn not to admire too much the things of man'.

Just as Tecmessa finally comes to Ajax pleading in vain, so
Tantalus came in vain to Niobe, hoping to comfort her and to
persuade her to live. . . . And even if we can never know the rest of
the tragedy, enough is certain. The *Ajax* and the *Niobe* belong to the
same genre.

But the similarities in external formal construction show up all
the more clearly the difference between the two poets' deeper

---

*[We have translated the text of H. Lloyd-Jones (Loeb Aeschylus ii), not
that used by Reinhardt.]

personal conceptions of tragedy. In Aeschylus the disaster falls on
the whole house; husband and father share in the downfall. . . .
Niobe represents the fate of her whole immoderately large family.
In Aeschylus a human being even in his downfall does not stand
only for himself or by himself. The ruined man is not μονούμενος,
an individual separated from the world that contains and sustains
him, before Sophocles. The fact that it is necessary to make room by
force for Ajax's monologue for the first time in the middle of this
drama, an indication of the break-through of a new mode of speech,
is at the same time the most powerful expression, and historically
the most memorable symbol of a new tragic consciousness which is
unknown before the time of Sophocles. The relationship between
the two poets is made clear by the fact that in Aeschylus' *Women of
Thrace* [fr. 83 Nauck[2] = fr. 252 Mette] which treated the same
material, there was still the traditional messenger's report instead
of a monologue, still a description of the unhappy death of Ajax
instead of the speech of the isolated individual who has prepared
himself for death.

But there is another innovation. We cannot understand the
deeper contrast between the nature of the tragedy of Ajax and the
tragedy of Niobe if we do not realize that each is conditioned by a
different type of deity. In Sophocles the goddess has her sport with
the mortal.[5] And this sport, and everything connected with it (on
the one hand the confusion of the madman trapped by his own
delusions, on the other hand the harshness and irony of the divine
will) is presented in a form which is more cruel than anything in the
Ajax saga or any other work known to us. Even more cruel than
anything in Aeschylus, despite the terrible things of which his gods
are capable. That a person's intentions and impressions should clash
with the reality of his nature and his surroundings, so that everything he does and says becomes a mockery of what he wants and
believes, is a peculiarly Sophoclean motif; it appears for the first
time—admittedly in a traditional form—in the prologue of the
Ajax, and it recurs in some form or variation in every later work.
And even if in the three late works, the *Electra*, the *Philoctetes* and the
Oedipus at Colonus, the clash appears playful and secondary rather
than terrible and central, nevertheless in the end it breaks out once
more with all its old power: for finally it creates one of the most
powerful scenes in the *Oedipus at Colonus*.

23   But what is later revealed within the bounds of a human fate
appears at the beginning in the form of the divinity in person (71
ff.):

Athena
> You there, who are binding fast your captives' arms
> With fetters, come outside! Ajax! Come out!
>
> . . .
>
> Ajax, I call you once again!
> Is this how much you care for your old ally?
>> *(Ajax enters with a bloodstained whip from the tent, where*
>> *he has been lashing, not Odysseus, but a ram.)*

Ajax
> Hail, Athena! Daughter of Zeus,
> Hail and welcome! How well you have stood by me!
> I shall deck you with trophies all of gold
> From the spoils of this hunting, in thanksgiving.

Athena
> Excellent. But tell me, did you dip
> Your blade well in the Greeks' blood?
>
> . . .

Athena
> Well, then, if your good pleasure wills it so,
> Do execution, carry out all you have in mind.

Ajax
> I must be at my work. Goddess, I charge you to[6]
> Stand always my ally as you have today.

If we listen to the goddess, Ajax is 'bad' and Odysseus good. But
this is only the judgment of the religion of humility—admittedly, a
Greek, not a Christian humility—whereas, if we disregard the voice
of this religion, Ajax is great, a hero, a colossus indeed in the
greatness of his heart no less than in his physical strength. Does this
mean that the goddess is blind to what Odysseus sees and feels? It is
obvious that the morality of the gods has nothing to do with their
power. For the function of the divine (leaving aside, that is, its
function in epic poetry) seems to be to define and limit the area
within which man can act, and which can be measured by the mind
of man.
    The figure of Ajax the outsider is developed by Sophocles

beyond the Ajax of the epic poems. Similarly, Odysseus, the figure
who stands in opposition to him, develops from the crafty fox of
the epic into a character of god-fearing resignation, who can recognize himself in his neighbour. What has happened to the age-old
contrast between the giant and the trickster, between the archer and
the warrior with his shield and spear, between the nimble, inven-
tive, adaptable Odysseus and the stubborn, steadfast, direct Ajax? It
has developed beyond Homer's representation of the spirit of two
types of warrior to become a contrast between two attitudes
towards fate.[7] On the one hand stands the tragically unprotected,
heroically rigid and inflexible Ajax; on the other, the protected,
perceptive Odysseus, well-adjusted to his fate. Sophocles sets the
intransigent Ajax, the man who wanted to massacre the Achaeans
out of wounded pride and ambition, and the humane Odysseus side
by side, thus foreshadowing the later contrast between the inflexibility of Antigone and the mildness of Ismene. Yet a comparison
between this situation and a later untragic and protected contrasting figure—for Creon too stands in the same relationship to
Oedipus—shows how the *Ajax* belongs to a quite different, earlier
stylistic phase: there is as yet no tension or conflict between the
opposites. Each stands alone, each holds his own fate within himself, each is self-sufficient, separated from the other—not seen in
relation to him. Sophocles was able to make characters stand out in
contrast with each other before he could relate them to each other
and involve them with each other.

The contrast between the victim of fate and the man who knows
occurs also in religious narratives, and these may well have influenced Sophocles. Odysseus' awe in the presence of the downfall of
human greatness is shared by Cyrus (Herodotus i. 86.6) when
he rescues his enemy Croesus—who 'was a fellow human-being'—
from the pyre, 'reflecting that nothing in the affairs of mortals is
secure'. But what a difference dramatic presentation makes! It concentrates the abstract opposition of fortune and misfortune into a
contrast between one individual in the grip of a daimon and one
untouched by any daimon.

In the *parodos* the fall of Ajax, their leader, is echoed by the fears of
his followers. The one is joined by the many, the great man by small
men, who are brought together by the bad news. Their urgent
questions bring Tecmessa from the tent. Expressions of fear con-

cerning the dangerous rage of the soldiers who threaten both the leader and his retinue alternate with the narrative of the behaviour of Ajax, first in his madness, then after he had recovered his senses. This gives rise to a dialogue in melic form, of a traditional type: it is no more than an extended echoing and invocation of the fate which has overtaken them all. The *parodos* of the *Trachiniae* is similar, though simpler and shorter. The form becomes more elaborate later.[8] For although there are already in the *Ajax* two voices which alternate in question and answer, the *mood* of the dialogue is still monotonous by comparison with the later, less static developed form. The outlook and attitude remain the same from beginning to end; there is no change. It is particularly noticeable that there is no final climax. On the other hand, the language, with its vividness, its lyrical description, its invocations and wealth of imagery, is as a result more continuously devoted to the central theme, the fate which they are bewailing. Sophocles' choruses reflect the stylistic development of the *epeisodia* which separate them. Just as the action is most compact, tense and well-rounded in the *Oedipus Tyrannus,* so are the choruses; and the same phenomenon occurs in the other plays. On the other hand, at the early stylistic level of the *Ajax,* there is a greater wealth of imagery, even in the dialogue, and the language is noticeably more heroic: for example, pathetic comparisons are found only in the *Ajax* and the *Trachiniae.* Indeed, an accumulation of assonance and imagery such as that at the very beginning, when the goddess reveals herself to Odysseus (7 ff.):

Athena
. . . You've coursed him like a keen Laconian hound. . .

and Odysseus answers:

Odysseus
Voice of Athena, dearest utterance
Of all the gods' to me—I cannot see you,
And yet how clearly I can catch your words,
That speak as from a trumpet's throat of bronze![9] . . .

—such wealth of assonance and imagery from the heroic age never occurs again in Sophocles.

26   The prologue portrays the mad Ajax; the first *epeisodion* portrays
him after his return to sanity. The prologue reported the madness
before the madman himself appeared; in the first *epeisodion* therefore the description of the tragic hero similarly precedes his appearance on the stage—this time inside his tent, revealed to the audience
by the *ekkyklema*, the wheeled platform. This lessens the emphasis
on the *transition* from madness to sanity, while stressing the two
points of time which affect Ajax's destiny—his state before the
transition and his state after it; the latter no less serious than the
former (259). For not only is there no dramatic representation of the
transition on the stage; but even the account of it (though told so
much more sensitively, tenderly and intimately by Tecmessa than
by the goddess in her more pitiless and explicit description) is still
concerned exclusively with the contrast between the *states* of madness and sanity (311 ff.)—not with the transition or the painful
awakening.

Tecmessa
   He sat so, without speaking, for some time;
   Then finally spoke those fearful, threatening words—
   What should befall me if I failed to say
   What had befallen him . . .
   Now, though, quite overcome by his misfortune,
   Refusing food and drink, he sits there motionless,
   Relapsed among the beasts his iron brought down.

Compare this with the madness of Euripides' Heracles, to take a
later example of the representation of insanity: we find in Euripides
what is lacking in the *Ajax*, the mental change as Heracles wakes
and opens his eyes, which forms the climax of the most important
scene. One might imagine that it was simply because the latter is
Euripidean, the former Sophoclean. But this is certainly wrong, for
there are plenty of transition and transformation scenes in other
plays by Sophocles: for example, the transition from error caused
by deception to truth in the *Philoctetes*, the change from the last
glimmer of hope to deepest despair in the *Electra*, the plunge from
27   illusion to discovery in the *Oedipus Tyrannus*, the transformation of
deepest gratitude to deepest shame in the *Oedipus at Colonus*, to
mention only a few. After the *Trachiniae*, change is sought, not

avoided, and takes place not off-stage but as the climax of the *epeisodia*. The *Ajax* and the *Trachiniae*, in which pathos is presented in a stationary form and in which no reversal of emotion occurs during the action, stand on one side, and all the other plays on the other. Both in language and in dramatic composition, a change has taken place between the two types of play.

Nevertheless, in this early work, once the tonality has been established, the stream of lyric poetry is more resonant, ranges more widely, and breathes more deeply and expansively than in any other play of Sophocles. The lament of Ajax, like Ajax himself, is colossal. It lacks changes and variations of mood, but the result is that its fixed contrasts resound on an unceasing note, and the horror of the circumstances can be expressed without restraint: the greatness of Ajax and his shame, the sense of his heroic being and the senselessness of his fate, the hero turning his hatred on the outside world and his misery on himself, locked in lament or shouting his heart out. . . . The first sounds issue from the closed tent, as he calls for his little son and his half-brother; then the *kommos* (lament) accompanies the revelation of the interior of the tent: the battle-field strewn with dead cattle, the hero seated in the middle amidst the laments of Tecmessa and the chorus: the *picture* turns into melic dialogue. . . . And what echoes and re-echoes in this scene, the slyness of Odysseus his arch-enemy, the falseness of the leaders of the army, the mockery of his soldiers, the landscape and the scenes of his glory . . . all these threads are woven into the harmony of the inevitable end of the *kommos* (364 ff.):

Ajax
   Here I am, the bold, the valiant,
   Unflinching in the shock of war,
   A terrible threat to unsuspecting beasts.
   Oh! what a mockery I have come to! What indignity!

Tecmessa
   Ajax, my lord and master,
   I beg you not to say such things.

Ajax
   Go away! Take yourself out of my sight!

                                        (*He groans*)

He is no longer worthy to lift his eyes to seek help from either gods or men. Where can he flee? Where can he stay? . . . (412 ff):

Ajax
O
Sounding straits of the sea
Caves by the sea's edge, meadows on the shore,
Long and long have you kept me here in Troyland . . .

What follows the *kommos* is very much the same in the static way in which it expresses the tragedy: it is just as much without crescendo, change, climax or descent. In the prologue Ajax and Odysseus had stood in contrast with each other without either penetrating the consciousness of the other; the same is true of Ajax and Tecmessa in the second *epeisodion*. There is no interplay of dialogue, there is not a single word which has the power to communicate and penetrate the wall between them. Each remains the prisoner of his own fate. Ajax's speech rings out as though Tecmessa were not present; and Tecmessa's plea, urgent and touching as it is, does not touch Ajax either by its vibrant tone or the power of its arguments. She does not even provoke him to contradict her. And when she pleads, she expresses herself only from her own point of view; and that is hopelessly out of touch with her husband's.

The speeches of both characters begin with the same emphasis on fate; both characters recall their fathers; both end with themselves—and again it is not a coincidence that in all the tragedies of Sophocles it is this passage that is most comparable in genre and attitude with the opening speech of the *Trachiniae*. Even if the chorus does hear Ajax's decision—let them hear it, they hear it only as the audience hears it. No advice, no directions, no words are addressed to him—Ajax's powerful survey of the hopelessness of his position, delivered to the world with such pathos, stands in isolation, unresolved (457 f.):

Ajax
And now, Ajax—what is to be done now?
I am hated by the gods, that's plain; the Greek camp hates me . . .

Tecmessa begins her speech with a solemn *gnōmē*, which is

followed by the account of her fate—her plea, too, develops into a narrative imbued with pathos (485 ff.):

Tecmessa
  Ajax, my master, life knows no harder thing
  Than to be at the mercy of compelling fortune.
  I, for example, was born of a free father;
  If any man in Phrygia was lordly and prosperous, he was.
  Now I'm a slave. Such, it seems, was the gods' will,
  And the will of your strong hand . . .

The rest of her plea, right down to the last detail, is based on Homer—Hector's farewell to Andromache in the sixth book of the *Iliad*.[10] But because the model is so clear, the difference that is revealed by the way in which Sophocles adapts it for the stage is particularly significant. In the epic (vi 407 ff.: the following excerpts give some idea of the content), Andromache laments:

And you have no pity on your little son, nor on me, who soon must be your widow. . . . For me it would be far better to sink into the earth when I have lost you, for there is no other consolation for me . . . since I have no father, no mother and they who were my seven brothers all went down into Hades, for Achilles slaughtered all of them, and my father too; my mother died at home, struck down by Artemis . . . Hector, you are father to me, and my mother, you are my brother, and my husband. Take pity upon me, that you may not leave your child an orphan, your wife a widow. . . .*

Like Tecmessa, Andromache speaks of herself and her son, but mainly because these are the two things most likely to persuade her departing husband to turn back. His reply also refers to them:

All these things are in my mind also; yet I would feel deep shame before the Trojans, and the Trojan women. . . . For I know there will come a day when Ilium shall perish, and Priam, and the people of Priam. . . . But it is not so much the pain to come of the Trojans that troubles me, nor even of Hecuba nor Priam, nor the thought of my

*[This is based on the translation by Richard Lattimore (University of Chicago Press, 1951), modified to correspond with Reinhardt's phrasing.]

brothers in their numbers and valour, ... as the thought of you, when some Achaean leads you off, taking away your day of liberty, in tears; and in Argos you must work at the loom of another, and carry water from the spring Messeis or Hypereia, reviled and dishonoured; and some day seeing you shedding tears a man will say of you: 'This is the wife of Hector, who was the bravest fighter of the Trojans, in the days when they fought at Ilium!' May the earth hide me under before I hear you crying and know by this that they drag you captive.*

30

Tecmessa's plea does not seem at first sight so very different (510 ff.):

> . . . And last, dear lord, show pity to your child.
> Robbed of his infant nurture, reft of you,
> To live his life out under the rule of guardians
> Not kind nor kindred—what a wretchedness
> You by your death will deal to him and me!
> And I no longer have anywhere to look for help,
> If not to you. My country was destroyed
> Utterly by your spear, and another fate
> Brought down my mother and my father too . . .
>   . . . Then what fatherland
> Shall I ever have but you? Or what prosperity?
> You are my only safety . . .

And yet how *different* the two speeches are. Take, for instance the slavery awaiting the wife—Tecmessa and Andromache alike, for the future of each will be the same—when one of the Achaeans takes her away as his booty, and the remarks that will then be passed around: 'See, this woman was once the wife of Hector' or 'this woman was the wife of Ajax, the greatest of all heroes.' In the epic it is the husband who thinks about this, a touch which enhances the tenderness of the situation; in the tragedy it is not the husband but the wife. That is, in the epic they speak to each other, in the tragedy they speak without communicating with each other, for each speaks his own language to which the other does not listen. The words of the wife die away without a syllable having reached her husband's ears, and vice versa. Ajax's thoughts of his father, his

*See note on p. 20.

home, his son, respect and shame (αἰδώς) are to him reasons for
committing suicide; but precisely the same ideas appear to Tecmessa as reasons for *not* committing suicide (ἀλλ᾽ αἴδεσαι μὲν πατέρα
. . .). But neither speech refers to the other, neither refutes the other;
they do not touch or lead to any argument for and against; rather,
they express two incompatible philosophies of life, each justified
from a different, totally separate standpoint.

Instead of replying, Ajax commands that his son be brought to
him.[11] Why had he been kept at a distance? When Ajax hears that it
was for fear that in his madness he might attack him too, he says
(534):

Yes, that would have been worthy of my evil genius.

31   And yet, when the child is brought to him, we forget for a
moment that the hero is standing, not among dead enemies, but
among dead cattle; the hero's farewell is like a farewell on a battle-
field; the dissonance between the hero and his fate, his soul and his
circumstances could not be more terrible (545 ff.):

Ajax
Lift him up, lift him to me. He won't be frightened,
Even by seeing this fresh-butchered gore,
Not if he really is my son.
                    . . .
My boy, have better luck than your father had,
Be like him in all else; and you will not be base.

He will not let the mother come near him. His solicitude for his
son, the heir to his heroism, is the only thing which brings him out
of the prison of his fate, the barrier erected around him by his
'daimon'.[12] But as though this were too great a sacrifice to sentiment, he has scarcely finished pouring out his heart when he calls
even more impatiently for the door of the tent to be shut, so that he
may retreat silently into himself again.

There can no longer be any doubt as to what will happen. The
chorus which concludes this scene ends like a lament over one who
has already fallen: they sing of how the mother of Ajax will cry
'woe' and beat her breast when she hears of the calamity that has

befallen her child. It would be better for him to be hidden in Hades; when he left his father's house he was the best of the Achaeans, and now he has gone so far astray. . . . But when in the *epeisodion* which immediately follows Ajax steps out of his tent, he is a changed man. And now, if we are not to misinterpret what follows, we must make use of comparisons.[13] Only by comparison can we grasp the formal structure and avoid being misled by perverse modern interpretations. Has a genuine transformation taken place? Can Ajax be lying? And if he is lying, why? Or do his lies change into truth? There are as many interpretations of this passage as there are possibilities. But before we indulge in speculation, we should bear in mind that the same phenomenon recurs in the *Trachiniae* (436 ff.), the play which comes next in chronological order. So we should start by making sure that the interpretation is valid for both the *Ajax* and the *Trachiniae*.

It is true that the two speeches, both that of Ajax and that of Deianira, are speeches of deception, obviously uttered to mislead another person. Both are equally unexpected in the mouth of a person who until that point, whether standing in silence, speaking or singing, had always remained rigidly enclosed in the world to which he is bound by his own fate, apparently incapable of any difference in conduct or any change of attitude. The characters plunge into both speeches with equal abruptness; neither is preceded by any previous deliberation; neither is directed towards any goal which has been mentioned before. They are thus both very different from any form of *intrigue*, either external and caused by circumstances, or within the mind. But in that case are we entitled to speak of deception? Indeed some scholars have concluded that we cannot. Yet in both cases the deception is revealed by the reversal which follows, in which the apparent truth of the speech is confronted with the real truth. In both cases we are completely unprepared for the reversal that reveals the real truth; its effect is like the impact of a shattering blow on the chorus in both plays, an impact similar to that caused by the reversal that had revealed the apparent truth a little earlier.

But the roots of the relationship between the speeches go even deeper. They both counterfeit the truth; but, more than that, in spite of the obvious deception involved, they both unfold a tale which is rendered so convincing to the ear by the wealth of its imagery that the will to deceive does not suffice to explain its pathos. In these speeches the individual, in his loneliness and isolation, comes to realize the truth about the way in which all things fit together, in an order which is valid not only for the community of which he is no longer a part, but as the very essence of Nature, which is valid both in heaven and on earth. So the individual who has been cast out exercises his own will in spite of the circumstances by which he is bound, and frees himself not only from the ordinances of society but also from the ordinances of all existence.[14]

33

The eyes of Ajax are suddenly opened, he recognizes the world, but he refuses to fit into it, to submit to its ordinances, to follow the rule 'Know thyself'. Rather, he sees in the world something alien and contrary to his nature, in which he could participate only if he were no longer Ajax: 'If I were to submit to this world and its gods, who tolerate nothing that is extreme or persistent, no final Yes or No, I would hate my enemy, but, bearing in mind that he may one day become my friend, I would limit my hatred accordingly' (he alludes to the saying of Bias [Ar. *Rhet.* 1389 b, 24–5]); 'and I would do good to my friend, bearing in mind that his friendship might not endure for ever' [679–82]. He has to perish, not only because he has detached himself from his heroic environment—that was already his fate in the epic—but because the world can no longer contain him. The comparisons which he makes between himself and the world of nature are more than a rhetorical device; they are more than the dignified language of tragic diction. While they stress change as a universal law to which all realms, both the macrocosm of nature and the microcosm of man, are subject, they bear witness to a feeling concerning the world close to that of Heraclitus: 'God is summer and winter, day and night . . .' [fr. 67 Diels-Kranz[6]]. But in the words of Ajax a discord can be heard underneath the noble praise of the order of the world, an undertone of revulsion, almost of scorn of that wisdom which is the wisdom of this world (646 ff.):

Ajax
  Strangely the long and countless drift of time
  Brings all things forth from darkness into light,
  Then covers them once more. Nothing so marvellous
  That man can say it surely will not be—

Strong oath and iron intent come crashing down.
My mood, which just before was strong and rigid,
No dipped sword more so, now has lost its edge—
My speech is womanish for this woman's sake. . .

. . .

From now on this will be my rule: Give way
To Heaven, and bow before the sons of Atreus.
They are our rulers, they must be obeyed.
I must give way, as all dread strengths give way,
In turn and deference. Winter's hard-packed snow
Cedes to the fruitful summer; stubborn night
At last removes, for day's white steeds to shine.
The dread blast of the gale slackens and gives
Peace to the sounding sea; and Sleep, strong jailer,
In time yields up his captive. Shall not I
Learn peace and wisdom? Have I not learned this,
Only so much to hate my enemy
As though he might again become my friend,
And so much good to wish to do my friend,
As knowing he may yet become my foe?

In this passage the deception grows from an irony which has
deeper roots than what we generally call 'tragic irony'; here the
irony arises from a dawning perception of an everlasting discord
between the hero and the way in which the world is organized.[15]

It is true that the speech of deception in the *Trachiniae* does not
employ the same wealth of comparisons with the world of nature as
that in the *Ajax*; but Deianira disguises her intentions in the same
way. She pretends to recognize and glorify a power which governs
mankind, the gods and the world; but this recognition is deceptive,
since she does not act in accordance with her words. Admittedly it is
not the same power as that in the *Ajax*; but it is as much in conflict
with the unchangeable nature of the loving Deianira as the law of
change is in conflict with the inflexibility of Ajax. What Deianira
pretends to recognize—that is, what she recognizes as valid for the
world, but not for herself—is the law of change, confined to the
only part of the world that she recognizes, her own world—Love.
Just as Deianira boasts of her insight (ἐπίστασθαι τὰ ἀνθρώπεια) at
the moment when she least possesses it, so Ajax pretends to fulfil
the law 'think as a mortal should: do not presume to go further'

34

(κατ' ἄνθρωπον φρονεῖν) when he is furthest from doing so [cf. *Trach*. 439, *Ajax* 677].

But in Ajax's 'speech of deception' his newly gained perception helps him to make a decision. The result of his perception was not deliberate dissimulation; similarly the result of his decision is not an intention to mislead. Rather, Ajax's own mind is the victim of self-deception to such an extent that, far from voluntarily intending to mislead, Ajax involuntarily *veils* his meaning: 'But you [Tecmessa] go in and pray to the gods that they may grant fulfilment of my heart's desire.' In this passage the words 'desire' and 'fulfilment' are both veiled; they are veiled allusions to 'the fulfilment of death' (τέλος θανάτοιο)—and this is an action as far removed from a trick as it is from the usual word-play of irony; it is not even ambiguous like the 'long sleep' which Schiller's Wallenstein plans, but is the attitude of a man hiding himself in darkness (687 ff.):

Ajax
And you, my friends, heed my instructions too,
And when he comes, deliver this to Teucer:
Let him take care for me and thought for you.
Now I am going where my way must go . . .

But the veiled language is at its most veiled when it comes to the thought of the suicide weapon, the sword. It is true that Ajax needs an excuse to move away with his sword without arousing any suspicion, but it is not merely this excuse which gives his speech a secret inner meaning: his intention outstrips his words, and the 'speech of deception' becomes a monologue; his words, instead of remaining within the play, break right through its framework and address the audience. They signify: this is Ajax, this is how he veils his words, here is a man who is turning away from reality to appearances, who is renewing his allegiance to the unreal, a man who is making atonement, who is in truth unteachable, who is shutting himself off from everything—for he does not begin to shut himself off completely before the lines which give an *appearance* of participation in society (654 ff.):

Ajax
But now I'm going to the bathing place
And meadows by the sea, to cleanse my stains,

In hope the goddess' wrath may pass from me.
And when I've found a place that's quite deserted,
I'll dig in the ground, and hide this sword of mine,
Hatefullest of weapons, out of sight. May Darkness
And Hades, God of Death, hold it in their safe keeping.
For never, since I took it as a gift
Which Hector, my great enemy, gave to me,
Have I known any kindness from the Greeks . . .

36   His thoughts circle around his death. The 'enmity' of the weapon, the 'digging' of it 'in the ground', 'Darkness' and 'Hades', the 'beyondness' (ἐκεῖσε) of the 'deserted place', the 'cleansing' of the 'stain': all these are just as valid as images of his inner self, but transposed from clarity into obscuring, veiling references.[16] Deception drives Ajax into the abyss: once more he draws around himself the disguising veils of this world and its hopes which have become alien and inimical to him.

This is the key to the relationship between Ajax's 'speech of deception' and his monologue, from which it is separated by the episode in which his followers go to look for him. The relationship is one of contrast between veiling and unveiling, between illusory participation in society and the nakedness of the solitary soul in the face of death. The cleansing of the stain, the enmity of the weapon, the hostility of the ground and the implacability of his hatred, everything that had previously been veiled, now stands as naked as the hero himself (815 ff.):

Ajax
He's firm in the ground, my Slayer. And his cut
(If I have time even for this reflection)
Should now be deadliest. For, first, the sword
Was Hector's gift, a token of guest-friendship,
And he of all guest-friends my bitterest foe;
Here, too, it stands, lodged in this hostile ground
Of Troy, its edge made new with iron-devouring stone.
And, last, I've propped it, so, with careful handling,
To help me soon and kindly to my death.
This preparation I have made. And now,
Making my invocation, as is right,
I call first, Zeus, on you . . .

The monologue with its sevenfold invocation embraces the entire world around him, the world in which he has his roots and from which he is departing; friend and enemy; Hector and the Atridae; Zeus and the Erinyes; his ancestral home and the scene of his exploits; Salamis and Troy; light and death. This invocation is arranged in accordance with the Greeks' view of the world as composed of pairs of contrasted antitheses. No lament, reproach, world-weariness, aversion, no hint of melancholy, not even the melancholy of a Brutus—none of the bitterness of renunciation; right up to the very moment of his death, the moment when he sets himself free from the ties of the world, he is unable to lose, either in love or in hate, his preoccupation with that same world which scorns him, and him alone, and which he, and only he, can no longer bear. Imagine the totally different way in which Euripides would have made Ajax put the blame on the world! Each of the invocations is followed by a final prayer, a final greeting—except that the invocation of death is broken off, and in its place comes a final greeting to light (854 ff.):

Ajax
Strong God of Death, attend me now and come.
And yet I shall converse with you hereafter . . .
O radiance, O my home and hallowed ground
Of Salamis, and my father's hearth, farewell!
And glorious Athens, and my peers and kin
Nurtured with me, and here all springs and streams,
My nurses, you that wet the plains of Troy,
Farewell! This last word Ajax gives to you;
The rest he keeps, to speak among the dead.

It is only in his speech of deception, taken in conjunction with his monologue, that Ajax is finally caught up in the incompatibility between two worlds—his private world and the everyday world. The inflexible fighter becomes the inflexible soul; the man deprived of his honour becomes the man deprived of the world, and, because he was too firmly rooted in his private world, he is punished. For the gods remain the guardians of this cosmos. The tragedy of Ajax does not take place in a world which is out of joint.

For the purpose of dramatic presentation, the contrast between

what is veiled and what is revealed is set in the context of a
rambling, changing inter-play of hope, awe and fear on the part of
those close to Ajax; a song of jubilation at his 'unhoped-for change'
(716–17) is followed by the news of the warnings of the seer, and
everyone hurries to look for the hero whom they now know to be
in danger. . . . The stage has to be empty to allow for the change of
scene—it appears that the *ekkyklema* was used for the second time at
this point:[17] now, suddenly, we are taken to a distant place, where
the sword is fixed firmly into the ground, concealed by the surrounding undergrowth, and the hero stands in front of it. There also
had to be provision for the actor who played the part of the living
hero to be replaced by the dummy representing his dead body,
which appears with the sword thrust through its chest. . . . After
that, the chorus, divided into semi-choruses, re-enter from either
side, with weary steps to indicate that they have come a long way in
their desperate search—and then Tecmessa stops with a sudden cry
at the place where the body has fallen. Now that the body has been
discovered, they all stand around it, and begin the lamentation over
the dead hero. His body has fallen foward, but Teucer lifts it up and
displays it, covered in blood. . . .

But this is more a question of stage-management, the outer
trappings of the play, an area in which the young Sophocles was
fond of innovation and experiment. Furthermore, the motif 'Too
late!' is not developed from the character of the fallen hero, and has
no connection with his fate; he is involved in it merely for the
purpose of the framework of the play. It is true that the speech of the
seer, as reported by the messenger, recapitulates, interprets, and
points to the future, but what a difference between this early work
and the language of the Tiresias scenes in the later plays! Instead of
arousing shudders of fear and unleashing threatening powers, it
adds no more to the play than an anxious warning and a didactic
explanation, which, in any case, after a gnomic opening, soon
reverts to the epic style of reported narrative. The anecdote about
the remark of Ajax which illustrates his lack of a sense of moderation is modelled on Odysseus' description of Achilles' departure
from home in the *Iliad* (ix 254);[18] and what follows is much the
same. There is no question in this scene, as opposed to those in the
later plays in which a prophet appears, of two different worlds
coming into contact with each other; the relationship between man

and god, as illustrated in this speech with examples from the past, does not go beyond the traditional framework of archaic ethics, the doctrine of moderation. Thus the traditional type of interpretation is juxtaposed in this early work with the power of the new style of tragedy just as sharply as the tremendous innovation of the monologue is juxtaposed with the old device of introducing a messenger within an *epeisodion* to bring news and to explain the situation. Scenes of this kind are no longer to be found in the plays of Sophocles' later style.

The second part of the play—the coda or whatever you like to call it, the dispute about the burial—is less concerned with purely theatrical considerations than the first. For it is certainly not just tacked on for merely external reasons, in order to make up the length of the play, as some have thought; nor is the relationship of this part to the whole satisfactorily explained by saying that the fate of the body was more important to an Athenian than it is to us. Not everything which is considered important is turned into drama. The purpose of the finale is rather to contrast the genuine greatness of the tragic hero who was fated to die with the spuriousness and conceit of those who opposed him, triumphed over him, and lived on—their ingratitude, pusillanimity, envy, meanness and arrogance.

39

Certainly we must take the play for what it is. There is no development or forward movement; instead, one set of circumstances simply succeeds another, and we watch a collection of contrasting figures who are united only by their relationship to the central figure of the hero. It is not that he has any effect on them or they on him: it is rather that they shed light on his character, in that their characters define his by contrast. We have already seen how Tecmessa, while embodying and foreshadowing her own fate, provided the contrast of feminine with masculine. Similarly Teucer defines Ajax's character by contrast: he is the noble bastard, who is to be driven out of his own country with curses by his father because he returns home without his greater, legitimate brother: for that incident too—which involves the same type of pathetic deliberation as Ajax's decision to die—is presented simply in the form of a lament of the surviving for the fallen, without being interwoven into the plot as 'action'. This preference for setting the fates of different characters in contrast with each other, and indeed the overall preponderance of demonstration, direct representation and didacticism over development and forward movement, the predominance of a series of relationships over dynamic action and gradual downfall, is the aspect of the play which more than anything else determines the character of the whole of the *Ajax*, not only of its last part. Thus, later, when Teucer becomes the mouthpiece of the poet, even the relationship of both friendship and enmity between Hector and Ajax is revealed as determined by fate (1034): when they exchanged the sword and the belt, what a difference between the meaning that they had both attached to the action and the meaning which in fact it was destined to have! Hector was dragged to death, according to Sophocles, by that same belt which Ajax had given him, and Ajax killed himself with that same sword. They had hoped to escape the fate that hung over them, but it used their behaviour as a means of fulfilling the divine will which operates above and beyond the human context (1034 ff.):

Teucer
Did not a Fury beat this weapon out?
And was it not Aidoneus, that grim craftsman,
40   Who made that other one? In my opinion,
That was the gods' contrivance, like all other
Destinies of men, for the gods weave them all.

Thus there would obviously be something lacking from the whole picture if there were no opportunity for that deceitful world which opposed Ajax, and upon which he wanted to take his revenge, to express itself; and it is the Atridae who speak for it. And the fame of the hero whom the gods overthrew is enhanced by contrast with the lack of moderation of the petty men who seek vengeance: the sententious complaint of the over-commanding sub-commander Menelaus, who preserves the morality of the *polis*—and yet is unable to get the better of Ajax to any great degree (much in his character already points to the Creon of the *Antigone*), and the explosively quarrelsome way in which the highest dignitary, Agamemnon, expresses his envy of Ajax's glory. Confronted with innate worth, outward rank, as represented by Agamemnon, can only adorn itself with jangling maxims about the wholesomeness of obedience and the stability of the state: orders must inspire fear in the army just as *nomoi* do in the *polis*, and so forth. Contrast this petty-mindedness with the final greatness of Ajax! Contrast this 'righteousness' of the little men with the 'wrong-doing' of the great hero!

But in order to round off the drama in this way, Sophocles made use of the old formal device of the *agon,* or set debate—indeed, as scholars have observed, an *agon* of a particularly antiquated type: the opponents enter to prevent the burial, one after the other, and exit again with threats or protests, as in the *agon*-scenes of comedy; word rebounds against word, reproach against reproach, maxim against maxim. There is so little attempt to disguise the genre that the *agon* is even described as such in the choral anapaests that introduce the second half (1163). Thus as a method of representing the opponents, the *agon* appears to our minds to be unduly restricted by the formal nature of its construction. Instead of situations which develop from the *nature* of the pervading hostility, there is a ready-made *schema*, a mere substitute for it, which has to be filled with the appropriate ingredients. Perhaps the lack of development, movement and progress is due to the traditional nature of the form. Even the grudging retractation of Agamemnon which is provoked by Odysseus makes no difference. The attitudes of the opponents at the end are just the same as they were at the beginning; the strife continues to rage in all its fury but it does not shift its ground—and in this too it is similar to the *agon*-scenes of comedy.

The tableau on the stage makes amends to us for this in one respect: all the time that the brawl is growing in intensity, Tecmessa and Eurysaces kneel in the background, guarding the body, a silent, motionless group. The child holds in his hand the hair-offerings of his family as a gift to his dead father, in the posture prescribed by Teucer (1180):

Teucer
    Take it, dear child, and guard it, and let no one
    Remove you, but cling fast, inclining over him . . .

At the end, the chorus divides, going away in groups to either side, as Teucer commands: to dig the grave, erect the tripod, fetch the armour. . . . Teucer and the boy remain by the dead man, they raise him—he is still bleeding. . . .

Thus there is much in this play that is unique. Methods which will be discarded by Sophocles in his later work stand cheek by jowl with others which point ahead to later developments. Above all there is the conception of a single figure who is presented in only one or two situations, which is unparalleled in the later plays. To a greater extent than any of the later works, the *Ajax* seems to have been composed around this central character; the rest of the characters are seen in the light of this dominating figure, whether they interpret it, look back at it, or stand in contrast to it. But the interpretation falls short of the conception, and the form of the play seems to conform to the religious drama of the older style rather than to rise from the heart of the work. It is not until the *Oedipus Tyrannus* that both form and content grow together so as to form a perfect unity.

II

TRACHINIAE

An earlier generation regarded the *Trachiniae* as a 'psychological drama' on account of its heroine, and therefore saw it in the light of Euripides' tragedies about women. In this play, as in none of his other dramas, Sophocles seemed to be trying to capture the problematical modernity of the man of the 420's. And if it was an imitation of Euripides, its date of composition had to be put much lower, at a date later than the *Heracles*, later than 415. Moreover, Deianira's femininity, both in the outburst of her passion and in her attachment to hearth and home, her sympathy, her good intentions, all the touching qualities which create around her a kind of private atmosphere, seemed to appeal to nineteenth-century readers as something familiar, almost like part of a novel, something after their own hearts. They saw Deianira as a figure taken from life. It is this closeness to life, too, which made Sophocles appear to be following more closely in Euripides' footsteps in this play than in any other, taking Euripides as the first tragic writer to break through myth into contemporary life and times.[1] Deianira was regarded as a sister of Euripides' Alcestis and Medea, even though her remark about the 'wicked deeds of daring' performed by 'women that I loathe' (582–3) seemed to be a direct reference to Medea.[2] But although the heroine's fate is that of a woman, more passive than active—she is, as it were, carried along, or helplessly swallowed up—it shows no trace of the conflicts and psychological strife of the Euripidean characters. In the *Trachiniae*, too, that which determines the centre, surroundings and conditions of a human life is very much the same as in the *Ajax* and the *Oedipus Tyrannus*, though it takes a different form. Even the touching element of intimacy is not included for its own sake, or as a 'slice of life' thoughtlessly inserted by the tragedian, but plays its part in the
unveiling of a universal fate, receives its meaning from the figure of the daimon and grows from the same root as the *Ajax*—though it is,

as it were, a tender shoot in comparison with the hardy shoot of the *Ajax*: for both are creations of the same poet.[3]

We must also guard against trying to interpret the plays by foisting upon them modern psychological or even sociological concepts. We are all too familiar with the force of invisible but relentless powers, either external circumstances or the depths of the 'subconscious', as an explanation for the bourgeois soul breaking through bourgeois barriers. But the soul which forms the subject of this drama is exposed to powers and dangers of a different kind: whereas the modern soul suffers from the clash between the human and the sub-human, in whatever form it may take, and from the discord between them, the suffering of Deianira is conditioned by the clash between the human and the super-human, between the voluntary and the daimonic; it is when a person is alienated from himself by his fate that he first understands himself for the being that he is.

The early style is again revealed above all in the way the speeches move. Here as in the *Ajax* the 'pathos' which *is generated* in each case by fate is greater than that which generates itself. In contrast with the later style, the words do not constitute action so much as reaction, wherein the tone may change according to the situation of the victim, but the words themselves do not create new situations by their continuation or by the power of their own developing movement. Thus one stroke of fate is set directly next to another, often with magnificent effect; the small-scale transitions take place outside the spoken words just as the large-scale transitions take place outside the visible action. The succession of situations in the *Trachiniae* may be compared with archaic sentence-structure in which ideas are strung in a row, in which one phrase is set next to another without link or connection, whereas a work in the later style, the *Electra*—to take another example of a drama about a woman—has no scene without its parallelisms, transitions, reverses and echoing of voices—in short, without a rhythm resembling that of a developed, syntactical period.

44   The action falls into two parts, the first, longer section dealing with the downfall of Deianira, and the shorter one at the end dealing with the downfall of Heracles. Even though the downfalls of the two are closely linked in the traditional story, and in fact the fate of the woman finds a place in the saga only because it is bound up with that of the man, yet in the *play* their two fates are not intertwined in

the course of the scenes; they are unfolded one after the other, without being connected with each other in any obvious way. It is true that Heracles' fate is approaching and threatening from the beginning; there is no lack of allusions to prepare us for it before it appears on the stage; yet the play as a whole does not portray a 'double fate' like that of Romeo and Juliet, or of Phaedra and Hippolytus, but, as might be expected from the outward division of scenes, the inner content too portrays *two* fates strung one after the other in a kind of rhythmic succession, one opposite in sense to the other. The true content of this drama is the isolation of *two* characters, the repetition of the alienation which separates and divides *two* figures from the protective unity of existence—two figures who, though they correspond with each other and are linked, are nevertheless independent by reason of their immanent daimons and who remain separate in their fates. If you want a formula, the drama portrays not two characters with one fate, but the fate of two in one whole.

The form of the characters' fate determines the form of the scenes. The basic tendency of the main characters, in the first as well as the second part of the play, is always to deliver monologues which are filled with the expression of their fate, even in their conversations together. The second speaker is only an accompaniment, either taking up and re-echoing the outpourings of the first, or, by a statement or a question, bringing new material to the speaker in his or her *pathos*, in response to which the latter plunges again into the current which carries forward both his fate and his words. On the other hand in this play there is as yet no conflict as such, no struggle between two souls, nor is there any type of scene which would be suitable for such a conflict. Drama is still no more than the unveiling of something darkly foreshadowed by an event which is now approaching step by step, something which is received, taken and suffered rather than desired, planned or contested; all action and suffering still runs in the same direction, without deviations, detours or digressions, almost without resistance. Admittedly, the mortal fondly imagines that he is taking the path which will avoid the end to which in fact he is hastening; but as yet even his confusion and error do not lead to any reversal of situation between success and failure, heights and depths. If we imagine a series beginning with the form taken by fate in Aeschylus' *Seven against Thebes* and ending with the form it takes in the *Oedipus Tyrannus*, there is no doubt that the *Trachiniae* would come between the two, but nearer to the *Seven* than to the more changeable, faster-moving *Oedipus*.

Just as pathetic narrative forms a disproportionate part of the whole play, so already at the very beginning it monopolizes the prologue and gives it its character. Now this deviation from Sophocles' own custom has been explained as an imitation of Euripides' manner, and regarded as mere 'exposition'.[4] But the rhythm which carries this woman's fate, which begins to be told in her opening lamentations, is already the same rhythm which recurs throughout the later part of this play: again and again an awareness of doom gives way to an unhoped-for stroke of good luck, which has no sooner appeared than it begins to reveal itself as the sinister source of the object of fear. In the same way that this recurs time and again even in the prologue, it recurs act by act in the drama: the form of pathetic narrative in the prologue already anticipates the outer form of the whole play as well as the inner form taken by the fate.

Thus what is essentially fairy-tale material is already caught up and swept along by the impetus of the daimon-driven soul. It is true that the fusion of saga material and tragedy of fate is not yet as masterly as in the *Oedipus Tyrannus*. The fairy-tale horrors of the primeval world press in on the pitiable soul and cause Deianira to suffer her anxieties, but the realm of the marvellous and that of the psychological do not overlap completely: the element of the marvellous, as though rejoicing in the bold language which is capable of expressing it, rejoicing for its own sake, towers over and encroaches upon the realm of the psychological more independently and in a stranger fashion than in any of these dramas. In addition, in the lyrics and narrative passages a fairy-tale uncouthness plays around the uncouth hero of the primeval world: hybrid river-monsters, coming as suitors to woo princesses, the horned god of the watery element wrestling with the champion, centaurs living on riverbanks as ferrymen . . . and all taken as seriously as in the formal art of the middle of the century (507 ff.):

Chorus
One was a strong river with the looks of a high-horned
four-footed bull,
Acheloüs from Oeniadae . . .[5]

Fatally self-engrossed, speaking in as much of a 'monologue' as Tecmessa approaching Ajax, and no less gnomic in her use of examples, the heroine begins (1 ff.):

Deianira
>   It was long ago that someone first said:
>   You cannot know a man's life before the man
>   has died, then only can you call it good or bad.
>   But I know mine before I've come to Death's house
>   and I can tell that mine is heavy and sorrowful.
>   While I still lived in Pleuron, with Oeneus my father,
>   I conceived an agonizing fear of marriage.
>   No other Aetolian woman ever felt such fear,
>   for my suitor was the river Acheloüs . . .

—then, after describing the monster, with its figure that is part bull, part man, part incarnation of the element, continuing in the rhythm which expresses and anticipates her fate—moving rapidly to and fro between fear of what is to come and unhoped-for relief, and back again to fear (15 ff.):

Deianira
>   I had to think this suitor would be my husband
>   and in my unhappiness I constantly prayed for death
>   before I should ever come to *his* marriage bed.
>   But, after a time, to my joy there came
>   the famous Heracles, son of Alcmena and Zeus . . .
>   . . . I do not speak of the manner
>   of their struggles, for I do not know. Someone
>   who watched the spectacle unafraid could tell.
>   I sank down, overwhelmed with terror lest
>   my beauty should somehow bring me pain.[6] Zeus of the contests
>   made the end good—if it has been good.
>   Chosen partner for the bed of Heracles,
>   I nurse fear after fear, always worrying
>   over him. I have a constant relay of troubles;
>   some each night dispels—each night brings others on.
>   We have had children now, whom he sees at times,
>   like a farmer working an outlying field,
>   who sees it only when he sows and when he reaps. . . .
>   Now he wins through to the end of all his labours,
>   and now I find I am more than ever afraid.

47

Ever since he killed the mighty Iphitus,
we, his family, live here in Trachis, a stranger's guests,
forced to leave our home. But no one seems to know
where Heracles himself can be . . .

But in order to bend the curves of fate towards their goal from
outside as well, and at the same time to link the fates of the couple
from the very beginning, the daimon of her own *pathos* is not
sufficient; it needs the outward confirmation of the oracle, but this
too is only hinted at darkly at first, as befits the style of gradual
revelation (46 ff.):

Deianira
Yes, this tablet he left behind makes me think
it must surely be some terrible trouble. Often
I pray the Gods I do not have it for my sorrow.

And, again, it is no coincidence that the content of the oracle, as it
is revealed at the end of the prologue (166 ff.), in its still rather
awkward form, and its emphasis on the critical moment, resembles
the warnings of the seer in the *Ajax* (756, 778):

Deianira
Then he would either die exactly at *this* time,
or, by getting past *this* time limit, he would
in the future live a life without grief . . .

Thus, from the very beginning, the action becomes the fulfilment
of a prophecy which has been made known at the outset. But the
inner and the outer world, the daimon of the mind and the daimon
of the surroundings, still run on separate paths, and there is still no
link or interaction between them, let alone anything like the
uncanny coincidences of the *Oedipus Tyrannus*. Nor is Deianira's
desire to ward off the daimon as yet a struggle against it. Oedipus is
the first who, while bringing a mortal daimon to fulfilment, also
possesses sufficient tension of will to form the bond and nerve of the
scene. In the *Trachiniae* there is still nothing comparable with the
concealed resistance in the *Oedipus* in the chorus, in the person of
Creon, of Tiresias; the nurse and the son, Hyllus, who still take it in
turn to join the heroine in the earlier style, so that the three never

take part in a three-sided dialogue, only serve to bring news of outward events to her. And so they come to the lamenting woman, the nurse with advice, Hyllus to be sent forth, but neither their inner nor outer relationship with her creates any kind of tension. The boy whom she sends forth will in the end bring back the father whose death she fears, but how differently from the way she imagines it in her fear! In contrast, the nurse, in her rôle of confidante and adviser, is here no more than a figure who helps and who facilitates trans-itions. How much more Euripides made of her later! How he altered and enriched her relationship with her mistress!

The brief first 'act' gives an equally archaic impression, turning as it does on the contrast of the change from fear to liberation, as already developed in *epeisodion* form by Aeschylus (e.g. *Choeph.* 212; *Suppl.* 911): after the revelation of the oracle which seems to foretell Heracles' death, a garlanded messenger announces his vic-torious approach, on the road from the castle of King Eurytus, which lies in smoking ruins behind him. The reversal still comes from outside, not from the potential or the disposition of inner forces. Even though Sophocles deliberately makes the presence of the daimon felt at the same time as the announcement, yet its effect does not yet penetrate the dialogue, or permeate the entire situation, in any way comparable with the unfolding of its power in the first scenes of the *Antigone* or the *Oedipus Tyrannus*.

Meanwhile the narrative in monologue form greatly surpasses the action on the stage in its expressive power. But the language, with its sombre colouring, its muffled echo of the fateful surround-ings of a character's existence, is already sure of its daimon; and alternating between *gnome*, tragic narrative and outbursts of *pathos*, develops a kind of premonitory understanding, which already begins to point to a significance that is wider than the obvious meaning of the words and the thoughts of the speaker (144 ff.):

Deianira
                    So the young thing
grows in her own places; the heat of the sun-god
does not confound her, nor does the rain, nor any wind.
Pleasurably she enjoys an untroubled life
until the time she is no longer called a maiden
but woman, and takes her share of worry in the night. . . .
                    . . .

so that I leap up from pleasant sleep in fright,
my friends, terrified to think that I may have to live
deprived of the one man who is the finest of all.

The second *epeisodion* is very much richer and more varied than
the first and is longer than any of the others. It is the first revelation
scene in Sophocles, or perhaps in all literature; 'revelation scene',
that is, in the sense of a scene of which the construction and outward
form arise from an inner clash between the drive to conceal and the
drive to reveal. It is true that there was revelation in the *Ajax*, but
only in the form of self-concealment and self-revelation, both of
which still resulted only in separate, short *epeisodia*, with no change
of attitude within themselves. But here one and the same *epeisodion*
is expanded to such an extent that deception and truth, concealment
and revelation follow one another without a break, and the whole
section is divided into two parts by a sharp break (between 334 and
335): it is rooted in deception until that point, and from then on
truth takes over. But in order to control a play of opposites of this
nature, Sophocles, more timid here than in his later revelation
scenes, made use of the usual stage device: the messenger. Or rather,
he uses two of them, one messenger of concealment and one messenger of revelation, and still places them side by side rather than
opposing them to each other. This means that the messenger of
revelation has to stand aside at first while Lichas, the messenger of
concealment, is speaking; at the very moment that he is taken
indoors, that is, at the moment at which in the normal way the
epeisodion would seem to be coming to a close, just as the queen and
the messenger are in the act of going into the house, the other
messenger steps forward, to speak and reveal, until the first comes
out of the house again. Then the two confront one another, Lichas
has to confess, and at the end we are left in the dark as to what
effect the revelation of the truth has had on the mind of the heroine.

Thus in this scene both deception and truth still make use of
narrative form, and this narrative has to bear most of the weight of
the play of opposites. What a difference between this and the later
Oedipus Tyrannus, where there is a completely different pattern of
deception and truth, and where the messenger-speech is avoided! In
that play, too, at the end, two witnesses stand face to face, but one

pushes forward and the other holds back. . . . But here there is
hardly a trace of the *dynamic* contrasts without which it is impossible to conceive a single scene of the *Oedipus*.[7] Truth and deception
do not come into conflict with each other, but stand apart, and are
divided so that only one appears in each account, like variant
versions in the story-telling technique of Herodotus. Indeed, what
is reported as true and what is reported as false are not even different
in kind; it is not the content which is true or false, but the way in
which events are linked together. Heracles, as King Eurytus' guest,
insulted and mocked in his drunkenness, cunningly avenging himself, flinging Iphitus from the walls of Tiryns, then at Zeus' command having to atone for the murder as the servant of Omphale,
and swearing vengeance on those who brought this humiliation
upon him—this is the same Heracles as the hero who, as King
Eurytus' guest, requests his host's daughter 'for his secret bed'
almost as soon as he sets eyes on her, and, when this is refused,
conquers the castle and takes the girl home as a prisoner of war.
Both are equally boorish, equally outside heroic society, and
equally immoderate; it is of little account whether he is acting out of
revenge or out of love. But at the same time this is the cause of
another difference between this play and the more developed style
of Sophocles' later deception-scenes: in this case it is not clear from
the report itself whether or not it is true, whereas in the *Electra* and
Philoctetes the deception can be seen to make more and more strenu-
ous efforts to appear outwardly credible the further it moves from
the truth; it even comes on to the stage as a character in the second
Oedipus. In the *Trachiniae* the deception, since it is presented in a
messenger's speech, does not take on the form of an actor in the
plot. And it is only because of their content, as a part of the saga
which is being told, that the reports of messengers and others have
any place in the whole; they rank no higher than a piece of
stichomythia or a chorus.

The opposition of true and false can be developed more freely
in the scene of the questioning, and already it is more a part of the
action. Lichas, the herald, is shaken roughly enough from his pretence of honesty, and his thinly-veiled dignity soon finds itself
painfully embarrassed by the vigorous questioning of the messenger, who acts as go-between (414, 429 ff.):

Lichas
I am leaving. I have been a fool to listen so long.
. . .
I said 'as a consort'? By the Gods, explain to me,
dear mistress—this stranger here, who on earth is he?

And, since the only effect is that the accusation is repeated all the
more vehemently (434 ff.):

Lichas
Please have this fellow leave. No sensible person,
mistress, wastes his time exchanging words with a madman.

Here we begin to see a contrast between the higher and the lower
elements in the action. But the play of opposites, between the
narrow, limited circumstances of those who are the tools of fate,
and the violence of the suffering of its victims, has neither the extent
nor the weight of the great witness-scenes of the *Antigone* or the
Oedipus Tyrannus. The lower element remains episodic, and the
tragic element is neither echoed by this other, lower tone of voice,
nor mirrored in the reflection of the non-tragic, everyday world.

It might even be asked whether all this carefully organized business of revelation is so essential. Since Lichas' deception is un-
masked when it has only just begun, is it not quite pointless and
ineffectual? And when it transpires that Lichas was lying not with
any malevolent intention but out of unintelligent devotion to duty,
in the hope of preventing what he was causing (in the same way that
the mistake made by poor Deianira in her preoccupation with her
own concerns causes exactly what she had feared)—would not the
same effect have been achieved if Lichas had carried out his errand
without lying? Was it only the dramatist's fondness for scenes of
revelation which led him to such roundabout methods? In fact the
opposition of true and false is hardly rooted in the substance and
basis of the action here. But it is only by this business that the way is
prepared for some incomparable situations: Deianira greeting Iole,
but veiling her feelings before Lichas. . . . It is only the deception
which brings her to the point at which she herself has to reveal her
own misfortune, which causes her failure to see her own fate in the
shape of the beautiful captive standing before her, which then leads

her step by step to break her way through to the truth; it is only through the deception that the noble self-control in her nature, her tenderness, can be revealed, that she can appear as more mature in comparison with the younger woman, and that her relationship with her rival can take on its own delicate tension (307 ff., 320 ff.):[8]

Deianira
   O unfortunate girl, tell me who you are.
   Are you married? Are you a mother? To judge by your looks,
   you have never known treatment like this, but you
   are someone noble . . .
   Then do tell us yourself, my poor child, for it
   would be a great shame not to know who *you* are.

Lichas
   It will be quite unlike her manner up to now
   if she begins to speak . . .

53   The isolated, enclosed, fatal situation in which a character is confronted with his own fateful strangeness is still, as in the *Ajax*, the chief means by which the tragic element is conveyed, the element that makes the most powerful impression and strikes the deepest roots, whereas the following-up, the unfolding, the leading along, in a word the dramatic *development*, is still in its earliest stages. But it would be a great mistake to see in all this no more than the revelation of mental states, no more than the dissection of a mental web: the meaning of this *inner* action, which answers and echoes the messenger's outer action, has nothing in common with Euripidean psychology, which depicts the soul, dissects the mind, and so forth. Down to the very last phrase and nuance it is about the conditioning and confinement of mortals by the inevitability of their daimon. And as for Deianira's moderation, discipline, self-restraint and sympathy, however much they may be misinterpreted on psychological lines, they still belong essentially to the attitude of warding off a threat, just as in those stories in Herodotus which show the working of fate. Because of this attitude the scene is imbued from the very beginning with a consistently dark tone, and attuned to a consistently anxious state of expectation of some future event (293 ff.):[9]

Deianira
> Yes, I should have every right to rejoice
> when I hear the news of my husband's great success.
> Surely my joy must keep pace with his good fortune.
> Still, if one gives it much thought, one knows a feeling
> of dread for the man who prospers so, lest he fall.
> For a terrible sense of pity came over me,
> my friends, when I saw these ill-fated women
> wandering homeless, fatherless, in a foreign land . . .
> O Zeus, who turns the tide of battle, grant that I
> may never see you come like this against *my* children.

In the unity of its muted fate-laden tones and premonitions, this dramatic style remains at a considerable distance from the later style of reversals and rapid twists and turns in the *Antigone* and the *Oedipus Tyrannus*—not to mention the works of Sophocles' old age. Thus the sudden change in Deianira's behaviour in the middle of this scene is all the more surprising. Deianira, who has been so hesitant, timid, fearful, asking others for advice at every step, suddenly takes up a perceptive, decisive stance which unites her outward purpose and inner state of mind in an amazing fashion (436 ff.):

Deianira (to Lichas)
> By Zeus who flashes lightning over the topmost glen
> of Oeta, do not cheat me of the truth! Speak,
> and you will find that I am not a spiteful woman
> nor one who does not know how it is with man—
> we cannot always enjoy a constant happiness.
> How foolish it would be to climb into the ring[10]
> with Love and try to trade blows with him, like a boxer.
> For he rules even the Gods as he pleases, and
> he rules me—why not another woman like me?
> You see I would be altogether mad
> to blame my husband, because he suffers from this sickness,
> or that woman. She has been guilty of nothing shameful,
> and she has done no harm to me. No, it is
> inconceivable. If you have learned to lie from him,
> then you are not learning honest lessons. If you school
> yourself in this fashion, you succeed only
> in seeming dishonest when you are trying to be decent.
> Tell me the whole truth . . .

. . . One man and many women—
Heracles has had other women before.
Never yet has one of them earned insults
from me, or spiteful talk, nor will *she*, even
if she is utterly absorbed in her passion,
for I pitied her deeply when I saw her because
her own beauty has destroyed her life . . .

. . .

55 *Lichas*
Well, dear mistress, I realize that you are not
unreasonable. You see things as we mortals must.
So I shall tell you the whole truth . . .

. . .

Deianira
Those are my feelings too, and so too shall I act.
You may be sure I shall not choose to add to my
afflictions hopeless resistance to the Gods . . .

Here too we have a deception comparable for its completeness
and plausibility only with that in the *Ajax*. Change does not appear
as action here any more than it did in the *Ajax*; there is no sort of
transition, either from the trusting to the disillusioned Deianira, or
from the sympathetic to the jealous, fearful Deianira. Note how
after the revelation (385) there is no plunge from one emotion to
another to create any contrast: throughout the entire act, in spite of
fluctuations, the same attitude—that of a woman timidly trying to
fend off disaster—is maintained.

Again, we can explain the inner enigma of Deianira's deception
only if we understand the form of this act. As in the case of the
'speech of deception' in the *Ajax*, what is disconcerting is that each
time that a character dissembles for an outward purpose it is linked
to a moment of true perception on their part: both characters, when
dissembling, are going with the way of the world, they perceive
their fate as a fragment of the destiny that surrounds them, they
understand the law 'of gods and men' even if only for this one
moment; and they illustrate the truth of this law so clearly that there
can be no doubt that their 'pathos' lies not merely in their dissembling but in their tragic destiny. Their insight raises them above
themselves, apparent deception brings them to the point where
they actually touch their own fate, grasp the truth as it were with

their own hands, and yet they cannot allow either their insight into the world and themselves, nor the attitude which gives rise to it, to emerge from their own being and become something which is true and effective for themselves. If they had been able to do so, Deianira would calmly conform, Ajax would become reconciled. . . . But the reversal brought by the next *epeisodion* in each play shows in a terrible way how far this is from being the case. The disguise that the character assumes makes it clear what he should have been like in order to escape his fate—and that he never could be like that. Thus the speech of deception itself becomes one of the protean forms which the character's basic daimon assumes, only to come upon him in ways which despite their strangeness and variety leave it essentially the same.[11]

The next *epeisodion* is completely filled with revelation, with monologues by Deianira in which she reveals and explains her secret plan to avoid disaster.[12] For here, as throughout the drama, the other partner in the conversation, in this case the chorus of women or the eldest of them, has only the function of acting as a background to the main character, as her echo; even when the other character appears in the rôle of adviser, it is only in order to bring out the heroine's attitude, without any development of a to and fro between conflicting forces in the speeches (586 ff.).

Once again the plan with which the heroine comes onto the stage has already been completely worked out; her attitudes succeed each other without any development, and the transitions take place off-stage.[13] Deianira is holding in her hands the garment of Nessus, which she is going to give to the messenger at the end of this *epeisodion*. But first she has to recount her adventure with Nessus. The material of the story as given by the saga forces its way into the action taking place in the present as something which is still quite alien, untamed, recapitulated and tacked on in the form of a narration. This 'pre-history' has no effect on the action, nor does its introduction bring about any new development such as occurs in the *Philoctetes*, the *Electra* and the *Oedipus Tyrannus*. The only thing about it which is dramatic in the true sense is Deianira's hesitation in the face of what is coming; and the more anxiously she seeks something to which she can cling so that she will not be carried away by her 'daimon', the more violently her future presses in on her (536 ff.):

Deianira
　For here I have taken on a girl—no,
　I can think that no longer—a married woman, as
　a ship's master takes on cargo, goods that outrage my heart.
　So now the two of us lie under the one sheet
　waiting for his embrace. This is the gift my brave
　and faithful Heracles sends home to his dear wife
　to compensate for his long absence!

57　　And yet (582 ff.):

　I am not a woman who tries to be—and may
　I never learn to be—bad and bold. I hate
　women who are. But if somehow by these charms,
　these spells I lay on Heracles, I can defeat
　the girl—well, the move is made, unless you think
　I am acting rashly. If so, I shall stop.

And this act draws to a close by completing the circle with another concealment after the revelation; it draws to a close in the transparency of passion which seeks to conceal itself; but the harder it tries, the more it betrays (627 ff.):

Deianira
　And, of course, since you saw it, you know the girl's
　reception—you know I received her as a friend.
Lichas
　Yes, I do, and I am astonished and delighted.
Deianira
　What else is there to tell him? For I am afraid
　you would be talking too soon of my longing for him
　before I know if *he* feels longing for me.

Thus Deianira's mistake stands at the centre of the tragedy, as the work of the 'daimon'. Regarded by itself and in isolation, this mistake would appear to be a pitiful, regrettable accident. But as part of the curve of her fate which we see starting to rise uncertainly at the very beginning, in the prologue, and already moving towards her downfall, her mistake becomes the necessary completion of her existence. The fact that her mistake, her haste, her lack of moderation, stems from nothing but her desire to be moderate, not to go astray, not to take revenge or to rebel, or to overstep the bounds of her surroundings—this is precisely what makes Deianira, just like Ajax, a dramatic example of human entanglement and limitation. The isolation and the loss of the connections which in each case nourish, protect and frame the existence of the character here take on the form of innocent guilt, by which the guilty person robs herself of the sense and centre of her own life. However much the characters and circumstances may differ, it is the same kind of fate. Just as Ajax loses his heroic status because he was too deeply devoted to it, Deianira, anxiously, most fervently intent on the 'control of her senses', must lose her *sophrosynē*, that very moderation that she sought to preserve. And even if their guilt is not the same, yet the human rigidity and preoccupation with self are the same and their result is the same: in both cases they lose their sense of the existence of the world outside themselves. And despite the variety and multiplicity of all that is embraced by this 'sense', in the *Ajax* a man's world, in the *Trachiniae* a woman's, it bears the same name in both cases (*Trach*. 721 ff.; [*Ajax* 479 ff.]):

Deianira
  I could not bear to live and hear myself called evil
  when my only wish is to be truly good.
Ajax
  Let a man nobly live or nobly die . . .

In the *Ajax* it is the report of the warning by the seer Calchas that is the forerunner of the catastrophe; in the *Trachiniae* it is the report of an omen. But here too the transition from error to truth, from hope to fear, is not seen to take place on the stage: the *epeisodion* which presents the catastrophe does not represent the change in dramatic action; instead it shows the succession of dawning recognition and final certainty; to create a sense of foreboding the omen which is the precursor of the downfall again takes the form of a revelation in monologue form. Deianira steps forward to recount the omen herself.

It is true that this omen is not so obviously god-sent as the signs in the *Antigone* or the *Oedipus Tyrannus*, and it might even appear natural if it were taken as a mere incident. But not only is it placed as a portent of the future at just the same point in this play as the appearances of Tiresias in the two other plays, but it is also decorated with such a wealth of figures of speech that there can be no doubt that it is a sign from the daimon (θαῦμ᾽ ἀνέλπιστον). At the same time the particular form that the omen takes is conditioned by the material and devised to fit the framework of the Nessus story. However, the omen itself is not peculiar to the story, but is characteristic of the type of tragedy to which this play belongs. It is an element artificially extracted from the Nessus story and transferred into the drama: the adventure with Nessus is now interpreted in a sense which is the reverse of the earlier, favourable interpretation (707 ff.):

Deianira
> From what possible motive, in return for what,
> could the dying beast have shown me kindness, when he
> was dying because of me? . . .
>   . . .
> I alone, unless my fears are fanciful,
> I, his unhappy wife, shall destroy him.

Admittedly, there seems to be an incongruity here between the potential form, the irruption of tragedy, and what is actually presented, which is still limited and coloured by the fairy-tale material, and not yet refined: here it is a small piece of wool which is destroyed, and considering that it *is* only a small piece of wool it is loaded with almost too heavy a burden of significance. (The remnant of wool comes from the garment in the fairy tale, just as the portent which is connected with it in the fairy tale is the effect of the gift.) (697 ff.):

Deianira
>   . . . as it became warm,
> it all ran together, a confused mass, and crumbled
> to bits on the ground, looking most like the dust one sees
> eaten away in the cutting of a piece of wood.
> Like this it lies where it fell. But from the earth
> on which it rests, clotted foam boils up
> like the rich liquid of the blue-green fruit
> from the vines of Dionysus, poured on the earth . . .

In the *Antigone* (1006) the omen speaks as it were in its own words through the mouth of the seer, appears in person and enters the debate; in the *Trachiniae* it remains part of an impassioned narrative. In the *Antigone*, obstinacy struggles against it, wavering for the first time. . . . Here, in the *Trachiniae*, there is still no comparable double *peripeteia*, that is, a *peripeteia* in the form of the whole scene which is accompanied by another in the consciousness of the victim, just as a large wave is followed by a smaller one. . . . In the later plays there is no longer any need for comparisons to heighten the effect: in the *Antigone* it is the solemn sacrifice and the whole sacral world of Nature with it which opens its mouth—no longer is a mere fragment of wool required to point to the future (*Ant.* 1008 ff.):

Tiresias
> No fire caught my offerings. Slimy ooze
> dripped on the ashes, smoked and spluttered there.
> Gall burst its bladder, vanished into vapour;
> the fat dripped from the bones and would not burn. . . .
> All of the altars of the town are choked
> with leavings of the dogs and birds; their feast
> was on that fated, fallen Polynices . . .
> These are the omens of the rites that failed,
> as my boy here has told me. He's my guide
> as I am guide to others.
> Why has this sickness struck against the state?
> Through your decision . . .

In the *Trachiniae* there is a great effort to achieve fearful premonition; in the *Antigone* premonition achieves speech and takes on visible form; in the *Oedipus Tyrannus* it breaks out of the realm of the daimonic to invade the mortal world of appearance with equal strength of language, meaning and dramatic effect.

Presentiment is followed closely by certainty:[14] from the mouth of Hyllus on his return comes the condemnation of the apparent wrongdoer. The daimon's way of viewing the world embraces a duality: a tension between something that is strange and beyond comprehension, and something that is one's own and can be recognized as familiar. That is why both are also present in Deianira's *anagnorismos* of the daimon, the strangeness and incomprehensibility, and at the same time the recognition (738 ff.):

Deianira
    My son, what has happened that I should be so hateful?
                         . . .
61   No, no, my child! What have you blurted out?
                         . . .
            How could you say it? Who on earth told you
            that I did this awful crime you charge me with?

The acceptance and incorporation of this strange element into her own being entails her own destruction (910):

She would call out loud to her daimon.

As a tragedy of blindness, the *Trachiniae* already points in the direction of the *Oedipus Tyrannus*. This, too, ends with the acceptance of what seemed alien at first, with the recognition of the 'daimon', although it is true that in that play the contrast between the alien and the familiar, in the form of the unwished-for, the unsuspected, or rather that which could not even have been suspected but must nevertheless be regretted and atoned for—this contrast is expressed much more forcibly in the *Oedipus*, and is indeed for the first time actually transformed into drama and visible action. At the same time, the similarity between the two plays shows how we must beware of applying our modern concept of guilt and responsibility even to the *Trachiniae*. In this instance, it would be idle to raise the question whether—or to what extent—'guilt' here implies no more than a causal relationship or to what extent it implies a sense of guilt involving intention or responsibility. It is no accident that no distinction is drawn between them.[15] Even though it may be possible, if one wishes, to find both notions, as yet undeveloped, in the concept of the daimon, yet the essence of this concept lies in the secret of a unity which it represents between the realm of men and the course of events, between will and fate. A distinction between intentional and unintentional guilt would not penetrate to the heart of the suffering (727 ff.):

Chorus
    But whenever we trip up unwillingly,
    the anger felt is tempered, and so it should be with you.

Deianira
  You may talk like this, since you have no share
  in the wrong; you have no burden all your own.

62 For a hidden unity of cause and consciousness appears visibly at the
end in Deianira's identification with the alien when she is ready to
die; and that is the form of fate the daimon takes here no less than in
the *Oedipus*.

However, in the Deianira drama the alien element is still presented in the early manner, in the form of the tragic narrative,
Hyllus' account of the effect of the fatal gift. At the same time the
narrative is a separate entity, a piece with its own tragic power,
neither addressed to Deianira nor intimately connected with Hyllus.[16] The pathos of the narrative is in contrast with the silence of
Deianira as she listens, just as Tecmessa's plea joins Ajax's self-
absorption to form a tragic harmony (813 ff.):

Chorus
  Why do you go off in silence? Surely you see
  that by silence you join your accuser and accuse yourself?
Hyllus
  Let her go, and I hope a fair wind blows
  to carry her far out of my sight . . .

In the *Oedipus Tyrannus* Sophocles again made use of the same
kind of exit. In the *Oedipus* Jocasta vanishes, silently acknowledging
her destiny, just as Deianira does here. We shall show later to what
extent the irony of the incongruity between the speaker and the
silent listener has increased between this play and the *Oedipus*.[17]

After a short *kommos* there follows the reversal of the misunderstanding in the form of the account given by the nurse as *exangelos*
[messenger from within]. (We see, in retrospect, why the nurse had
to appear with Hyllus in the prologue—because these two have to
take it in turn to recount the catastrophe.) But although it is presented in narrative form, her death is already a drama in itself, and,
even if not of equal greatness, comparable in significance with the
death of Ajax. Like Ajax, Deianira takes her leave by turning once
more to the places, things and people which were around her, and
saying farewell to them; except that her surroundings are more

63 limited and the objects closer, so that instead of calling to them from afar and giving them her last requests as Ajax does, she touches them and, weeping, presses them to herself. No less than Ajax, she stands for the last time enclosed in her own world (900 ff.):

Nurse
> When she went into the house, alone,
> and saw her son in the courtyard, arranging a cushioned bed
> to take with him as he went back to meet his father,
> she hid herself where no one might look at her[18] and groaned,
> falling against the altars, that now they would be
> deserted; and whenever she touched some household thing
> she used to use before, the poor creature would weep.
> Here and there, from room to room, she kept turning,
> and if she saw some servant of the household who was
> dear to her, she would look at her sadly and weep,
> and she would call out loud to her daimon and to
> her house that would have no children any more.
> Then she stops all this, and suddenly I see her
> rushing into the bedchamber of Heracles,
> and secretly, from the shadows, I keep watch
> over her. I see the woman casting sheets
> and spreading them upon the bed of Heracles.
> Then as soon as she had finished, she leapt up
> and sat there in the middle of her marriage bed,
> and, bursting into torrents of hot tears, she said:
> 'O my bed, O my bridal chamber, farewell
> now for ever, for never again will you take me
> to lie as a wife between these sheets of yours.'

What had previously been the entire meaning of their existence has now lost its relevance for both of them—homeland and scenes of glory for the inglorious hero, house and bed for the involuntary betrayer of her husband. For both had been rooted equally deeply in their home ground. And the 'house' is not yet a separable, bourgeois entity, not an environment, such as it begins to become in Euripides, but is the primal realm of the person and therefore part 64 of his 'daimon'. It has been remarked often enough how closely Deianira's death resembles the death of Euripides' Alcestis (158 ff.); but in Euripides the strong links between the whole fate of an individual and the final situation are lacking, and his drama is by no means so confined to the house as the whole drama of Deianira: the night fears (29), the growing children whom the husband hardly glances at (31), the last arrangements (155), the 'housekeeping money' which the faithless man sends her (542) and so forth. In the *Alcestis* the house becomes a mass of touching detail built up around the figure of the queen; her farewell to the household objects is more touching even than her farewell to her husband. And yet her husband is there, near at hand, so that we are almost amazed that so much attention is paid to the objects of the household rather than to him.[19]

The first part of the play ends gnomically, with the same reference to human frailty and mortality as at the beginning (943):

Nurse
           If anyone
counts upon one day ahead or even more,
he does not think. For there can be no tomorrow
until we have safely passed the day that is with us still.

That the finale is an intensified variation on the first part and its tragedy, is made completely clear by the retrospective *gnomai* at the very end of the play (1276 ff.):

Chorus
    You have seen a terrible death
and agonies, many and strange, and there is
nothing here which is not Zeus.

But at the same time, if we observe their scenic form, the contrast between the downfalls of the two characters is strongly emphasized: the silent fading away of Deianira is followed by the storming and violent struggle of Heracles, an extremely willing departure is followed by one that is extremely unwilling: unlike Deianira, who hides herself from everyone's view, the dying Heracles calls all his relations to crowd around him (1147). . . . His call has no effect: none are there. It remains without result for the 'action' but it is necessary for the sake of the contrast between the two characters. So what is 'inside' (943) in the case of Deianira is contrasted with the invasion of the 'outside' in the case of Heracles: thus fear and anxiety are contrasted with placing oneself in danger, faithful watchfulness with wild adventuring, loving care and protection with all-destroying desire, 'home' with roaming abroad.

The finale, the tragedy of Heracles, takes up only a single *epeisodion*, but it is an extended one, with a double development: one development from the sleep of the suffering hero to a state of madness in which he is oblivious of himself, and another from misunderstanding to recognition of the truth about himself. With soft steps, accompanied by song, the attendants enter with the litter. We do not know whether the man lying on it is asleep or dead (969; cf. 806). The awakening follows in non-iambic dialogue; in the alternation of the voices, lamentation is contrasted with the command to be silent, and fear with outbursts of rage. This is followed, in a dialogue in iambic metre, by the reversal from error to truth. In the interpretation of the much later *Philoctetes*, we shall show to what a limited extent, in the *Trachiniae*, even suffering and madness are communicated to others or penetrate to them; instead it is engrossed in itself, remaining locked up in the same, fateful, 'monologue-type' reserve, like all *pathos* in this drama. Similarly it will only become clear when we examine the *Philoctetes* how far this early play is from being 'dramatic' in the sense that the later one is; here conflict and contrast such as that between reserve and outburst do not actually become part of the interplay of dramatic action.

But to prevent a misunderstanding, we should perhaps say something at this point about the kind of interpretation to which this scene has been subjected in the secondary literature and for which it has become notorious among scholars. For although there could be no doubt that the outward features of the treatment of the lines and the dialogue placed the *Trachiniae* in the early period, scholars still believed they were dealing here with the older poet following in the steps of his younger rival: his 'sleep scene' was to be regarded as an imitation of the 'sleep scene' in Euripides' *Heracles*. And indeed, if no attention is paid to the nature of the two scenes, their content can be taken to be the same—sleep can be paralleled by sleep, rage by rage, and awakening by awakening—and the 'sleep scene' in the *Heracles* will indeed seem to be repeated in the *Trachiniae*. However, if one examines the significance and the context, the scene in Euripides' drama will be found to express the cracking-up of a man under the strain of man's inhumanity, either as embodied in his circumstances or in his own person in the form of the 'irrational', or whatever name you like to give it, which is effective within the person but sent by the 'gods', i.e. by blind forces; whereas Sophocles' scene shows the outburst of a heroism untamed and beyond man's measure. In the *Heracles* the awakening signifies a transition from intoxication and madness to a deathly sobriety (and that is why in Euripides the awakening no longer takes place in the course of the melic dialogue); in the *Trachiniae* the awakening signifies the surging development of the hero's misunderstanding of the truth about himself and his transgression of the bounds of moderation. And just as in the first case the sobering down is uniquely Euripidean, comparable with the sobering down after intoxication and madness in the *Bacchae*, so here the surging development is exclusively Sophoclean, comparable to the scenes of growing and developing in the *Antigone* or the *Oedipus Tyrannus*. Awakening, sleep and madness, used together as a progression of events by two different poets, have little more in common than any other common motif, cunning, revenge, death. . . . There are many such cases where it is impossible to decide which is the model and which is the copy simply by applying the scholars' favourite argument of a contradictory element which is not self-explanatory or does not fit. To say that in Sophocles this course of events is un-Sophoclean, inorganic, and therefore derived from a model, as some scholars have tried to show,[20] is to come close to the methods of Homeric criticism. In the search for guidelines to establish which are models and which copies, such concepts as 'reinterpretation', 'intensification', 'cutting up', 'shaping material to a climax', 'abridgment', 'tautening' and so forth will take us further than the employment of the notion of deliberate misjudgment, because the former are at least concepts which do not start by regarding a piece of poetry as something which is not poetry. It can scarcely escape anyone's notice that in this matter Euripides makes far more of the corresponding situation, that it is seasoned to his taste, intensified and brought to a peak in his own manner. But if we look at it from the other direction, it is hardly possible to take the corresponding situation in Sophocles as a tautening and pulling-together of Euripides' scene: there is nothing in Sophocles comparable with the whole play of opposites which we find in Euripides' drama of discord, his opposition of hallucination and reality, love and murder and all the other elements that play their part in it. In the *Trachiniae* sleep and awakening, as the opposites of rest and torment, serve merely as a transition and as the menacing foretaste of what is to come, and have no significance in the scene; they take place during non-iambic dialogue and are quite uninvolved, straightforward, and meaningful only as a prelude to the beginning of the finale. It may be that Euripides, seeing the situation in Sophocles through his own eyes, developed it in his own spirit. The reverse is scarcely possible.[21]

So the 'daimon' overpowers Heracles, the male character contrasted with the feminine Deianira. Just as Ajax lost himself and his senses when he lost his glory, so Heracles in his torment is beside himself, but with this difference, that the former took leave of life, while the latter breaks out into Herculean ravings. The root of the life of which he is being deprived is not heroic fame but the unruly and nobly vital exuberance of his nature (1105 f.):

Heracles

I
who am called the son of the most noble mother,
I who claim to be begotten of Zeus in the heavens.

Like Ajax in his madness, Heracles in his pain fails to recognize the power which has brought it upon him, seeing only 'blind disaster' (τυφλὴ ἄτη, 1104), since he is only able to measure the present by the standards of what his life up until that day had appeared to tell him made sense (1058 ff.):

Heracles
Neither the spear of battle, nor the army of
the earth-born Giants, nor the violence of beasts,
nor Greece, nor any place of barbarous tongue, not all
the lands I came to purify could ever do this.
A woman, a female, in no way like a man,
she alone without even a sword has brought me down.

And just as his environment consists of his deeds, which are incompatible with these sufferings, his narrower self is his body and his limbs; just as Ajax calls upon light, homeland and the plains of Troy, and Oedipus calls upon Cithaeron and upon his father and

mother, in other words upon his origins, and Deianira calls upon
her bed, and each calls upon the place from which he has been
uprooted—so Heracles calls upon the equivalents in his own life
(1089 ff.):

Heracles
                    O my hands, my hands,
O my back, my chest, O my poor arms, see
what has become of you from what you once were.
The lion that prowled the land of Nemea, that scourge of herdsmen,
that unapproachable, intractable creature,
with your strength once you overpowered it,
and the serpent of Lerna . . .

He calls once more upon his whole career as a conqueror, his
whole life—this one, truly Herculean passage embraces practically
all the twelve labours, and becomes thoroughly Herculean even in
its manner. And just as he twists in torment and cannot keep his
body still, so his thoughts twist and turn between the enemy who
has done this to him, and his own situation; his failure to understand
his own fate increases to a terrible misunderstanding of his innocent
wife; he calls to Hyllus (1066 ff.):

Heracles
Bring her from the house with your own hands and put
her in my hands, that woman who bore you, that I may know
clearly whether it pains you more to see *my* body
mutilated or *hers* when it is justly tortured.
Come my child, dare to do this. Pity me,
for I seem pitiful to many others, crying
and sobbing like a girl, and no one could ever say
that he had seen this man act like that before.[22]

He wishes to meet and conquer the poor woman just as if she
were his last enemy and the worst monster in his fabulous world
(1107 ff.):

Heracles
But I tell you this, even if I am nothing,
nothing that can even crawl, even so—
only let her come who has done this to me—

69

these hands will teach her, and she can tell the world: alive
I punished the evil, and I punish them in death.

When he hears how she has died by her own hand this is the cry that
he utters (1133):

Ah! She's dead too soon. She should have died by mine.

Regrets have been expressed that Deianira's quiet demise loses its
effect because of this passage of horror at the end.[23] How nice it
would be to have a Heracles who suffered but did not behave so
badly! But it is not so much the characters as the opposition of
surroundings and environment which creates this behaviour
which, it is clear, is almost intolerable in classical terms. His nature,
and its relation to what happens to him, means that Heracles can
hardly do otherwise than act as wrongly as he does. This hair-
raising end, as a possibility, is not a product of the emotional
rhetoric characteristic of Seneca,[24] but is rooted in the character's
tragic make-up, of which the centre is to be found in such an
extreme position that it is incompatible not only with those of the
other tragic characters involved but even with the structure of
events, 'divine will' itself.

The tragedy of Heracles remains a fate apart to such an extent that
even when it changes course it does not turn back or look back, that
even when the hero realizes what has happened he feels no remorse
for his loving wife. His failure to understand himself increases,
mocking every attempt at contradiction—until the name 'Nessus' is
heard. That name sounds like a prophetic omen in the ear of the
demented hero, and his raging against his external enemy suddenly
collapses. From now on there is no room for anything other than
the thought of his death and his last wish.

In the conflict of Hyllus, who is on his mother's side yet wishes to
be his father's son, the two spheres, the mother's and the father's,
clash once more, but the image of his dead mother is not evoked
again. Hyllus' resistance, the last piece of dramatic tension, is part of
the passing of the conqueror, just as the farewell to Eurysaces is part
of the passing of Ajax; the last thought of each concerns the heir of
his blood. When his son resists, his resistance serves only to heighten the greatness of this last act of conquest, in tragic acceptance

which springs from knowledge of his fate. (In the saga Heracles begs Poias to light his funeral pyre, whereas in the drama, although Hyllus must be prepared to bring his father's body to Oeta at his request and to pile up the pyre, he refuses out of awe to set light to it himself: that, too, is not so much drama as dramatization). Hyllus is not of any importance as a character in his own right, but only serves to give voice to the resistance which the conqueror finally overcomes not externally but in his own nature: 'and make an end of this unwanted, welcome task' (1262–3).

Thus this last *epeisodion* is the only one in the whole drama which swings around in the middle, and by its reversal from blindness to sudden illumination seems to equal those later reversal scenes in which Creon or Oedipus plunge from the heights of folly to the abyss. But what a difference in the way that those victims of delusion hurtle down! In the *Trachiniae* error and recognition alternate as two stationary emotional states. The fateful name of Nessus rings out like a cue, at which one note gives way to the other. And Hyllus, far from having the force of a Tiresias, or even of a Haemon, is so weak an opposing force that he himself has no idea of the significance of the omen that he utters; the omen only, so to speak, makes use of him as its agent, as though anyone would have served its purpose. It is true that anger now gives way to contemplation, but the sign itself does not yet have any dramatic presence, let alone any speech of its own. To transform it into a dramatic motif, a narrated anecdote has to be inserted and attached to the cue, and, moreover—significantly in view of the monologue character of the scene—it takes the form of an emotional account placed in the mouth of the victim. The intervention of the daimon does not develop as a drama, or obey the special laws of drama; one feature is singled out from the narrative and made to carry dramatic momentum, while the rest remains undeveloped. The story-telling style can still be seen beneath the dramatized form. Herodotus iii 64 may serve as an example:

> Then Cambyses asked what the city was called. And they replied: 'Ecbatana'. Now it had previously been prophesied to him in the city of Buto that he would die in Ecbatana. But he had believed that he would end his days in Ecbatana of the Medes at a great age and in possession of all his treasures. The oracle, however, had meant the

Syrian city of the same name. When he now asked and was told the name of the city—as he was already shaken by the disaster which had come upon him because of the Magus, and by his wounds—he perceived the truth, understood the oracle and said: 'Here Cambyses, son of Xerxes, is fated to die' . . .

A similar narrative could be made out of Heracles' end in the *Trachiniae*—indeed, Sophocles has actually narrated it and put it into the mouth of his hero: 'Listen then: . . . my father gave me an oracle which promised relief from my labours, and I had believed I would have better fortune, but in truth it meant my death.' (Herodotus iii 64: ὁ μὲν δὴ . . . ἐδόκεε . . ., τὸ δὲ χρηστήριον ἔλεγε ἄρα . . .; cf. Soph. *Trach*. 1171 f.: κἀδόκουν . . ., τὸ δ' ἦν ἄρ' οὐδὲν ἄλλο πλὴν θανεῖν ἐμέ.) For the sake of the error and the recognition of the truth Sophocles needed an oracle which showed how man's imaginings conflict with divine will. Hence the 'relief', misunderstood as a life 'without trouble'.[25] The ethos of this second oracle, which is added to the older oracle taken from the saga, is less in the spirit of the story of Heracles than in the style of later anecdotes, such as those about Croesus, Cleobis and Biton etc.[26]

Thus the *Trachiniae* is dependent on the art of the story-teller in the same way as the *Ajax* is dependent on the epic. In the *Antigone* Creon's change of mind can no longer be narrated as that of Cambyses or Heracles had been: 'then the seer came, and Creon began to be afraid . . .'. Afraid of what? we would ask. And to answer that question we would have to present a whole drama. This is the first time that the intervention of the daimon is made visible in word and deed, the first time that rapid action taking place in the present occupies the stage, and there is no further need for the aid of narrative.

Sophocles, balancing the death of Heracles against that of Deianira, has made it into a tragedy of knowledge in the sense of the Delphic maxim 'Know thyself', and in so doing he has departed from the sense of the saga. For according to the saga Heracles' self-immolation was only the means of his departure, and his last torment and victory were the beginning of his elevation to the gods. It is striking how much more powerfully this sense is reaffirmed by a chorus in the *Philoctetes* than here at the end of the *Trachiniae*, where no divine splendour falls on the sufferer to redeem and transfigure him.[27] The *Trachiniae* ends in gloom, as it began. The deification remains outside the play, at an unspecified distance, and has no connection with the human fate represented within it. The 'relief from labours' which is promised is not Olympus, but death. The meaning of the saga is almost reversed. Since little was said in the saga about the raging of the hero and his subsequent transgression of human limits, his death by fire in the saga scarcely signifies change to a state of acceptance of what at first appeared as utterly alien, senseless and intolerable. Here the form of fate by which the tragedian was obsessed in his early period has triumphed over the saga.

III

ANTIGONE

73 As we have seen, Sophoclean tragedy has its starting-point in the positioning of the vital centres of its main characters and in their remoteness from the centre of the divine or—what comes to the same thing—the daimonic forces that surround them. Hence this tragic discrepancy can develop into drama either by a single, violent downfall and destructive isolation—as in the *Ajax* and the *Oedipus Tyrannus*; or the centres of two human beings, both equally remote, may move around the same invisible central point, each equally thrown off balance and off course. The unity of action is then no longer to be seen in the isolation of one figure, but in the relation of each to the other and the relation of both to the centre of the daimonic ambience, which remains invisible, and can only be guessed at and hinted at. This second type is the basic form of those tragedies which may be grouped under the general heading of tragedies dealing with a double fate, of which the *Antigone*, as well as the *Trachiniae*, is an example.

On the other hand, the usual concepts and categories, with which there has been such a struggle since the time of Hegel to penetrate to the true nature of the *Antigone*—the victorious and the defeated cause, plot and counterplot, right against right, idea against idea, family against the state, tragic guilt and atonement, freedom of the individual and fate, individual and society (state, *polis*)—all these are borrowed from the aesthetics of the late eighteenth or early nineteenth century, and they are either so general that they are just as applicable to German drama—which means that they are too vague; or they seem to fit the *Antigone* but then do not fit any other of the surviving tragedies of Sophocles—which means that they are too precise. It is no good thinking up a formula for the *Antigone* which breaks down when applied to the other plays.[1]

Now it is true that the difference between the *Trachiniae* and the
74 *Antigone* as tragedies of double downfalls is that in the former play

the contrast between the two human centres remains restricted to the sphere of what is vitally heroic: home and abroad, house and adventure, feminine and masculine . . . whereas in the *Antigone* the contrasts are so extended and deepened that now on the one side we have what is to our way of thinking a very diverse collection—family, cult, love for one's brother, divine command, youthfulness and unselfishness to the point of self-sacrifice; and on the other side imperiousness, the maxims of the state, the morality of the *polis*, pettiness, rigidity, narrowness of heart, the blindness of age, insistence on the letter of the law to the point of breaking a divine commandment. In the face of such a variety of themes it is understandable that it has been thought that what appears to us diverse should perhaps be traced back to some unity, some single idea, in fact to a clash of ideas—traced back to a conflict of two principles each justified in itself, as if Sophocles were a dramatist like Schiller, Kleist or Goethe.[2] And yet the opposing sides in this drama, personified in Antigone and Creon, have no conflict within themselves; one side is not in itself attacked by the other, nor does one side convert the nature, law, idea of morals of the other to its own —as Goethe's Tasso, Kleist's Prinz von Homburg and Schiller's Wallenstein do. Antigone is not a sacrifice which Creon has to force himself to make for reasons of state, nor does Antigone have to fight against her own nature and innate tendency to obedience to make her self-sacrifice. Still less does Creon come to perceive that in the case of Antigone he had disregarded a law which was alien to him and directed against him. Thus his final downfall comes about not because the tangled events were just (in human terms), or because it is necessary to atone for the blood spilt by him, but because his own blindness as he loses all sense of moderation drives him into *hybris*. Nor is the theme of the *Antigone* a conflict of norms, but the tragedy of two human downfalls, separate in nature, daimonically linked, following one another as contrasting patterns.[3]

And yet there was some justification for the satisfaction which the Hegelian thirst for dialectic discovered in this play. Instead of the human ways or centres of existence separating from each other, suffering because of each other, without suspecting that they are sending themselves to destruction, remaining alien and unaware of each other, like Ajax and Tecmessa, Heracles and Deianira—instead of this, in the *Antigone*, and in the *Antigone* alone, a conflict develops, one nature is opposed to another, the pros and cons are presented, and at the same time the opposing spheres are more extensive, more real, more far-reaching (downwards as well as upwards), and their conflict touches on the difference between mortal and immortal commandments, the laws of a particular state and eternal laws. Thus this conflict too emerges finally as a kind of 'dialectic' in spite of everything; but that is not something to be assumed in advance, but rather something which follows from the special nature and position of the two centres.

Now we must forget for a moment our threadbare contemporary theatre if we are to realize what a new phenomenon in the Attic theatre this conflict is: no longer an *agon* like the stationary debate in the *Ajax*, but an advancing, continually shifting, changing collision, driving towards an obscure goal; no longer is it a matter of attitude set against attitude or fate against fate, but will set against will, strength against opposition, deed against deed. Compared with both the *Ajax* and the *Trachiniae*, the *Antigone*, taken together with the *Oedipus Tyrannus* and the plays which follow, belongs to a new phase as regards its scenic form. From now on one can take any scene from any play and compare it with any scene from the two earlier plays or indeed any earlier play, and see a changed aspect, discover a changed structure; now for the first time the drama of the older style has become a play in the sense familiar to us. Now for the first time there arises out of a drama of contrasts a drama of *developments* which takes control not only of the whole but also of each single feature, not only of the greater series of scenes but also of the lesser transitions from one reply to another. Developments: that means that there is now not only what there has been since Aeschylus —a movement up and down and to and fro, hope and anxiety, announcement and appearance of what is feared, hesitation and final decision—but a gliding advance from one position to another, with continuous change of the dramatic constellation, from act to act, scene to scene and from the beginning of each scene to its end.

76   The *Oedipus Tyrannus* is thoroughly permeated by the new form right down to its smallest detail, but the *Antigone* is already strongly in its grip. For what is to become a mere recipe for scene structure in modern drama is here still the outpouring of a religious and poetic passion. The new dramatic style arises because the daimonic ambi-

ence begins to treat the self-absorption of human nature with irony.
What moves, what creates the reversals, what drives the centres
around each other, is not the poet's assured command of his theatrical technique, nor the dramatic deployment of the inner conflict of a
mind suffering as a result of internal or external causes, but the
experience of that sport by means of which the gods love to show
up the human as human and to change human intention and purpose into fate and destiny.[4]

Even the beginning of the prologue is governed by an action of
reversal. It opens with a harmony than which nothing could be
more heartfelt:

Antigone
My sister, my Ismene . . .*

The news of the new ruler's prohibition is clothed in the form of a
question full of expectation, imbued with the emotions of Antigone, who has tremendous hopes of support and is ready for
anything: 'Have you yet heard? . . .' But because of this hope of
unity, discord arises all the more violently, the separation of two
entire types of existence follows all the more abruptly: the way of
Ismene who clings faithfully to the familiar, and the way of Antigone who sacrifices herself for an extreme, ultimate purpose. What
the one calls madness, the other calls sanity (47 ff.):

Ismene
O hard of mind! When Creon spoke against it!
Antigone
It's not for him to keep me from my own.

Antigone's contact with an alien nature, as soon as it is recognized
as such, is enough to transform her warmth to coldness, her pleading to aversion. The more gently her sister's loving incomprehension speaks to her in the familiar second person, the more abruptly
her insistent ego sees itself repulsed. And the game of reversal is all
the more fascinating for being played between such young girls (69
ff.):

*[Reinhardt here cites Hölderlin's translation: 'Gemeinsamschwester-
liches, o Ismenes Haupt! . . .']

Antigone
>   I wouldn't urge it. And if now you wished
>   to act, you wouldn't please me as a partner.
>   Be what you want to; but that man shall I
>   bury. For me, the doer, death is best.
>   Friend shall I lie with him, yes friend with friend,
>   when I have dared the crime of piety.
>   Longer the time in which to please the dead
>   than that for those up here.

The only effect of her sister's objections is steadily to intensify her aversion, until it culminates in a cry of woe (82 ff.):

Ismene
>   Oh my poor sister. How I fear for you!

Antigone
>   For me, don't borrow trouble. Clear your fate.

Ismene
>   At least give no one warning of this act;
>   you keep it hidden and I'll do the same.

Antigone
>   Dear God! Denounce me. I shall hate you more
>   if silent, not proclaiming this to all.

In the end the reversal has put Ismene in the place of Antigone as the unsuccessful pleader. . . . And yet her closing words, after the rupture, have the sound of a gentle harmony (98 f.):

Ismene
>   Go, since you want to. But know this: you go
>   senseless indeed, but loved by those who love you.

But the sport of the gods does not become perceptibly the content of the new form of scene until the entrance of Creon. When the new occupant of the throne comes before the leaders of the community, the phrases and maxims with which he introduces himself are neither resounding platitudes nor the exposition of a moral or political principle. Creon is neither merely an example of the swollen *hybris* of a tyrant,[5] nor a representative of the claims of state, nor

78

of the idea of the *polis* in opposition to the individual and the family. No principle, no moral or idea is speaking through his mouth; he is a human being confined within his own orbit, and subject to his own limitations to the point of blindness.[6] But the circle in which he moves, although it is illuminated by no higher principle, is not merely empty illusion from the beginning either: it is well-known to us as a political reality from the history of the sixth and fifth centuries. In Creon's world, Polynices' campaign of vengeance no longer has the significance of the old feud between brothers that it had in the epic,[7] but is the enterprise of a hostile party of political exiles. And as usual in such cases, here too there are apparently secret alliances between the enemy of the country and a discontented underground faction within the city. But now, after a successful defence, it is a question of attacking those citizens who had been the undercover supporters of the vanquished enemy; and his aim is, if not to annihilate them, at least to keep them in a state of such fear that there will be no future attempt at an uprising.

Creon begins with his own situation, but in such a way that one has to draw one's own conclusion from every word. His declaration contains a veiled threat: 'It is impossible to know a person's soul, temper and intention until he has made it manifest in law and office.' Even if this is primarily intended to be applied to himself, all the same the leaders of the community who face him are in the same position: I am this—and what are you? And step by step, as his suspicion develops, so too Creon himself develops. Hidden at first behind the gestures and words of a leader, his aim, his nature, his identity are gradually revealed. For he is one of those who are not what they make themselves out to be, and this can be seen by the way in which he speaks, and from the situation in which he speaks.[8] Out of the first enigmatic, general phrases, 'best decisions' (ἀρίστων βουλευμάτων), there suddenly emerges the specific threat of a politician who has diagnosed the situation with which he finds himself confronted. Beneath the noble, statesman-like words we can hear as it were the undertone: 'Don't think that I don't know you!' As the feeling of superiority which he entertains from the beginning becomes threatened by insecurity, he tries to assert it at any price.

What he now fears, soon regards as proven and seeks to attack, is two-fold: undercover resistance, and the secret or open support of the party which has been defeated at the gates (184 ff.):

Creon
So I—may Zeus all-seeing always know it—
could not keep silent as disaster crept
upon the town, destroying hope of safety.
Nor could I count the enemy of the land
friend to myself, not I who know so well
that she it is who saves us, sailing straight,
and only so can we have friends at all.

When the command to honour one of the fallen brothers and dishonour the other is put into this context, it no longer means the same as it had done in the epic; it now becomes a touchstone of political allegiance. The treatment of the dead is to be the gauge and yardstick for the 'punishments' and 'rewards' which the survivors are to expect from their ruler (207 ff.):

Creon
Such is my mind. Never shall I, myself,
honour the wicked and reject the just.
The man who is well-minded to the state
from me in death and life shall have his honour.

Just as misfortune (ἄτη) and the welfare of the city (σωτηρία) are contrasted here, a distinction is also to be made between 'friend' and 'foe', between different political standpoints, and between 'good' and 'evil', and no liaison or allegiance (no κτᾶσθαι τοὺς φίλους) should dare to bridge this chasm. The order to dishonour the dead is no longer an expression of blind revenge but has now become a means of uncovering the obviously concealed attitude of the nobility of the community. What effect will it have? After the solemn proclamation with its sanctions the ruler continues watchfully, almost as if he were lying in wait—watching all the more closely the more openly he is answered (215 ff.):

80   *Creon*
Now you be sentinels of the decree.
Chorus
Order some younger man to take this on.

Creon
Already there are watchers of the corpse.

Chorus
What other order would you give us, then?

Creon
Not to take sides with any who disobey.

Chorus
No fool is fool as far as loving death.

Creon
Death is the price. But often we have known
men to be ruined by the hope of *profit*.

So this 'profit', the motive so often decried in feuds and party struggles, the means of corruption employed in revolutions and coups, is what the new ruler and *strategos* who has only just assumed power, imagines is at work against him. His last phrase betrays the aim of his whole speech. But at this point he is interrupted.

The game which the gods play with man the more he takes refuge in his own cleverness begins straight away with the arrival at this very moment of the fateful news, begins indeed with the appearance of the secret opposition in the foolish figure of the cringing watchman, miserably squirming. With him there enters a whole area of humanity which undermines high office by its mere existence. This is how the mighty man looks, suddenly seen from below!—seen by a creature who shrieks and shakes, is chosen by lot, dilly-dallies, and comforts himself tragically with 'fate'. . . But just as all this depends on the mighty man's nod, the mighty man himself feels dependent on it and does not know in what way. . . The sport of the gods is continued in his first, bewildered question, in which the two worlds which are soon to come into collision are already beginning to separate (248):

Creon
What are you saying? What man has dared to do it?

It continues in the description of the discovery, which has something about it of a riddle, of a miracle (249 ff.):

81   *Guard*
      I wouldn't know. There were no marks of picks,
      no grubbed-out earth. The ground was dry and hard,
      no trace of wheels. The doer left no sign . . .

What is to be reported is no longer something in the past which
has now been caught up with and is now tacked on like the reports
in the *Trachiniae*, but something which thrusts its way in, creates a
situation and is itself charged with the quality of a situation.
Although it takes the form of a report, there is not a single word
without significance for the present, without a meaning which adds
to the tension arising from the clash of forces.

The gods have their sport, and man, who is always made in such a
way that he fits divine nature as a hollow mould is filled by its
content—man, in the belief that he can penetrate the mystery before
him, rushes still further into blindness; now his suspicions begin to
speed ahead with a full wind, sails swollen by everything he hears
(278 ff.):

Chorus
      Lord, while he spoke, my mind kept on debating.
      Isn't this action possibly a god's?
Creon
      Stop now, before you fill me up with rage,
      or you'll prove yourself insane as well as old.
      Unbearable, your saying that the gods
      take any kindly forethought for this corpse.
      Would it be they had hidden him away,
      honouring his good service, his who came
      to burn their pillared temples and their wealth,
      even their land, and break apart their laws?
      Or have you seen them honour wicked men?
      It isn't so.
      No, from the first there were some men in town
      who took the edict hard, and growled against me,
      who hid the fact that they were rearing back,
      not rightly in the yoke, no way my friends.
      These are the people—oh it's clear to me—
      who have bribed these men and brought about the deed.

82   The game intensifies: a new, more forceful oath. . . The talk of

'profit' as the chief danger to the city, that masterpiece of political rhetoric, thrusts its way with its threats into a vacuum; the further it reaches out and the more moral its tone becomes, with its inflated appeals to law and state as though it were a question of the preservation or destruction of the *polis*, the less it corresponds with reality. And again, the further it thrusts its way into a vacuum, the more forcefully the oath with which the ruler concludes rings out, as if his overstrained voice were beginning to break. . . . Here the gnomic style, in its failure to correspond with the reality to which it is applied, itself creates a dramatic situation. The chorus, to whom the speech is addressed, makes no reply. Instead, interrupting and spoiling the effect of the ruler's powerful peroration, to his great annoyance, there comes the voice of the cringing agent: 'And what will become of me? . . .' The dignity of the scene can only just be saved by a further brief threat and a rapid exit. The cringing guard, suddenly finding that he is no longer under fire, makes off while the going is good. His exit is the ironic reply to Creon's.

Although what thwarts Creon, what crosses his will, is the deed of a human being, the *manner* in which it crosses his will and plays with him does not belong to the deed in its human aspect—for the woman who performed the deed was thinking of very different matters—but is a part of the divine setting which acts on human beings through the deed. To confuse human cleverness still further, to enmesh the mighty man more tightly in the game, the sense of the human situation is actually violated, and the burial, instead of being performed once, which would have sufficed to satisfy tradition, has to be performed twice. For it is only by the repetition of the deed that the attitude of the man of power is mocked and his limitations revealed.[10] And when the chorus fears that what has happened could have been brought about by the gods, they are wrong in so far as they believe in a miracle, but in essence what they say is only too true. Admittedly the sport of the 'gods' with men had been shown and exemplified in the *Ajax*, but there it had not as yet given rise to a drama with human content. It is not until the *Antigone* that the irony of the divine begins to permeate the action on the stage.

The next *epeisodion* is divided from the one that precedes it by a chorus in praise of man's glory which, however, contains allusions to the earlier scene; the new *epeisodion* again stands in the relation-

ship of a complete reversal to what has been revealed so far. Just as
the rapid return of the messenger is a repetition of his first entrance,
but with its tone reversed, the inquiry which follows is very much
the reverse of the ruler's unhappy pronouncement about 'profit'. In
the agent himself there is shown—concealed, but all the more
noticeable for that—the hand of the elusive opposition. And the
beginning of his speech is gnomic and explanatory in a way
reserved previously for the most serious matters: it takes the same
form as Tecmessa's and Deianira's opening words, but now (388
ff.):

Guard
   Lord, one should never swear off anything.
   Afterthought makes the first resolve a liar.
   I could have vowed I wouldn't come back here
   after your threats, after the storm I faced.
   But joy that comes beyond the wildest hope
   is bigger than all other pleasure known.
   I'm here, though I swore not to be . . .

(The agent now feels as proud and happy as he had previously
stood bowed and outcast. And—this is perhaps even more
ironic—Sophocles places the most wonderful words of praise in his
lowly mouth.)[11] For again the deed is a sign. But whereas previously
the person who had done it had left no trace, there now appears
from out of the commotion of all the spaces of the divine universe,
from the dust flung up by the midday whirlwind, the girl, lamenting—that is how in Sophocles divine power can be revealed! (421
ff.):

Guard
   . . . We shut our eyes,
   sat and endured the plague the gods had sent.
   So the storm left us after a long time.
   We saw the girl. She cried the sharp and shrill
   cry of a bitter bird which sees the nest
   bare where the young birds lay.

Next the interrogation shifts to the silent captive. But here too
matters turn out contrary to expectations. Power had been expect-

ing to meet with resistance here; instead a voluntary sacrifice presents itself. She denies neither the deed nor the knowledge that it was forbidden. Instead, in her actual confession there is the beginning of a kind of resistance on a different level, coming from a now unattainable region. The divine sphere which mysteriously frames the human world in each of Sophocles' tragedies is here for the first and last time acknowledged in the dialogue, by a human speaker, to be incomparably superior to the human sphere (450 ff.):

Antigone
For me it was not Zeus who made that order.
Nor did that Justice who lives with the gods below
mark out such laws to hold among mankind.
Nor did I think your orders were so strong
that you, a mortal man, could over-run
the gods' unwritten and unfailing laws.
Not now, nor yesterday's, they always live,
and no one knows their origin in time.

Separated from its context, that might almost be a theological pronouncement—if it were not spoken by the girl, who loses nothing of her own nature even when the poet speaks through her mouth. By comparison, it is remarkable how little of the theological element in the *Ajax* stemmed from the true nature of Athena. And this is so very much Antigone's own tone of voice! It is not a case of a god possessing her, nor of another voice speaking through her. How easy it would have been for another poet to reach for the types of ecstasy which lay ready to hand in this situation! But Sophocles seems opposed to everything of that kind. In contrast with Aeschylus and Euripides, his plays keep away from any kind of divine possession.[12] His seers have knowledge, it is true, but are not possessed by ecstatic 'enthusiasm'. Unlike the other two dramatists, Sophocles did not write about the forms of interpenetration of man and god, supernatural visions and 'divine madness', Bacchae and Cassandras. It is only the second Oedipus play that is, to some extent, an exception, but it would be a misapprehension of the unique significance of this last work, written as death was drawing near, if we expected to find in the earlier works the new rapprochement, finally achieved, of the divine and the human which we find in the *Oedipus at Colonus*.

Nor is Antigone, although like Cassandra she is sacrificed in the service of the gods, possessed by the god as a driving force within her. What permeates her is indeed some kind of knowledge; this knowledge of hers tells her that just as human society has its own justice which punishes offenders, so do the gods have theirs—she leaves it vague where and when; if she were to be more precise she would be transferring the terms of this world to the world beyond.[13] But this is very far from making her into a martyr or a saint. Guarantee and surety for that other order does not come to her from above; her knowledge is not from heaven, nor does it emerge from subterranean, mysterious depths; it rises from her own ties of blood and her own nature. What does injury to the divine is identical with what inflicts torment upon the nature of man (465 ff.):

Antigone
And so, for me to meet this fate, no grief.
But if I left that corpse, my mother's son,
dead and unburied I'd have cause to grieve . . .

Is she concealing a secret which has been revealed to her alone? There is nothing to indicate that. When she commends herself to the divine, the eternal totality, when she remains obedient both to Zeus in heaven and Dikē in the underworld, and fulfils the unwritten law—then what she does for her brother, or, as she puts it even more clearly, her 'mother's son', fits into that divine order, and what arises from her nature receives its universally valid significance. What she names together with Zeus and Dikē, heaven and earth, is the all-embracing, the whole, of which this deed of hers is a part. ('Zeus' and 'Dikē' are the two terms of a polar expression here.)[14] And the unwritten law here is none other than that of which the chorus in the *Oedipus Tyrannus* (865 ff.) sings the praises:

. . . in word and deed
prescribed by the laws that live on high:
laws begotten in the clear air of heaven,
whose only father is Olympus;
no mortal nature brought them to birth,
no forgetfulness shall lull them to sleep . . .

There is no indication that this law is valid only for blood relationship or only for the relationship between the living and the dead; it is enough that what her dead brother demands is also subject to the universal order. And this is again no more than what the nature which she shelters within her desires. And even when this demand finds itself in the position of a higher duty opposed to the mere will to live, it does not entail any command of 'Thou shalt' unless that command also comes from the voice of her own nature, knowing itself to be at one with her neighbour. Is that too simple for us? That is Greek religion.

But the clearer, the freer it all is, and the brighter the proclamation of divine truth, the more the circle of human power closes in. Whatever opposes it must be *hybris*, revolt, and anything which does not fit in appears as a cloak and extenuation for *hybris*. As if it were a question of defeating an equal opponent, the ruler surrounds himself with the images of his world—the overheated steel which becomes brittle, the horse which will not obey the bridle—without realizing how his own nature is being reflected. His own narrowness drives him on, the captive of his own oath, and subject to his own proclamation. For the sake of self-assertion Creon must humiliate the opposition, bring it down to his own level and attack it with the means at his disposal. This is not right against right, idea against idea, but the divine, the all-embracing with which the young girl knows she is in harmony, against the human, which appears as limited, blind, self-pursuing, self-deceiving and distorted.

The sudden demand for her accomplices, the ruler's command that Ismene (whom he had seen inside the house and believes to be in despair) should be brought out to him, also spring from the strong man's need for some resistance against which to direct his anger (493 f.):

Creon
The sly intent betrays itself sometimes
before the secret plotters work their wrong.

Thus the cut-and-thrust dispute (*stichomythia*) which follows is not a conflict of rights and principles either. Although the two characters use the same words when they speak and develop their pros and cons, the content of their speeches does not result in an antithetical relationship. Rather, the opposition is between two *realms*: word for word, and meaning for meaning, they *separate* from each other. Creon presents the concepts of his first speech again, but now he comes up against something that blunts his weapon. What he calls 'dishonour' is holy to his opponent; what he calles 'pious' is not so to her, and the same with 'friend' and 'foe' and 'good' and 'bad' (514 ff.)

Creon
Your act of grace, in his regard, is crime.
Antigone
The corpse below would never say it was.
Creon
When you honour him and the criminal just alike?
Antigone
It was a brother, not a slave, who died.
Creon
Died to destroy this land the other guarded.
Antigone
Death yearns for equal law for all the dead.
Creon
Not that the good and bad draw equal shares.
Antigone
Who knows that this is holiness below?[15]
Creon
Never the enemy, even in death, a friend.
Antigone
I cannot share in hatred, but in love.

88   It is only when we realize that the inner form of this conversation is a parting of the ways that we discover how it leads up to the last couplet. In the assonance of the last two lines (οὔτοι —οὔτοι) the two realms face each other in utter opposition for the first time; the division between them is brought to its sharpest form. For even the much-quoted saying about love and hate does not defend one ethical principle against another; its meaning is 'I was not born into the circle which believes "Hate your enemy", but into the one

where love between blood-relations knows itself to be in harmony with its like.'[16] Not that Antigone is the personification of love, but her hate and her love spring from a different level from that which produces Creon's friendships and enmities. Moreover, in Greek 'love' is the same word that in Creon's world stands for a band of men of like-minded political views; and what we translate as 'hate' is the same word as 'enemy'. Thus, though outwardly they echo each other, the contrast of the different meanings tears the two spheres all the more sharply asunder.

But at the end, when Ismene is brought forward, the ruler finds himself faced with something which he finds completely incomprehensible: instead of the breakdown which he expected, the two girls engage in a dispute which is the prologue in reverse, a dispute over precedence, a real girls' fight, before his very eyes, about the right to have done the deed and to be allowed to share the consequences. . . Creon, with his authoritarian mind, can only draw the conclusion (561 f.):

Creon
One of these girls has shown her lack of sense
just now. The other had it from her birth.

*   *   *

If one considers all the many contradictory attempts to characterize and categorize the figure of Antigone, to pin down its essence by psychological or metaphysical, sociological or ontological methods, one is forced to the conclusion that she does indeed present an enigma—an enigma which has baffled others besides Creon. But if there is one thing that helps to illuminate the darkness around her, it is the great scene containing the lyrical dialogue between Antigone and the chorus and then Antigone's speech, which stands in the middle of the tragedy, just as the monologue of Ajax stands in a central position in his play—Antigone's final lament in the face of death.

But here we see that the nature of the foundations beneath her actions of entering, deciding and departing, the supporting, deeper, more general basis which gives rise to her particular action, is something no less fundamental than the nature of Deianira, or Ajax, or Heracles; only in this case it is something more remote from our way of thinking: the cult of the dead and myth of the dead of the classical period. If we turn to Attic funerary *lekythoi* and grave reliefs with their scenes from girls' lives, we meet Antigone in person. In the plays of Aeschylus, on entering the realm of the dead, we come, as it were, into the presence of archaic statues of heroes. Here it is as if we were looking at a scene of farewell or lamentation in a work of art in the style of the middle of the fifth century. And just as in the pure forms by which death is depicted in this style, forms set free from magic and fear, we find that rite and nature and cult and kinship are interwoven, so too the all-embracing world with which Antigone's figure is linked partakes of the same sanctity and humanity both in this life and in the life beyond. It hardly matters whether one speaks of race, family, love, rite, religion, right, or ethical idea. None of them is wrong, yet all of them together are not enough. In the nobility of this cult they are all one, and deepest awe, the legacy of former times, is joined in them with the relaxation and freedom of the newly-awakened realization of the beauty of existence.

Perhaps we find it easier to imagine and to listen to the saints, blessed ones, martyrs and brides of God, who are in possession of heaven, and yet are defeated by the power of this world. For the images of Christianity are closer to us than the myth of the ancient world.[17] But Antigone has none the less a sphere of her own, even though it is not heaven which opens to her but the much more restricted fellowship of those from whom she comes and to whom she goes.[18]

What are celestial ecstasies, glories descending from heaven, deathbed visions, compared with this attitude to death? The images are melodious but simple: the shore of Acheron, Hades who puts all to sleep. . . The burial chamber as bridal chamber and Acheron as bridegroom are scarcely even metaphors: it all grows to such an extent out of the living popular tradition in which the world of death was depicted. It was an Attic custom to place wedding vessels on the graves of the unmarried dead.[19]

But death becomes dramatic—that is, it becomes not just the drama of a person dying, but of death itself, represented, it is true, by the case of one girl—only when life breaks in upon the inevitability of a fate she has already voluntarily accepted, and the two realms, life and death, struggle against each other. As in the German song where death the enemy suddenly turns into death the friend, death here finally changes from being the force that separates and tears a person abruptly from existence, and becomes something obscurely protective and welcoming.[20] Such comforting things as the Christian heaven provides are not, it is true, part of the welcome. But in the vacillation, hovering, to-and-froing between the two abandonments, that of life which is rejecting her, and that of death which awaits her, it is the latter which seems in the end the gentler. The dead do not exclude, they set no bounds to love.

It is in the lament, the *kommos*, that we first hear the mournful note that comes from a sense of having been abandoned. For even the rock-chamber grave in which Antigone is buried alive, which belongs to the traditional story, becomes an image of her halfway position, her rootless hovering. To have been abandoned by all—that means in the first place to be judged by everything to belong somewhere else, in life and death at the same time. In this Antigone resembles the dying Niobe, who turned to stone but still wept. . . But then the abandonment becomes a state of being nowhere, neither in life, in contact with the living, nor in death, among the dead (842 ff.):

Antigone
O city of wealthy men.
I call upon Dirce's spring,
I call upon Thebe's grove in the armoured plain,
to be my witnesses, how with no friend's mourning,
by what decree I go to the fresh-made prison-tomb.
Alive to the place of corpses, an alien still,
never at home with the living nor with the dead.

The hereditary curse of her family, too, here takes on the meaning of her rejection and abandonment (862 ff.):

Antigone
My mother's marriage-bed.
Destruction where she lay with her husband-son,
my father. These are my parents and I their child.
I go to stay with them. My curse is to die unwed.

The four short strophes of the chorus alternate with the lament: not echoing, not reinforcing, but standing out in contrast—a kind of frame, or like two banks on either side, between which the lament runs like a stream, or like groups of people standing on the bank and following with their eyes someone who is being snatched away by the current. That is how the chorus stands in safety and watches, participating, but outside. And among themselves, too, there is a contrast, between two voices, each taking up two strophes—warnings, each of which is no less right than the other, but both of which seem wrong in the face of the sacrifice. The approximate meaning of the first two is: what you are suffering is praiseworthy, unique, you are undefeated, you are master of your fate, as a mortal you resemble the gods. The sense of the next two: what you are suffering has to be, is according to the order and rightness of things, has been incurred by your family and by your-self: piety may be pious, but government is government; it will not tolerate transgression. . . And in between, after the first pair of strophes, the cry of the victim:

Antigone
    Laughter against me now. . .[21]*

92   But the more that life rejects, the more and more receptive death becomes, and thus there begins, after the more emotional tone of the *kommos*, the more composed utterance of Antigone's speech—also sombre in tone (891 ff.):

Antigone
    O tomb, O marriage-chamber, hollowed out
    house that will watch forever, where I go
    to my own people, who are mostly there;
    Persephone has taken them to her.
    Last of them all, ill-fated past the rest,
    shall I descend, before my course is run.
    Still when I get there I may hope to find
    I come as a dear friend to my dear father,
    to you, my mother, and my brother too.

[*Reinhardt here cites Hölderlin's translation: 'Weh, närrisch machen sie mich! . . .']

All three of you have known my hand in death.
I washed your bodies, dressed them for the grave,
poured out the last libation at the tomb . . .

But this last speech, too, still stands on the border between the
two conflicting realms: the nearer the loving welcome of the dead
and the higher the duty which she has carried out, the more bitter
and accusing becomes her final backward glance at the realm and
government of the living which is expelling her (916 ff.):[22]

Antigone
So now he takes and leads me out by force.
No marriage-bed, no marriage-song for me,
and since no wedding, so no child to rear . . .

To consider briefly the 'calculation' in Antigone's last speech
which so disappointed Goethe (*Conversations with Eckermann*, 28
March 1827): what surprises us about it is not the precedence which
she gives to her love for her brother over everything else. That a
brother counts as one's closest relative, not necessarily because of
any particular devotion or excess of sisterly friendship, has been a
matter of experience since the earliest times. That in comparison
with a brother even a husband, indeed even one's own child may
appear replaceable, a matter of chance, is a similar observation. But
if the preference which singles out the brother is not to be arbitrary,
it must be based on a *nomos*. If it were only psychological, only an
individual case, it would have no place in a Sophoclean tragedy. The
question of the *nomos* is important enough to be given a central
position in this most emotional speech. Antigone's urge to explain
her action can only be satisfied by referring the present example to
the general rule. Admittedly, in establishing this *nomos* Sophocles
follows a Herodotean anecdote.[23] But even in its changed context in
Sophocles, the 'calculation' is not as 'illogical' as commentators
have thought. For it is not this one particular action of Antigone,
but the *nomos* of her action that is based on the fact that husband and
child can be replaced, a brother not. The *nomos* remains, whether
brother or sister are alive or dead. And if we disregard Goethe's
psychological drama, if we transfer ourselves to the world of this
very different play of 'centres of existence'—if this expression may

be used for the sake of brevity; if we grant the validity of the human and general circumstances which make sense in the light of the *nomos*, then the 'calculation' yields to a proof which can hardly be disregarded any longer: just as Antigone follows divine law, and her own nature, so too she follows the *nomos* of love for her brother. For Sophocles the one embraces the other.

The dying Ajax called once more upon the light of day, the sun, his whole world; turning back for the last time to life, he entered into death. By contrast, Antigone stands facing the realm of death: as Ajax had called on the light and the landscape, she calls on the bridal chamber of Hades and the dead of her own blood; that is her realm. A generation later Sophocles depicts death again—not merely a person dying, but death as something which receives a man—as the end of his second Oedipus play. What death was to mean to him in the end—that is something to which we shall return later.

*   *   *

In between and after the sacrifice of consideration for the gods, which leads to disrespect, rebellion and 'madness' in the eyes of men, the rest of the tragedy shows the sacrifice of consideration for men, leading to disrespect, rebellion and madness in the eyes of the gods. But in order to link the first sacrifice with the second, which is its reverse, and to join both with a causal link, Sophocles here, as in the less developed *Trachiniae*, makes use of an intermediary figure, who without himself being of equal significance to either has a share in the fates of both. Haemon is linked with both Creon and Antigone, as Hyllus was with Heracles and Deianira. But as a character he is not necessary either for Antigone's fate in itself, nor for the ruler's fate in itself, for that too runs its own self-absorbed course. Although Haemon is betrothed to Antigone and is Creon's son, as a character he does not make Creon into a tragic father nor Antigone into a tragic lover. In the epic, the Sphinx demanded Haemon as Creon's 'most youthful, most handsome son' as a final and most cruel sacrifice. Of this Sophocles has left him the youthfulness—he is still Creon's 'youngest son' (627)—the handsomeness, and the early death, but has placed him in a new position between the fates of the two main characters. Just as it is only through him that Antigone's deed finds an echo in a youthful heart, devoted admiration and imitation, so it is only through him and his death that the ruler's deed rebounds onto the doer. We need only compare Haemon with Hyllus in order to see how much more pregnant with fate, how much more definite, how much richer in emotional appeal and how much closer to the other characters this supporting figure has become, in comparison with the colourless and inactive character of the typical son of the earlier play.

Two dialogue scenes, the first containing the defiance of the young man, through which at the same time the voice of the *city* makes itself heard, the second containing the defiance of the old man, Tiresias, through which at the same time the voice of the *gods* makes itself heard, hang like a pair of pendants, as it were, on either side of the laments sung by the victim as she is led to her death.

Creon's speech of admonition to his son is, in its weight and extent, a repetition of his official speech, but at a higher level, in a heightened version; just as in the former speech Creon the ruler struck the wrong note before his nobles, so now does Creon the father. And his speech again starts with an attempt to anticipate an imaginary danger: he speaks as if it were a question of warding off an evil which is threatening father and son alike. This is the speech of a man who has to feel himself in agreement, and tries to enforce agreement by a demand, a man half intimidating, half seeking a foothold, becoming more and more morally perverse—what he commands will be accomplished, but in a way very different from that which he has in mind—(653 f.):

Creon
    Oh spit her forth for ever, as your foe.
    Let the girl marry somebody in Hades.

Once again law and obedience and the well-being of the whole city, in war and peace, seem to depend on one thing: just as before they had depended on the prohibition proclaimed in a single announcement, so now they depend on the punishment which rests on a single decision. Once again the *stichomythia* which follows brings a reversal, when the appearance of harmony develops into such disharmony that two people are thrown off course. Two types of blindness confront one another, the noble blindness of youth and the corrupt blindness of age. Or rather two kinds of blindness on each side. Haemon's first blindness, his false idea of his own strength, is that he believes he has the power to teach this father of his a lesson; his second blindness is that he believes that his father's mistake is simply the result of not knowing something that he, the son, has discovered, and that he believes that he has to do no more than mention it. . . Without this blindness he would not go astray, fly into a passion and plunge to his death. In Creon's case also his first blindness is his false idea of his own strength, when he thinks himself equal to the *polis* and his judgment equal to *nomos*. But he believes this only so long as the idea exalts him; as soon as there is a danger that it may bring him down he reverses his position and pits himself and his strength alone against the whole city. Thus his argument goes round in circles and cancels itself out. Shaken out of state morality, which sounds well but is false when it comes from his mouth, he flings himself into *hybris*, rather like Xerxes in Herodotus, in that he too needed the large cloak to disguise his own pettiness from himself. It is unfortunate for those who see this as a drama of 'principles' that they have to take their *polis* principle from this speech where the speaker is so grievously deluded.[24]—Creon's second blindness leads him to suspicions of his son's sincerity, as if the latter were speaking under the spell of a Circe. Suspecting his motive, he tries to shuffle off a truth which he cannot allow to be a truth. Thus blindness fights against blindness; each misses the other with his thrusts. And yet Sophocles needed only to have let the lover, as well as the son and youth, speak—as Euripides did afterwards in his *Antigone*—and the two would have had common ground on which to fight. But then they would not each have been separated from the other's world and have escaped each other, to hurtle to their extremes.—Scenes of this kind had not been possible in the *Ajax* or in the *Trachiniae*, if only because of their language. It is not until this play that the conflict ends not simply because the contestants have had enough, but also because the end of the scene has become a literal separation, and this separation, instead of being merely the ending of the speeches, becomes their aim and consequence.

Whereas the argument with Haemon had developed into *hybris* in the sight of men, the argument with the seer Tiresias soon develops into *hybris* in the sight of the gods. It is again a question of 'teaching a lesson' to the unteachable; before, the lesson had come from the bold approach of the young man, now it comes from the painful advance of the blind old man, leaning on the boy who guides him. What was true of the form of the scene with Haemon is also true of this scene. As on the one side fear and respect are transformed into accusation and mockery, so on the other side benevolent encouragement is transformed into angry condemnation. Once more the second half of the scene becomes the reversal of the first half. The relationship between line 997:

Creon
    What is it? How I shudder at your words!

and line 1055:

Creon
    Well, the whole crew of seers are money-mad.

is the same as that between the words of Tiresias (1031):

    I speak for your own good. And I am right. . . .

and its reverse (1084 ff.):

    A bowman, as you said, I send my shafts,
    now you have moved me, straight. You'll feel the wound.

What has been prophesied no longer lies in the background, it breaks out, with the effect that it is the seer's anger that seems to be calling forth the immediate future: his words develop into a curse. And here, too, it is characteristic of the difference between the two centres, which simultaneously attract and repel each other, that the same word is used in two meanings. Like 'friend' and 'foe' in the argument between Antigone and Creon, 'profit' (kerdos) here has two meanings, in one case the sense of sordid advantage and monetary gain, and in the other the sense of true salvation (1031 ff.):[25]

Tiresias
    I speak for your own good. And I am right.
    Learning from a wise counsellor is not pain
    if what he speaks are profitable words.

Creon
. . .
Make profit, trade in Lydian silver-gold,
pure gold of India; that's your chief desire.
But you will never cover up that corpse.
Not if the very eagles tear their food
from him, and leave it at the throne of Zeus . . .

Unlike the forms of *hybris* in the two earlier plays, the arrogance
of a boorish conqueror and of a hero who falls victim to the daimon
of blind obsession with fame, Creon's *hybris* is of a later, riper form
appearing in the garb of soundness and rightness. The sentence in
which it culminates is of such a kind that the enlightened propa-
ganda of Xenophanes or Euripides might have made brilliant use of
it, in fact did make use of it in order to distinguish the truly divine
from its counterfeit, the *physis* of the divine from its *nomos* (1043):[26]

Creon
. . . For I know
no mortal being can pollute the gods.

98   What would delusion be if it did not surround itself with the
appearance of truth? But just as this passage already hints at forms
of human delusion which will not be developed more fully until the
Oedipus Tyrannus, that play is already foreshadowed here by the
way in which a firm tread gives way to slipping and sliding; and it
is also foreshadowed by the persecutor's outbreak of delusion, as
though he alone were being persecuted; and again by the increasing
number of signs of human frailty revealed by Creon in his lack of
moderation when he tries to secure and fortify his own position
(1033 ff.):

Creon
Old man, you all, like bowmen at a mark,
have bent your bows at me. I've had my share
of seers. I've been an item in your accounts.

Whatever differences there may be between the figure, the intention and what we call the character in each case, yet the sport of the

daimon and the nature of man's limitation is identical both in this play and in the *Oedipus Tyrannus*.

Taken as a whole, the end of the Tiresias scene unites three motifs, which have also occurred, singly or in pairs, in the *Ajax* and the *Trachiniae*: first the prophecy, the divine sign, secondly the change from delusion or *hybris* to fear and awareness, and thirdly the motif of 'too late'. If one compares each of these three from the point of view of form, then in each case the first two examples clearly prefigure the more developed use of them in the *Antigone*.

In the *Trachiniae* the warning sign had to be exhaustively explained in narrative (678 f.):

Deianira
  . . . I want to tell you this
  in detail, so you may know the whole story.

The two earlier plays were both characterized by a development away from the forms of report and narrative, a development which was not yet complete. The new departure whereby in the *Antigone* the omen itself becomes drama has already been pointed out in the chapter on the *Trachiniae* (cf. 51, above); it is not until the *Antigone* that Sophocles holds both the divine and the mortal *sphere* within his grasp, that the long explanatory speech comes to invade the present, and that the person who delivers the message becomes an incarnation of the forces themselves.

In so far as the Tiresias scene presents at the same time a prophecy and its *interpretation*, it is comparable with the prophecy of Calchas in the *Ajax*. But in the *Ajax* the prophecy and the interpretation did not form a unity, nor did the interpretation and the visible figure of Ajax. The interpretation did not grow out of the events on the stage, but was tacked on to recapitulatory narratives of previous events. If we turn to the *Antigone*, we find a very great difference in the way in which the character of the person concerned now grows out of the action and pervades the prophecy. Now it becomes part of the tension, part of the conflict; kept back until this moment, called forth by the insult, the revelation comes pouring forth from the old man's lips: this is what you are and this is what you are doing! What he prophesies for the future does not differ from the present, but is only the future shape of what now is; and his language takes on some of the colour of the mysterious nature of the sacral (1064 ff.):

Tiresias
　Know well, the sun will not have rolled its course
　many more days, before you come to give
　corpse for these corpses, child of your own loins.
　For you've confused the upper and lower worlds.
　You sent a life to settle in a tomb;
　you keep up here that which belongs below,
　the corpse unburied, robbed of its release.
　Not you, nor any god that rules on high
　can claim him now.
　You rob the nether gods of what is theirs . . .

　　The seer's abrupt conclusion, his departure, is itself the last and deadliest of the arrows which he sends to their mark. In what earlier play had an exit ever achieved this effect? Left alone, Creon stands at first perplexed, then embarrassed, he vacillates, asks what he should do, stoops, loses control. . . Just as the 'tree-trunk' must first 'resist against the storm' if it is to be broken (713), just as the 'sail', before it 'overturns', must first be overstrained (715), so Creon has overstrained himself; his breaking-point was already contained in his overstraining, his weakness and anxiety in his abuse. And now, too, his 'yielding' is no longer the kind of yielding spoken of, the action of prudence, but the beginning of his downfall.[27]

　　But this is the first time that Sophocles has achieved this degree of creativity. In the *Trachiniae*, the change from delusion to awareness remained concealed in the narrative form;[28] no supernatural sphere forced its way through. The *Ajax* contained the prolonged argument about the burial, but did not use the power of words to call upon the sphere of the divine; the 'law of the gods' demanding burial was touched on only once, when it was mentioned in passing during the *stichomythia* (1130); it was fame and honour that were the subject of the furious quarrel. Here, in the *Antigone*, even the Erinyes, whose approach is foretold by Tiresias, no longer appear as the vengeful spirits of a man or a corpse, as they are generally conceived, but as 'avengers of Hades and the gods' (1075), i.e. avengers of a wrong done to the spheres of the divine, instead of to an individual. 'Hades and the gods' is just as much a polar concept for the whole as 'above' and 'below' had been shortly before.

And so we have almost already arrived at the main point about the motif of 'too late'. It is true that in the *Ajax* the seer already brings about a decision within a limited period of time, a fate is contracted to a moment on the razor's edge (*Ajax* 786; cf. *Antigone* 996). But this was not something which grew naturally out of the drama itself; in order to be presented, the time factor had to take on narrative form, and the sequence of great emotional scenes did not yet bear the stamp of the concentration in time imposed by the daimon. It is true that this motif of 'too late' had already appeared in the *Ajax*, but only for those who were afraid for the hero; it entered into the contrast of tones and outward tensions, linked the hero to the chorus, but still was not linked to the hero himself and to his nature. Creon, on the other hand, both by his own nature and in his appearance on the stage is the 'man who learns too late' (ὀψιμαθής);[29] a human being with his mortal limitations he is by his own nature in the power of time and the daimon, and the motif of 'too late' is part of his character just as much as it is in the case of Xerxes in Herodotus (vii. 14). Creon comes 'too late', not because things develop more quickly than could have been foreseen, nor because he goes to the dead Polynices first instead of straight to the burial chamber: the daimon peers out from behind every word as he speaks and as he breaks off; Creon comes too late because he is such a limited person; and what follows is only the outward consequence of what was already determined by his breakdown (1102 ff.):

101

Creon
   This is your counsel? You would have me yield?

Chorus
   Quick as you can. The gods move very fast
   when they bring ruin on misguided men.

Creon
   How hard, abandonment of my desire . . .

But his closing words when he at last decides to make haste only reveal again how deluded he is in his belief that human will can 'set free what it has bound' (1111 f.):

Creon
>   Now my decision has been overturned
>   shall I, who bound her, set her free myself.[30]

The end of the tragedy then concentrates on raising this fate—the fate of a man who realized too late—as far as possible to the level of a symbol, an example of the survivor, the desperate man who stands between his dead son and his dead wife, the victims of his own blindness. The messenger's speech takes the continuation of the scene between son and father as far as the catastrophe: the two meet once again, as in the drama, but this time in the rocky tomb, next to the dead girl, Creon begging and beseeching, Haemon raging and rushing upon the man who has slain his beloved, then taking the sword which he had drawn against his father and plunging it into his own body. Eurydice hurries up to hear the terrible news and then hastens away (her exit is a weaker repetition of Deianira's departure)—but here, where blindness and error are to develop into fate and action, it becomes obvious that the main figure of the second half lacks the support of the myth to sustain him.[31] Nor can all the piling-up of the forms of narrative and *kommos*, all the profusion of tragic means of expression, make up for the loss of the myth, which takes its revenge, as it were, on the drama for being overlooked. The survivor, full of self-accusation, weeping uncontrollably between the dead, enters, alive, but living a life which is no better than death (ἔμψυχον νεκρόν, 1167). 1272 ff:

Creon
>   . . . It was a god who struck,
>   who has weighted my head with disaster; he drove me to
>   wild strange ways,
>   his heavy heel on my joy.

It makes no difference whether he blames his own stupidity, or a god: here the daimon's work does as little to make Creon innocent as it does in the *Oedipus Tyrannus* to make Oedipus guilty. And yet Creon is piled around with misfortune rather than struck at in the root of his being. Ajax, Deianira, Heracles lost what they were; Creon lost only what he possessed, and his possessions had not previously appeared as being dearest to his heart. The other consequence of his blindness, the revolt in the city, is hinted at (1080 ff.) without being developed into drama.

But there is one respect in which Sophocles should not be reproached with the emptiness of this conclusion: it is the very emptiness of this fate that makes it into the opposite of the fullness of the other. Thus at the end Creon stands in contrast to Antigone exactly as the two kings in the *Ajax* stood in contrast to the dead hero—except that they had no fate in that early play—and exactly as Heracles stood in contrast to Deianira. But how much deeper, more powerful, more embracing the contrast has now become! It is not until the *Antigone* that the play of realms of meaning enters into the play of fates. It is not until now that the figures are surrounded by a contrast of spheres, an above and a below, and divine significance is set in contrast with human insignificance. The fullness of Antigone's death invests her life with human fullness; like a woman conscious of having a mission, she is justified and dedicated. . . . By contrast, Creon ends as the personification of nothingness. For if we go by the actual words, the tragedy ends not so much with a judgment on the guilty person nor with his atonement for the evil deed he has perpetrated, but rather with the picture of the useless survivor, the ungodly fool.[32] He is driven to his downfall not by a single offence, but by the nature of his being. His empty lament rings out in response to the last, and very different, lamentations of his victim.

IV

OEDIPUS TYRANNUS

In contrast to the static scenic form of the earlier plays, we have seen that practically every scene of the *Antigone* portrays a reversal, which entails the development of a situation into its opposite. The *Oedipus Tyrannus*, taken as a whole, constitutes a reversal of the same kind, but on a larger scale, the scale of the whole drama.[1] Of course the fall of kings from their power and glory was nothing new to the Athenian stage. But what a difference from the downfall of kings in Aeschylus, in the *Agamemnon* and the *Persians*! Aeschylus prepares for the coming event from the beginning. What anxiety in hope, what presentiments and affirmations from the choruses! What forebodings in the dialogue, how the downfall lies in wait in every word from the very beginning! And in Sophocles too, in the earlier *Trachiniae*, we could see how the tone imparted a presentiment of the approaching ruin, how the gloomy note struck by the very first words foretold it and prepared its way. And what a difference in the case of the *Oedipus Tyrannus*, where the beginning and the end, both of equal power and breadth, stand in contrast to each other! The beginning holds up one example, and the end another. At the beginning, a man who is everyone's shield and protection, at the end a man who is cast out from everywhere and everything, even from his share of the light. Between the two states there develops the play of the daimonic constellations as they glide forward, no longer separate, sharply divided, independent entities as they still were in the *Antigone*, but in a single movement, which begins slowly, then rushes with ever-increasing speed into a whirlpool of motion.

Little as we know of Aeschylus' *Oedipus*, we may nevertheless conclude that it did not portray this kind of reversal. That play formed the central section of the trilogy which Aeschylus produced in 467, where it was flanked by the *Laius* and the extant *Seven Against Thebes*. Now, since in the *Seven Against Thebes* the grandson

falls victim to the family curse inherited from his father and grand-
father, the *Oedipus* of Aeschylus must have had a different approach
and a different tone. Moreover a dramatic technique involving
development, which alone makes Sophocles' *Oedipus* possible, is still
quite unknown in the *Seven Against Thebes*.

To complete the contrast between the beginning and the end, to
show before the uprooting both the roots and the soil from which
this royal tree is to be torn—roots of such strength that their
uprooting comes near to being an uprooting of all human foundations—Oedipus appears at the beginning not as what he had
once been in the saga, the son of Tyche, the lucky man favoured by
fortune who comes and wins a kingdom, but as the man blessed by
grace, leader, helper, saviour, the regal figure sustained by the
favour of the gods, who stands not for himself but for all, and who
speaks on behalf of all. Furthermore, to add to his stature and
increase his greatness, he is surrounded by a procession of suppliants who are in awe of him as though he were a god: by aged
priests and also by a crowd of boys, so that his speech, which is
addressed to them, begins like that of a father:

Oedipus
    Children, young sons and daughters of old Cadmus . . .
    What do you fear or want, that you sit here
    suppliant? Indeed I'm willing to give all
    that you may need; I would be very hard
    should I not pity suppliants like these.

The tone and attitude of this opening are taken up and carried on
in continuing waves, as it were, by the solemn petition of the priest
of Zeus (15 ff.):

Priest
    You see our company around the altar;
    you see our ages; some of us, like these,
    who cannot yet fly far, and some of us
    heavy with age . . .
                    . . .
    We have not come as suppliants to this altar
    because we thought of you as of a God,

106   but rather judging you the first of men
         in all the chances of this life and when
         we mortals have to do with more than man . . .

                 . . .

         In virtue of no knowledge we could give you,
         in virtue of no teaching; it was God
         that aided you, men say, and you are held
         with God's assistance to have saved our lives . . .

Sophocles has here achieved a kingliness of diction matched only by Aeschylus in the *Agamemnon*. In the strains of the royal speech in the *Agamemnon* there is sublime knowledge of the forces of fate which hover around the royal power, but here in the *Oedipus* the words are those of a king bound by an inherited public obligation (59 ff.):

                 . . . I know you are all sick
         yet there is not one of you, sick though you are,
         that is as sick as I myself.
         Your several sorrows each have single scope
         and touch but one of you. My spirit groans
         for city and myself and you at once.[2]

The first breach of the security of this situation does not come, as the saga might lead one to expect, from a reminder of the old Delphic oracle given at the birth of the outcast, which said that he would kill his father and violate his mother. On the contrary, very much in contrast with the rôle of the old prophecy in the *Trachiniae*, the oracle is kept well away from the opening of the play and is not mentioned until security has already been shattered and trust already broken—not until the quarrels with Tiresias and Creon (791). The first attack comes rather from a new directive from the Delphic god, to purify the land from the pollution caused by the blood of Laius—i.e. not from an oracle belonging to the saga but from a directive such as Delphi frequently issued in historical times. It set the searcher the task of finding himself. The task, no sooner set 107   than performed, pervades the solver and soon begins to transform him, to bewitch him like a draught of some potion, to become for him a test of his existence. He is seized by an overwhelming desire to pledge himself, to discover—even before the return of Creon, who had been sent to consult the oracle (76 f.):

Oedipus
But when he comes, then may I prove a villain,
if I shall not do all the God commands . . .

And even more as soon as Creon enters (86 ff.):

Oedipus
What is the word you bring us from the God?
Creon
A good word—for things hard to bear themselves
if in the final issue all is well
I count complete good fortune.
Oedipus
                What do you mean?
What you have said so far
leaves me uncertain whether to trust or fear.
Creon
If you will hear my news before these others
I am ready to speak, or else to go within.
Oedipus
Speak it to all;
the grief I bear, I bear it more for these
than for my own heart.

Thus, from the very beginning, Oedipus is the mighty revealer, open in every gesture and every word, the same Oedipus who at the end shouts for the doors to be torn open so that all the world may see him.

But the suspense for which this play is famous is not maintained simply by the unrelenting breathlessness of a discovery which comes in regular stages, nor simply by the cat-and-mouse game played by a fate lying hidden in the past upon a victim who as yet suspects nothing,[3] nor by an interplay of deceptions such as occurs in an interrogation or in the course of a trial—in short, not by any of the devices with which so many subsequent dramas of revelation have been crammed. Schiller referred to the *Oedipus* as a 'tragic analysis' (a phrase which has been quoted far too often since), and said 'Everything is there already and has only to be unravelled . . . Furthermore, what happens is far more terrifying in its nature because it is inevitable . . .' (letter to Goethe, 2 October 1797). But he was looking at the play from the point of view of his own work on his *Wallenstein*, and was concerned too much with the mechanics of construction and too little with the essential. For Sophocles, as for the Greeks of an earlier age, fate is in no circumstances the same as predetermination, but is a spontaneous unfolding of daimonic power, even when the fate has been foretold, and even when it is brought about by means of an order immanent in events and in the way that the world goes. Fate as predetermination does not exist before the Stoa and the victory of astrology.[4] So too the essential basis of the *Oedipus* is not the irrevocability of a past as revealed in the course of the play—there is no place in the *Oedipus* for the concept 'Even if it were possible, I could no longer do what I wished.' On the contrary, it is an actively pursued struggle for escape, self-assertion and defence on the part of a threatened world of illusion, a world which is human—indeed inextricably conjoined with an essentially human greatness; and from the point of view of this world and of its order, its 'truth' and its preservation, the boundaries between reality and illusion have to be reversed. The *Oedipus* is by no means distinct from other Greek tragedies in being *the* tragedy of human fate, of which it has ranked for so long as prime example—taking 'fate' as in the period of classicism in Germany as being inseparable from 'liberty', the liberty 'which elevates' at that.[5] It would be much nearer the truth to say that it is distinct from other Greek tragedies in being *the* tragedy of human illusion, in which illusion implies reality, just as Parmenides' *Doxa* implies *Aletheia*. It should have struck critics before now that not one of all the choruses in the *Oedipus* sings about fate, though enough sing about it elsewhere, whereas one chorus in a prominent position sings about human 'illusion' (1189 ff.):

What man, what man on earth wins more
of happiness than a seeming
and after that turning away?

The fight and the defence on the part of illusion begin at first

109 unobtrusively, but certainly as early as the start of the investigation ordered by the god. It begins with a strange diversion rightly observed but wrongly criticized by the logical Voltaire.[6] After an enquiry into the facts seems already to have been planned, after the question 'Is there a witness?' has already been asked, and after this question has been answered in the affirmative (118)—the word 'robbers' is heard, which suddenly arouses suspicion, supplanting the idea of an inquiry: how would robbers have dared to do that if they had not been bribed 'from here'? 'From here' would mean from some quarter in Thebes. The question, put after the murder of a king and by a king, is understandable. The question is addressed to Creon. Creon seems to evade it: the suspicion which naturally arose could not, he says, be followed up after the deed. Why not? The Sphinx came . . . With that the suspicion seems to rest for a while. But from now on, attention is directed not towards the scene of the deed, nor the course of events, nor the weapon, but towards the instigators, in Thebes—until suddenly, after the argument with the refractory and apparently malevolent prophet, the suspicion is confirmed, the link between Creon and Tiresias is established and a whole web of conspiracy stands confirmed as certain truth.

A fragment of Aeschylus' *Oedipus* [fr. 173 Nauck² = fr. 172 Mette] happens to have survived (the only extant fragment, in fact) in which a witness, obviously the sole survivor, tells us of the 'place where three roads meet'. That must have been followed by the revelation, or a part of the revelation. In Sophocles there is no such interrogation in the whole play. The fragment of Aeschylus is enough to show what it was that Sophocles displaced by his diversion and its consequences, so as to make room for other things.

For as a result of this diversion, the original, inevitable and, so to speak, innate illusion is joined by a new illusion in the shape of a delusion. And the way in which this new illusion is introduced, in the form of a suspicion of bribery and a secret conspiracy within the city against which it is directed, shows the influence upon the *Oedipus* of the dramatic and scenic form of the *Antigone* and the outward cloak by means of which illusion took control of the figure of Creon in that play.[7] There the suspicion of bribery was at first only hinted at by a single word—κέρδος (222)—only to be pushed aside by intervening matters, and then it suddenly appeared fully fledged (290 ff.), to be expanded in the scene with the seer. So too in

the *Oedipus*. Except that in the *Antigone* the suspicion had already
been suggested to the new ruler by the outward state of affairs when
he took over, after the death of the heir to the throne and shortly
after the defeat of the exile. . . In that play, the suspicion already lay
hidden in the first proclamation, prohibiting the burial of the enemy
of the country. In the *Oedipus*, the ruler makes his entrance before
his people as a man universally honoured, surrounded by all his
subjects and warmly greeted by them—not announcing his own
arrival like Creon—so that the threat hardly seems to have any
foundation in the outward situation. And yet here too there is the
same suspicion, at first not directed at any particular person, which
hovers until it settles, by way of Tiresias, on Creon. In other words,
in the *Oedipus* the threat enters the human, subjective sphere,
presses into the domain of the spirit, is sensed and felt from the
daimonic incomprehensibility of the task rather than deduced from
the outward circumstances. And the suspicion is attached to the
wrong person because the victim of illusion must have an enemy, a
tangible enemy, so as not to lose his own sense of security. For
Creon the transgression of his prohibition did not in itself signify
any danger to his own existence; for Oedipus everything is in the
balance, even before he begins to guess what he stands to lose: his
realm of illusion, which sees itself threatened, not at this stage by
reality, but only by the illusory products of its own creation
(137 ff.):

Oedipus
  For when I drive pollution from the land
  I will not serve a distant friend's advantage,
  but act in my own interest. Whoever
  he was that killed the king may readily
  wish to dispatch me with his murderous hand.

The irruption of truth – one can hardly speak of reality in this
context, since Oedipus does not at first live in illusion but in a world
of objective falsity and appearance—the irruption of truth into the
structure of appearance occurs from two successive breaches in the
wall, the first at the edge, the second in the centre. The first breach
follows from the question 'What is this hidden thing that confronts
me, which it is my duty to bring into the open?'; the second from

the question 'What am I, and what is my own true existence?' For a while the second question lies hidden behind the first, then both run parallel for a time, in secret harmony, and at the end they come together. Both times, the structure tries to preserve itself and throws its forces towards the point from which the threat comes.

The first defence against the enemy, who is as yet unknown, is the proclamation of outlawry, and, together with this proclamation, the curse. And Oedipus knows how to curse. He curses with the power that his position bestows on him. As soon as cursing takes hold of him he speaks the words which carry their own fulfilment, the words which are simultaneously public and personal; he curses with priestly dedication and at the same time as if with ruffled plumage. . . We need only look at the curses in Euripides, for example those of Theseus in the *Hippolytus*, to see how little contact Euripides has with this kind of speech and action. But an almost greater disappointment comes if one compares the fragment of the old epic, the *Thebais* (fr. 3), which has been preserved by chance: there, nothing at all of the curse comes through into the written word—the narrative says that 'he cursed' . . . and no more. [7a]

The clearer it becomes that the curse is directed at none other than the unwitting curser himself, the greater the force of the speech which calls down the curse becomes. Creon's curses in the *Antigone* were similarly directed against the speaker, but the effect of recoil in the *Oedipus* is far more pregnant with fate. This curse has in common with Creon's speeches in the *Antigone* the dynamic force of its acceleration: each has a gentle opening, and then the speech begins to hurtle along like a man who is in danger of falling victim to a delusion. And again there is a reversal between the first part and the last, though in the *Oedipus* it takes place not in the course of the dialogue but in the twisting movement of the curse-speech itself. The moderate tone with which the speaker began, promising impunity if the wrongdoer were to confess, disappears as soon as outlawry has been solemnly decreed; the power of the curse and denunciation itself takes control of the speaker, the more he himself is implicated in the riddle that he wants to solve (244 ff.):

112   So I stand forth a champion of the God
    and of the man who died.

Upon the murderer I invoke this curse—
whether he is one man and all unknown,
or one of many—may he wear out his life
in misery to miserable doom!
If with my knowledge he lives at my hearth
I pray that I myself may feel my curse . . .

After the opening, where the new king still stands outside the unknown and almost forgotten event, he finds himself becoming uncannily involved in things alien to himself, as if they were his own. Although he is unaware of the relationship, he is already making himself the son of his real father; in the daimonic sphere of illusion his own true nature has already magically seized upon him in anticipation of things to come. At the opening he speaks as an outsider (219 ff.):

. . . what I say to you, I say
as one that is a stranger to the story
as stranger to the deed. For I would not
be far upon the track if I alone
were tracing it without a clue. But now,
since after all was finished, I became
a citizen among you, citizens—
now I proclaim to all the men of Thebes: . . .

He is just as much an outsider as he had been before (103 ff.):

Creon
My lord, before you piloted the state
we had a king called Laius.

Oedipus
I know of him by hearsay. I have not seen him.

But from being an outsider he begins to involve himself more and more intensely (258 ff.):

Since I am now the holder of his office,
and have his bed and wife that once was his,
and had his line not been unfortunate
we would have common children—(fortune leaped
upon his head)—because of all these things,

113

I fight in his defence as for my father,
and I shall try all means to take the murderer
of Laius the son of Labdacus
the son of Polydorus and before him
of Cadmus and before him of Agenor.[8]

He has ended by giving a complete list of the ancestors of the present representative of the family. That is how kings name their ancestors when taking an oath, as Xerxes does in Herodotus (vii. 11): 'If I do not take revenge on the Athenians, let me not be called son of Darius, son of Hystaspes, son of Arsames, son of Ariaramnes, son of Teispes, son of Cyrus.'[9]

Indeed, both are cases of tragic irony—the apparent lack of blood relationship and the apparent adoption of the same (the true adoption comes only at the time of the catastrophe). But even though this is only an apparent adoption, despite all its stormy impetuosity which leaves behind everything that is merely material, it is not until this adoption that reality and appearance are irrevocably twisted and woven together. It is only from this grappling together, which is no longer external, no longer pragmatic, but daimonic, embracing the whole being, the soul itself and language itself, that there arises the tragedy of the man hurled down from his realm of appearance, a tragedy which is also the answer to the question: What would Oedipus be to us if he did not happen to be the son of Laius? or: How is the exceptional case in the legend made into the symbolic figure in the drama? The daimonic, continual and unconscious reaching over out of the realm of appearance into the realm of truth is the human element which was not supplied by the legend and had not been linked with the figure of Oedipus before Sophocles.[10] This also forms the irony which is usually described in modern aesthetic theory by the inaccurate and overgeneralized technical term 'tragic irony'. For here it is not a case of the spectator knowing the truth while the character on the stage gropes in the dark, so that the character's speech bears a different meaning for the spectator, but it is a case of man standing in confusion between appearance and reality. Moreover, appearance and reality are not simply apportioned to stage and audience, or even the other way round; still less are they apportioned to the writer on the one hand and the world that he has created on the other: on the contrary, both

of them are seen in each and every word and gesture of the confused
hero. It is not the writer, making use of his own world of appearance or of theatrical appearances, but the invisible gods, operating
in the background from their position of unattainable remoteness,
who are playing games with human appearances.

After the secret, unconscious conflict which points to the future,
another conflict breaks out in the Tiresias scene—an open conflict
between truth and appearance. No longer is it a conflict between
truth and error. If we speak of error we do not imply that error is
inevitable, as it is here; it is not merely the intellect, but the whole
structure of a man, both internal and external, that is at fault.
Deianira in the *Trachiniae* found herself in a state of tragic error:
something overcame her, and, as soon as she realized it, she felt
remorse; in ths same play when Heracles raged he was in a state of
tragic error. . . Tragic error is something which overwhelms a
man. But the world of tragic appearance in which Oedipus finds
himself is without any doubt characteristic of deeper tragedy: it
contains and conditions the human state from the beginning,
including a man's nature and aims, and his rôle as king, husband,
leader, protector; it is his power and security, it is everything which
preserves him. In the *Antigone* Creon was driven into a position of
falsehood and appearance; Oedipus *stands* in a world of appearances,
and is hurled down from it.

There is something about the human vehicle, the vessel of truth,
the seer Tiresias, which is hard to comprehend, and not only for
Oedipus when he misinterprets him.[11] Half of Tiresias is super-
human, half only too human; half of him possesses secret knowledge
and is infallible, half of him is indecisive and forgetful, coming and
yet anxious to go, concealing and yet revealing; he is half a ca-
pricious, irritable old man, half—in the midst of his anger—possessed of second sight; he is a walking enigma, 'nursing the truth that
makes him strong' (356)—part of the whole mysteriousness and
paradox in the prophetic admonition, 'Neither speak nor hide',
seems to be personified in him. The paradoxical nature of his character certainly goes beyond that of Tiresias in the *Antigone*; he represents a further development of the figure of the seer in the earlier
work. There is no longer any need to point out his blindness, or the
boy leading the blind leader of the blind; instead, it is the paradox of
the prophetic phenomenon itself which speaks. It is the same paradox

115

throughout, something which, seen only from the point of view of the character, is totally incompatible with itself: the fusion of a self-willed, limited existence with a daimonic influence from the world beyond—yet this fusion does not make the man unambiguously ecstatic, an instrument of the god, an inspired prophet. It is a paradox of the same kind which dominates everything in the last work of Sophocles' old age, and when it is intensified to an altogether inconceivable degree by the firmness and breadth with which the character is drawn, it takes control of the aged Oedipus. If the mystery of this paradox is still lacking in the *Antigone* it is easy to infer that it was still beyond the reach of Sophocles when he wrote that work.

In the Tiresias scene in the *Antigone*, the fear and respect of the beginning gave way at the end to mockery and accusation. It is the same here. But now the transition is more violent and the content less rational. The first great speech of Oedipus to Tiresias, which not only shows royal respect for the seer as a person but also bows before the mystery of his office, is simultaneously a sincere attempt to win him over and an expression of trust in him. Thus it already goes beyond the *Antigone* in its noble gesture (300 f.):

Tiresias, you are versed in everything,
things teachable and things not to be spoken,
things of the heaven and earth-creeping things . . .[12]

In the *Antigone* the conflict amounted, more or less, to a warning, which was ignored, and an accusation, which was followed by the revelation of the accuser, but it still took the rational form of an argument about right and wrong, about *hybris* and *sophrosynē*. In contrast, Oedipus comes up against a mysterious resistance in the seer himself, an obscure refusal to obey, a barricade set up against the means of salvation, the question on which everything hangs. . .
116   And instead of right and wrong, it is 'light' and 'darkness' which clash and accuse each other in turn, the former developing from obscurity at the beginning to an increasingly bright and evil clarity, and the latter from readiness and receptivity to an increasingly passionate deafness; each is carried along into new extremes by the other.

The conflict soon reaches its first peak (334 ff.):

Oedipus
   You would provoke a stone! Tell us, you villain,
   tell us, and do not stand there quietly
   unmoved and balking at the issue.

The attack on the resistance of the seer is combined with the
attack on the resistance of the enigma which from the beginning,
ever since the message came from Apollo, has secretly endangered
and threatened the world of appearance surrounding Oedipus:
Tiresias is accused of being an accomplice to the deed. And this
attack, like the verbal battles in the *Antigone,* brings with it a conflict
between two spheres. Just as in the Tiresias scene of the *Antigone* the
argument was about the word 'profit', κέρδος, which had two
meanings, human salvation and the search for material advantage,
here too the argument is about an ambiguous word; but it is a much
fiercer argument, since it is about 'truth' and 'darkness'. For one
speaker, 'truth' and 'light' mean something which he is conscious of
having done, something which he surveys, something which submits to his will and perception; to the other it is something which is
hidden and denied to him. For the former it falls within the human
sphere, for the other it forms the limits of the human sphere. From
an objective point of view, Tiresias and the audience know a fact of
which Oedipus can have no knowledge; to that extent the conflict is
an example of tragic irony in the conventional sense. But from the
point of view of a man's existence it is not a confrontation of
knowledge and ignorance of a certain fact, but of one mode of
existence and another: what is 'light' for one is 'darkness' for the
other (362, 368 ff.):

Tiresias
   I say you are the murderer of the king
   whose murderer you seek . . .

Oedipus
117   Do you imagine you can always talk
   like this, and live to laugh at it hereafter?

Tiresias
   Yes, if the truth has anything of strength.[13]

Oedipus
It has, but not for you; it has no strength
for you because you are blind in mind and ears
as well as in your eyes.

Tiresias
                    You are a poor wretch
to taunt me with the very insults which
every one soon will heap upon yourself.

Oedipus
Your life is one long night so that you cannot
hurt me or any other who sees the light.

The clarity in which Oedipus lives, which 'nurses' him, which is
in and around him, the same for him as for all who 'see the
light'—without the appearance of this clarity this conflict would be
a dialectical conflict in the Euripidean manner. This is the kind of
clarity which has to label everything that threatens its existence as
'darkness'.

The threat becomes more intense until the god is named (376 ff.):

Tiresias
It is not fate that I should be your ruin,
Apollo is enough; it is his care
to work this out.

Oedipus
                    Was this your own design
or Creon's?

The threat from the god is immediately replaced by an equivalent
threat from man, in order to maintain the structure of the world of
appearances. It is true that there have been attempts to use external,
concrete associations to explain this association, which is however
an association made within the framework of a human mind.[14] And
Sophocles certainly has at least some pragmatic motivations in his
work: as we have already said, it was Creon who suggested consulting Tiresias (288). But it is only possible for something like this to
be taken as grounds for suspicion at all because of the general frame
of mind of the person in question; the frame of mind is the given
factor, and once suspicion has flared up there is no further talk of

external factors whatever. The mention of Apollo is the dividing
line, after which illusion has to become delusion and blindness in
order not to surrender. From a basis in the world of appearance
there immediately springs a whole world and a whole world-order
of delusion: Creon, the seer and the deed—a strange combination!
And indignation has found an object to attack. Passion unburdens
itself in the gnomic apostrophe with which Oedipus addresses this
world (380 ff.):

Oedipus
   Wealth, sovereignty and skill outmatching skill
   for the contrivance of an envied life!
   Great store of jealousy fill your treasury chests,
   if my friend Creon, friend from the first and loyal,
   thus secretly attacks me, secretly
   desires to drive me out and secretly
   suborns this juggling, trick-devising quack,
   this wily beggar who has only eyes
   for his own gains, but blindness in his skill.

The threat develops into an essential part of a newly forming
system—the past, too, is now dragged into service to support
appearances: where was the seer's wisdom at the time of the
Sphinx? . . . But is this view of the world false? Is it not right? What
would appearances be if they did not present their own appearance
of truth? Creon in the *Antigone* also justified himself on the grounds
of something which was not false in itself. But in that play the
relation between general truth and the reality of the moment had
something repulsive and mean about it; in this case the disparity
belongs to Oedipus' nature; it is a necessary part of his self-assertion
and self-justification.
   Again, the reply of the Tiresias of the *Oedipus* has something in
common with the prophetic speech of the Tiresias of the *Antigone*:
both combine a prophecy of the future with an interpretation of the
present (412 ff.):

Tiresias
   Since you have taunted me with being blind,
   here is my word for you.

You have your eyes but see not where you are
in sin, nor where you live, nor whom you live with.
Do you know who your parents are? Unknowing
you are an enemy to kith and kin
in death, beneath the earth, and in this life.
A deadly-footed, double-striking curse,
from father and mother both, shall drive you forth
out of this land, with darkness on your eyes,
that now have such straight vision.

119

'Where you live': the words 'live', 'settle' and so forth are favourite words at this stage to designate a place in the order of things, the place where a man's activity belongs. It is not to be taken as an affectedly mystical circumlocution for something which could be expressed by a single word; the meaning is not simply 'Thebes is your home, Jocasta your mother', although that is factually true. Origin, dwelling-place and friends, or in other words 'whence', 'where' and 'with whom', together form an expression of the whole of human existence; and in Sophocles, in so far as human existence is tragic, it is always embedded in its context by nature yet tragically isolated. But as things are in this case, the seer's vague phrases describe matters more accurately than more precise words would. 'You do not know with whom . . .' is an interpretation of a set of circumstances. 'You do not know that Jocasta is your mother' would only be enlightenment about a single fact. But the sense is: you think you belong, yet you are in fact alien to everything to which a man belongs. 'Beneath' and 'on the earth' are the two polar extremes which stand for the whole range of blood relationships, as in the prophecy in the *Antigone* [1068–73], where the totality of all nature is expressed by the phrases 'above' and 'below', 'the living' and 'the dead'. The final condition which Tiresias prophesies will again be no more than the making perceptible of what Oedipus already is in his true nature, although this is not as yet apparent. It is only from the standpoint of the daimonic sphere, which first makes itself felt in the seer's enigmatic utterance, that the condition in which a man finds himself can be defined. With the enigmatic, vague element in the seer's speech, what was in the legend simply an unrolling of the action and a pressing forward into the future, is brought into the present, into existence, and placed as a truth in that

world of appearances, that darkness, which is inseparably linked
with Oedipus.

The next *epeisodion*, the clash between Oedipus and Creon, stands
in contrast with the Tiresias scene in more or less the same way as
the clash with Haemon does with the Tiresias scene in the *Antigone*:
after the obscure, mantic world of darkness and the irrational, there
enters the rational man, who sees that he too, in his own very
different kind of stability, is threatened by the attack upon the seer.
(Compare the two adjacent argument scenes in the *Ajax*: at that
early stage there is hardly any contrast at all between them.) But the
two argument scenes are now linked: the second is a continuation of
the first. They take the action further and further from its objective,
from the task of self-recognition, until we discover that what on the
human level is a diversion leads, in the daimonic context, to the
objective. That is how oracles usually reach their objective; they
prefer roundabout paths, they tend to come true at the very
moment at which a man seems to have escaped them. But here it is
no longer a case of Sophocles' having taken over in his drama a
few external, formal elements from archaic stories about oracles,
as he did in the *Trachiniae*; instead, he has seized and dramatized
the experience and the deeper human roots which give rise to
the oracular detours. In the *Oedipus* the oracle is no longer, even
formally, the lever of an action of the impetus towards a self-
recognition as it was in the *Trachiniae*. Rather, it is the subsoil of the
oracular, the roots which it strikes in the mind, which also serves as
the ground from which the drama grows.

In the *Oedipus* there is no repetition of the continuous crescendo
which characterized the argument scenes of the *Antigone*. Instead of
developing from a position where both parties wrongly believe that
they are in agreement, the argument is waged from the very beginning with great vehemence. One man storms on to the stage full of
anger; the other soon clashes with his opponent in an even plainer
state of fury. The static and immobile nature of the scene is shown
by the parallel accusations, of equal violence, from each side. But
this duel is different in nature from those in the *Ajax*—between
them lies the phase of dramatic technique involving development
which we saw in the *Antigone*. For the battle, stationary at first, soon
begins to twist, to turn and to vacillate—it is a fight in which one
opponent exhausts himself in reckless assaults, while the other

121   parries his thrusts with a scientific defence. (That is why Creon has
to appear on the stage first, so that Oedipus can come upon him)
(532 ff.):

Oedipus
You, sir, how is it you come here? Have you so much
brazen-faced daring that you venture in
my house although you are proved manifestly
the murderer of that man, and though you tried,
openly, highway robbery of my crown? . . .

That is how he opens his attack. What had first arisen merely as a
fleeting suspicion—the unexplained question of why the seer had
said nothing after the deed and why the investigation was called
off—is now turned against the enemy in what seems to be a successful investigation. But immediately after this first blow, the inter-
rogator loses his lead in the *stichomythia* to Creon, the man under
interrogation, who throws in a counter-question which has the
effect of a counter-attack. In this his weapon is his rational lucidity,
his knowledge of his own innocence and lack of guile. For him the
fight is easy, for he has no deep roots, no lofty aspirations, and never
reaches the borders of a superhuman sphere. He has no drives
except those which he can consciously control and sensibly fulfil,
no relationships except those which bring an 'advantage' (τὰ σὺν
κέρδει καλά), no qualities except those which can be calculated and
entered on a 'balance sheet'. His 'balance sheet', his λόγον διδόναι,
may remind us of that of Euripides' Hippolytus (δοῦναι λόγον, 986).
But the difference is that in Euripides the balance, the *ratio*, is no
longer shackled to the totality of man, but belongs to man's essential nature; man is divided into *ratio* and passion; whereas in the
Oedipus the *ratio* serves only as an outside obstacle against which the
truly human element can crash and break up. The figure of Creon
who opposes the tragic victim represents the rational, enlightened
bios of the age, all the more aware of himself for being on trial,
neither capable of nor needing further self-knowledge through
suffering, summing himself up: 'This I am, that I am not; this, in
consequence, I am capable of doing, that I am not capable of doing',
and not making a single mistake about it . . . For there are such
people, besides the tragic figures. Always, in the works of Sopho-

122

cles, the great tragedy can be unfolded only against the background of the non-tragic: that is why the generals and Odysseus stand in contrast with Ajax, Ismene with Antigone, the world of the watchman who saves his own skin in contrast with Antigone and her self-sacrifice . . . and this too is how Creon stands in contrast with Oedipus: in contrast with the leader, the ruler, the man of the highest aspirations, the first in all things, stands Creon, the man of faultless reputation who shrinks from every risk and danger to his own person, who protects himself, makes attachments, is satisfied with profit rather than power, is reasonable in a mediocre way, born to come second in everything. It is easy to see who wins: it is Creon, who gets the first halves of the lines and who has the last word before Jocasta separates the combatants. Oedipus is secretly wounded, bleeding internally from the consequences of his own blind charge against an oppostion that stands its ground, rather than wounded by any particular verbal attack: at the end he is fighting only within his own enclosed world, he hardly sees whether his blows strike the target (618 ff.):

Oedipus
  When he that plots against me secretly
  moves quickly, I must quickly counterplot.
  If I wait taking no decisive measure
  his business will be done, and mine be spoiled . . .

How well this would serve as a defence against Oedipus' conduct! How ill matched it is to the 'balance sheet' to which it is the answer! The threat of the death penalty, too, is much more a burst of anger, a violent release of feeling, than a decision: it is as if the world of appearances in which Oedipus stands holds him fast and does not allow him to exercise any influence upon the world of reality. A threatened king, who could defend himself, a powerful man who in the end is left with nothing, is lost, and can only cry [629], 'O city, city!'[15]

In the *Antigone* the opponents disagreed only to separate at the climax of their quarrel. In the *Oedipus* the disagreement is calmed down, almost lulled to peace by the short lines which the chorus exchange with the speaker and the influence of their rhythm on the stormy spirit. And no less soothing is Jocasta's entry into the

123 quarrel between her brother and her husband. The last part of the *Ajax* has already given us an example of a quarrel which finishes in this way, with the entry of a third person who settles the matter. But here in the *Oedipus* we find that there has been a great development from the earlier type of scene. We have already noticed with regard to the external, technical aspect of the play that Sophocles has at last learnt to write a proper conversation for three characters. Indeed, one would look in vain in the *Trachiniae*, the *Ajax* or even the *Antigone* for an exchange such as we have here between Jocasta, Oedipus and Creon. But the real significance of achieving a dialogue for three actors lies in a change of style rather than in a mere technical advance. If we cast a glance at comedy, we find even in the earliest play of Aristophanes, the *Acharnians* of 425, written when he was still quite young, a succession and mixture of conversations and interchanges as varied as anyone could wish for even on the modern stage. So it was not an unprecedented achievement. But this achievement would have made no sense in a Sophoclean tragedy. For in Sophocles' plays, even at a later date, the purpose of the speeches is not to give details about the characters, or to establish the milieu, or even to give scope for conversation, as in nineteenth-century drama. Nor is there in Sophocles any society, or court, or anything like that, of the kind that sustains a conversation between several people in Shakespeare's early plays. Thus the first dialogue for three persons in the *Oedipus* is one of the signs of an individual style of scene-construction which Sophocles has only just achieved. In the *Ajax*, Odysseus intervened between the quarrelling heroes just as Jocasta intervenes between Oedipus and Creon. But the result was merely a dialogue between different pairs of speakers who took it in turns to confront each other; there was no true conversation *à trois*. The static confrontations by which the archaic type of emotional scene was presented would have been weakened, not strengthened, by a conversation between three persons. It is only in the interplay of shifting movements and changes, in a kind of emotional scene that does not stand still, but turns this way and that under the pressure of the daimon, that dialogue for three can express tragic content; for this form of dialogue, with its changing relationships, is itself one of transitions and transformations. Here, as always, it is the inner form which shapes the external form or, in other words, the technique. The arrival of the third person, and the

appeasement she brings, does not in this case constitute a conclusion but a reversal, a *peripeteia*; not a sharp break but an ascent to the main peak of this unusually long *epeisodion* with all its twists and turns—an *epeisodion* which, in addition to the contrast of the large areas, also contains a wealth of transitions, half-lights and flickering intermediate states.

Although the accused gets away free, and anger releases its victim, this brings about not relief and ease but an even more oppressive anxiety. For now the anger is turned inwards, the wound festers under the scar. The victim of accusation, now set free, can say to his accuser, and obviously with justification (673 ff.):

Creon
   I see you sulk in yielding and you're dangerous
   when you are out of temper; natures like yours
   are justly heaviest for themselves to bear.

When he has lost the certainty of his goal, the pursuit of the accuser turns into a new awareness that he himself is being hunted, and of a monstrous injustice of which he is the victim. The unity of the world without and the world within, of action and emotion, vanishes. The illusion which forms the basis of his certainty still exists, but it has already collapsed inwardly and been undermined subconsciously even before a convulsion from outside, starting from a point that had almost escaped notice, tears down the whole structure.

Anyone who considers that the accused is not guilty is heaping suspicion upon the royal accuser himself (658 f.):

Oedipus
   I would have you know that this request of yours
   really requests my death or banishment.

These are the only possible alternatives, so certain is he of the guilt of the man he has accused. That is the extent to which the deluded Oedipus has staked his honour and rank on his mistake. Yet he is prepared, by releasing the man he supposes to be the traitor, to take upon himself another's guilt—established by his own deluded 'either/or'; prepared to represent himself as the inno-

125 cent victim of persecution and suffering so that he can bitterly reproach the other persons present (669 f.):

Oedipus
Well, let him go then—if I must die ten times for it,
or be sent out dishonoured into exile . . .

What has happened? Logically it is absurd.[16] But as Oedipus hovers between apportioning and accepting blame, wounded in his soul, his illusion shattered, he grasps the truth without realizing it, just as previously he had adopted his own family without realizing it. . .[17] What first came into his mind as an 'as if' now actually becomes reality. The daimonic does not invade it from outside except in so far as it has caused the anticipation of possibilities in Oedipus' own mind to make it receptive to a fate coming from outside.

Thus the turning-point is prepared, and truth forces its way in, no longer in the guise of a foreign enemy who presents a threat from the borders, but from the innermost centre of the very core of his own being. And here again it begins with a state of transition, an uncertainty. Creon left. Will not Oedipus leave too? Will the queen not lead him away, fatally mistaken as he is? But she still has one question to ask: what has happened? When the chorus of old men, who are standing by, evades this question, she finally puts it to the stricken, silent Oedipus—who thereupon reveals himself, already almost more as a son would to his mother. . . Transitions such as this had never been known before.

The blood relationship is not spelt out in situations specially designed for it,[18] but is more like a soft accompaniment which can be perceived in the tone of the words and the manner of address, (700, 772 f.):

Oedipus
                    Yes, I will tell you.
I honour you more than I honour them.
          . . . .
                              Whom
should I confide in rather than you, who is there
of more importance to me who have passed
through such a fortune?

She is the rescuer, he is the lost one. But the more assured Jocasta becomes in speaking words of comfort, the more precipitously Oedipus is plunged into despair. Like Creon's *hybris* in the *Antigone*, her words of comfort are summed up in a *gnomē*, in the form of a generalization [724–5]: it is based on an enlightened belief in divinity. [19] But as in the *Oedipus* the danger to man lies not in the *hybris* of human self-assertion but in the *hybris* of seeming as opposed to being that is innate in his nature—a deeper danger—, what is amiss in her attempt at consolation is not the arrogance of the individual will but the fact that the consolation is grounded in appearance and not in reality. Since the time of A. W. Schlegel it has been usual to speak confidently of Jocasta's 'levity' or 'blasphemy'. [20] But what kind of pious respect could she be expected to accord to the belief that the oracle to which she had had to sacrifice her son had none the less come true? Has the sacrifice been in vain, the sacrifice that was her fate? And what good has that been to Laius? He has been murdered by robbers! Again, if Tiresias is asserting obvious impossibilities, is it 'levity' for her not to believe in them? Is she 'godless' because after this news her doubt is directed, not against the god himself, but only against his priest? After all that has happened, is she not, like Oedipus, living in an objective, necessary world of appearance? Her words are brief and definite (σημεῖα σύντονα, 710), dispersing at a stroke, as she believes, the whole cloud of impossible suspicion which has gathered around him (707 ff.):

Jocasta
  Do not concern yourself about this matter;
  listen to me and learn that human beings
  have no part in the craft of prophecy.

               . . .

  So clear in this case were the oracles,
  so clear and false. Give them no heed, I say;
  what God discovers need of, easily
  he shows to us himself.

The revelation, which in the *Oedipus* of Aeschylus came from outside, by means of an account given by an eye-witness, is shifted by Sophocles to an intimate scene in which two souls reveal themselves to each other. The monologue form, which was used in the

127 *Trachiniae* when the tragic self-knowledge which sprang from the fulfilment of an oracle cried out in its agony to the world—the same monologue form which was used at the end of Aeschylus' *Seven Against Thebes*, when Eteocles, Oedipus' son, recognizing the heritage of his blood, accepted his fate—has given way here in Sophocles' *Oedipus* to a movement to and fro, an exchange between souls driven onward by the daimon. Instead of moving in the manner of an emotionally charged messenger's speech, the narrative rushes along in staccato sentences, seeking relief under heavy pressure, with no room for decoration, no room for metaphors. (Contrast the language used in the revelation by Heracles in the *Trachiniae* (1157 ff.), the circumlocution for 'not living, but dead' (1160 f.), the piling up of epithets to denote the holy place (1167 ff.), the emotive pleonasm of the phrase referring to the present (1169), etc. There is nothing of this sort in the *Oedipus*.)

As in the *Trachiniae* (1141), however, it is again the unintentional utterance of a *word* which leads to the revelation: in that play the word 'Nessus', here 'the place where three roads meet'. The latter had already been named in a similar manner in the *Oedipus* of Aeschylus (fr. 173 Nauck² = fr. 172 Mette)—the scholia on Sophocles comment on the fact. But when it was named in Aeschylus, it was clothed in such a display of tragic splendour! It took three lines to strike the fateful note:

'We were coming on our way to the place where three
highways part in branching roads, where we crossed
the junction of the triple roads at Potniae . . .'²¹

In using an abundance of decorative epithets to convey pathos, Aeschylus does not scorn to double almost every expression. It is obvious that after this there could be no further questioning, corroboration, or doubt. There remained only the emotional unburdening of the hero as he saw the truth. (To attribute the surviving three lines to Oedipus himself instead of to an eye-witness would surely be to take too little account of their form.) In the *Trachiniae* (1143 ff.) the hero also comes to self-knowledge as soon as the fateful word has been uttered, apostrophizes himself and unburdens himself in a similar way; as indeed Eteocles had done before him in Aeschylus' *Seven Against Thebes* (640 ff.) when he saw his father's curses being fulfilled. In Sophocles' Oedipus there is no apostrophe, no self-indulgent word, nothing left of the tragic unburdening which belonged to the older manner of expressing pathos. Instead there is an interplay of ignorance and apprehension, incomprehension and self-discovery, hesitation and certainty . . . For the first time the exchange of lines in the dialogue becomes the expression of an oscillation between salvation and destruction (how different from the monologues in the *Trachiniae*!), the expression of an uncomprehended fear, so paralysing that it scarcely dares to speak. The restrained emotion here is more effective than emotion which unburdens itself without restraint; the hesitating 'maybe', 'it seems', the word as yet unspoken, as yet unnamed, runs ahead of the clear revelation of the terrible truth, and in place of the earlier imagery and sound-effects there appears the simple, unadorned movement of the dialogue (729 ff.):

Oedipus
> I thought I heard you say
> that Laius was killed at a crossroads.

Jocasta
> Yes, that was how the story went and still
> that word goes round . . .

Oedipus
> What have you designed, O Zeus, to do with me?

Jocasta
> What is the thought that troubles your heart?

Oedipus
> Don't ask me yet—tell me of Laius—
> How did he look? How old or young was he?

Jocasta
> He was a tall man and his hair was grizzled
> already—nearly white—and in his form
> not unlike you.

Oedipus
> O God, I think I have
> called curses on myself in ignorance.

Jocasta
> What do you mean? I am terrified
> when I look at you.

Oedipus
> I have a deadly fear
> that the old seer had eyes.
> . . . If it happened there was any tie
> of kinship twixt this man and Laius—

Here at last the man and the woman are clearly seen to be united in their involvement in the same fate. But even closer than this visible unity is their unseen unity: they are both fighting to preserve the same world of appearance, which at one and the same time links and divides them; and when one of them stumbles, the same action or word makes the other imagine that he is standing all the more firmly. For this scene is the reversal of the one that follows. First Jocasta believes herself and Oedipus to be safe, just when he is falling headlong into the truth as though into a chasm; and similarly Oedipus struggles up again into his world of appearance and thinks that he can save himself, just when Jocasta is falling headlong into her part of the truth.

For what has begun to be revealed is still only half of the truth; and, because it is only half, it allows the structure built by belief to seem even more precarious at first than it did when appearances held full sway. The half-demolished world of illusion stands within the half-truth like an overhanging building of which part has collapsed. But Oedipus, still terrified by the collapse, is already at work propping up what is still standing, by prayer, by intelligence, by will-power, by his readiness to flee, from Thebes, from Corinth. from every danger that threatens (824 ff.) . . .

One hope remains, weak though it is: the hope of preserving his world of appearance, which, from man's point of view, is the same as preserving his very existence. While everything around him is calculated to bring him insight into his deed and himself, there remains a contradiction in the number! The number—for according to the account of the eye-witness, several men were responsible for the death of Laius; indeed, because of the contradiction in the number it has been suggested that the whole of the *Oedipus* is built on a trick.[22] As though the number were not merely something to which illusion can cling! and as though every illusion, on the point of sinking beneath the water, did not reach out to find something to hold on to! Is it contrary to human nature for a man to cling with all

129

his intelligence to a hope, however faint, and argue desperately on
the strength of it (839 ff.)? For in such cases intelligence is guided by
instinct. And is it contrary to human nature for a woman, with her
more powerful instinct, to try to drive her intelligence more violently and forcibly than a man? (848 ff.):

Jocasta

Be sure, at least, that this was how he told the story. He cannot unsay
it now, for every one in the city heard it—not I alone. But, Oedipus,
even if he diverges from what he said then, he shall never prove that
the murder of Laius squares rightly with the prophecy—for Loxias
declared that the king should be killed by his own son. And that poor
creature did not kill him surely,—for he died himself first. So far as prophecy goes, henceforward I shall not look to the right hand or the
left.[23]

It is not that, as has been suggested, Jocasta's 'levity' has increased
in the meantime—it is surely too much to ask that she should make
distinctions between god and prophet at this point; the difference
between this and what she said earlier in the same *epeisodion* is rather
that instead of the voice of unquestioned certainty that we heard
previously, we now hear a most vehement defence. Here, in the
guise of ingenious argument, is Jocasta's defence of her very existence, the feminine will to live and to preserve, for the man's sake,
rather than any inadequacy of character. It remains true that this
leads to *hybris* in the face of the gods. But if this is true, it is much
rather because it springs from the roots of human nature itself than
because it belongs to the particular nature of one particular human
being.

If proof were still needed that doubt and reason are here nothing
but means of defence, weapons used by an existence which feels
itself to be threatened, and are not to be confused with the attitude
of the freethinkers in the age of the Sophists, then it is provided by
the beginning of the third *epeisodion*, when Jocasta offers prayers
and sacrifice to the very same Lycean Apollo (whose image stands
next to the door of the house) whose oracle she has doubted. For
now she feels fear, even if not in herself and for herself, a terrible fear
nevertheless: fear of Oedipus' fear (915 ff.):

Jocasta
>   . . . not conjecturing,
> like a man of sense, what will be from what was,
> but he is always at the speaker's mercy,
> when he speaks terrors . . .

131

But instead of unburdening herself of her distress in loud lamentation or in pleas, as she might have done in a scene in Sophocles'
earlier style—in the way that, for example, Tecmessa or Deianira
unburdened themselves—her sacrifice is followed by a silence; and
into this silence, with an incredible effect of an intrusion from the
world outside, comes the messenger with the news of the death of
Polybus. According to the laws of the earlier style, to which the
Ajax and the *Trachiniae* still conform, some warning of this new
element should have been given before it entered. But here something completely strange suddenly rushes in: it is the daimon cutting across the action with an irony very similar to that with which
the watchman in the *Antigone* interrupted Creon's pronouncement.[24] Jocasta has scarcely turned to pray—when lo and behold, by
chance, yet miraculously, and quite independently of her volition,
there enters something which appears to put an end to all her
troubles as though by divine command (946 ff.):

Jocasta
>   . . . O oracles of the Gods, where are you now? It was from this man
> Oedipus fled, lest he should be his murderer! And now he is dead, in the
> course of nature, and not killed by Oedipus.

There now begins a series of developments which it has long
been customary to compare with moves in a game of chess.[25] But
even this outward interplay of circumstances, some of which are
introduced artificially, plays its particular part in the whole, and
sheds its particular light in the general gloom, only because it
unrolls in an atmosphere of spiritual breakdown, against a background of inner confusion. Two-thirds of the play, in fact nearly all
of it, is already over, before the outer constellation of the facts
impinges upon the inner constellation, that of the spiritual conflicts.

For everyone who has joined Oedipus on the stage up to this point—Creon, Tiresias or Jocasta—has basically been no more than an expression, result, helper or hindrance of Oedipus' own searching, straying, and illusion, and has joined him only to the extent that Oedipus' own illusion called for it and came forward to meet it. But now the action of messengers from distant cities, and the introduction of events, some very recent, some from long ago, form a barrier of linked chains around the turmoil of Oedipus' spirit. And how clearly Sophocles shows that this element is introduced from outside! The good old messenger reels from shock to shock: it is not the news that Oedipus has inherited the throne of Corinth but the news of the death of Polybus which is regarded as almost incredible, has to be proved point by point, and unleashes jubilation as though it brought relief from dire distress. . . And soon he is even less certain of what confronts him; he hesitates—shall he or shall he not? But it is his own good fortune that it is the king's greatest good fortune to learn from his lips that he is not the dead man's son! So as the bearer of good news he is brought into the conversation as a third person (989), and his account swells with the happiness of an old man who has at last been allowed to reveal how he rescued the king as a foundling—so that in his joy he does not even notice that he has changed his solemn mode of address (1008):

132

> Son,
> it's very plain you don't know what you're doing.

A homely expression like 'very' in the Greek here would still have been impossible in, for example, the *Trachiniae*, in spite of the lengthy dealings with messengers in that play;[26] the style ruled it out. For the representation of pathos in that play still gave no hint of any ironic contrasts between outward events and inner suffering, so that a clash between them could not be mirrored in the language. On the other hand, the representation of the lower orders is another point of resemblance between the *Oedipus* and the *Antigone* (232 ff.).

The contrast between the two old people who rescued Oedipus as a child, one happily pressing forward, the other suddenly afraid and holding back, echoes in the tones of the common people the contrast between the two main tragic figures as they come to recognize themselves (1131 ff.):

Herdsman
Not such that I can quickly call to mind.

Messenger
That is no wonder, master. But I'll make him remember what he does
not know. For I know, that he well knows the country of Cithaeron,
how he with two flocks, I with one kept company for three years—each
year half a year—from spring until autumn time and then when winter
came I drove my flocks to our fold home again and he to Laius'
steadings. Well—am I right or not in what I said we did?

Herdsman
You're right – although it's a long time ago.

Messenger
Do you remember giving me a child
to bring up as my foster child?

Herdsman
                    What's this?
Why do you ask this question?

Messenger
                    Look old man,
here he is – here's the man who was that child!

Herdsman
Death take you! Won't you hold your tongue!

Oedipus
                    No, no,
do not find fault with him, old man. Your words
are more at fault than his.

Herdsman
                    O best of masters,
how do I give offence?

Oedipus
                    When you refuse
to speak about the child of whom he asks you.

Herdsman
He speaks out of his ignorance, without meaning.

The contrast between the two old men who give evidence here,
one in fear and the other in joy, one denying and the other convict-
ing himself, is quite different from the contrast between the messengers in the play of intrigue in the *Trachiniae*. What this interplay
added to the main tragedy in the *Trachiniae*—in which a messenger

was similarly convicted of deception, and there was a similar incongruity between the noble dignity of the task entrusted and the vulgarity of the man to whom it was entrusted—was only the questionable nature of human relationships: false appearance and presumptuous though well-meaning deception could not prevail. . . In the *Oedipus* the two messengers are indeed in themselves, in their fears and expectations, good, honest, even if self-centred, servants, but in the context of the whole merely unwitting, ignoble instruments of divine fate. The irony which sets them in contrast is the irony of the intrigue by which the divine will interweaves higher and lower things in order to manifest itself in the instability of human greatness.

Structurally, the third *epeisodion* is also divided into two. First it climbs steadily from fear to a gasp of relief, the victory of certainty—here Jocasta is the leader; and then, with a sudden new wave of anxiety, it climbs again from fear to certainty—but this time Oedipus is the leader and Jocasta counterbalances him in her fall, her entreaties and her final departure. But there is also an inner reversal between the beginning and the end. At first it was Oedipus who could not shake off his fear, and Jocasta who urged him to trust to 'fortune', 'chance', life in whatever form it presents itself (εἰκῇ κράτιστον ζῆν, where εἰκῇ means, not 'frivolously', but disregarding the mysterious and obscure, not opening up the depths which make life problematic, for it is the gods who make man problematic): soon it is Oedipus who, taking refuge in his world of appearance for the last time, calls himself the 'son of fortune', at the very moment that Jocasta despairs of him and her life is torn from the rock to which it clings. Her action at this point has already been foreshadowed in the *Trachiniae* (815) when Deianira, suddenly breaking off and leaving the others in error about herself, made her exit. In that play too the chorus had made questionable conjectures and had been rebuked for it. But whereas in the *Trachiniae* the scene had been cast in the form of narrative report typical of the old style, filled throughout with the sustained emotion of the speaker, here Jocasta herself is seized and expelled by her own daimon, which sinks and rises, soars and collapses. And just as her disappearance signifies her fall from a false sense of security, so too the misunderstanding that she leaves behind her is disproportionately more cruel and ironic than that to which Deianira fell victim: in Deianira's case the misunderstanding consisted only of the misinterpretation of quiet actions and a noble nature; here, in the *Oedipus*, it is an ironic outburst of the daimonic latent within the person, a monstrous error springing from an innate obsession with a world of appearance—for at the same time the world of appearance establishes itself in its own ruins, as if it were fashioning a new, final vehicle of deception out of its own broken timbers (1074 ff.):

Chorus
    . . . I am afraid that trouble
    will break out of this silence.

Oedipus
    Break out what will! I at least shall be
    willing to see my ancestry, though humble.
    Perhaps she is ashamed of my low birth,
    for she has all a woman's high-flown pride.
135   But I account myself a child of Fortune,
    beneficent Fortune, and I shall not be
    dishonoured. She's the mother from whom I spring;
    the months, my brothers, marked me, now as small,
    and now again as mighty. Such is my breeding,
    and I shall never prove so false to it,
    as not to find the secret of my birth.

In the *Ajax*, deception arises from insanity sent by the god; it is something external to the man, something interposed by fate against the course of nature; it is this deception which, through the power of the god, crushes the hero's existence; he does not bring about his own destruction. In the Deianira-drama of the *Trachiniae* the pitiful mistake comes with Deianira's loss of normal awareness when her grief-laden, fearful, loving spirit is troubled. In the *Oedipus*, deception is something in the atmosphere, something hovering around, the daimonic fate in the nature and surroundings of Oedipus himself. Although these different degrees of failure to recognize the truth do not form a progression, it is not easy to imagine them in any other sequence, or to regard the much more limited tragedy of recognition in the *Trachiniae* as the more mature.

    The last two short *epeisodia* of the action are richer in movement than any other even in Sophocles. But even the final contrast of the final rise and fall would never have been possible were it not for the contrast of the two human lives here sinking to their ruin, and the deeply felt contrast between the woman's attitude to fate and the man's. For *she* is made to fear or to hope not by truth in itself, not by the true situation , but by the man she loves, by his situation and his moods. In security or fear, her relationship with the truth is *indirect*, but her relationship with life and instinct is all the more *direct*—even her good sense is instinctual. Whereas Oedipus acts with 'pathos', in the original sense of suffering, she acts with sym-pathy in the same sense. That is why she also outdoes him in joy and hope, when she is triumphant, to the point of *hybris*, and when she collapses, to the point of self-destruction. Thus she counts it as victory if he can only begin to hope again, even though his hope is vain, and her final defeat lies not in seeing her own true position but in seeing how he will see his (1060 ff.):

Jocasta
　　I beg you—do not hunt this out—I beg you,
　　if you have any care for your own life.
　　What *I* am suffering is enough.
　　　　　. . . . . .
　　O Oedipus, God help you!
　　God keep you from the knowledge of who you are!

Is Jocasta really to be characterized as 'a frivolous woman'? Hardly. For it is only the difference between the two centres of existence, those of Jocasta and Oedipus, and the difference between their relationship to life, that makes possible the interaction, cross-currents and the intensification of the tragic waves which roll through the last part of the *Oedipus*. *Her* monstrous fault, which springs from *her* distress, is her readiness to accept even this last illusion, even if it remains no more than an illusion, for the sake of life, his life. Similarly, *his* monstrous fault is to accept even such a life—the life of a blinded, accursed man—if only it is the truth. The real action does not lie in the chess-like moves of their external fates, but in their reception of the truth as it impinges upon two different types of nature and behaviour. Therefore, although the break-through to recognition had already taken the same form in the fate of Heracles in the *Trachiniae* (1143: ἰοὺ ἰοὺ δύστηνος etc.) as it now does in the *Oedipus* (1182: ἰοὺ ἰοὺ τὰ πάντ᾽ ἄρ᾽ . . .), nevertheless the self-recognition attained by Heracles still remains within the confines of his preoccupation with himself, in so far as it is no more than recognition of his own approaching death; for even if Heracles does rise out of it to perform his last act as a conqueror, he still fails, in his finite, limited existence as a hero, to see himself as he is. Thus in his case even the sudden light of recognition takes the form of self-address, self-pity and sorrowful subjectivity (1143 f.):

Heracles
Woe, woe is me! This is my miserable end.
Lost! I am lost! I see the light no longer.

137 But in the case of Oedipus the recognition no longer takes the form of an expression of his own pain, felt only by himself. While his pain is by no means diminished as a result, Oedipus' recognition sums up a total existence of, as it were, universal validity (1180 ff.):

Herdsman
            . . . But he saved it
for the most terrible troubles. If you are
the man he says you are, you're bred to misery.

Oedipus
O, O, O, they will all come,
all come out clearly! Light of the sun, let me
look upon you no more after today!
I who first saw the light bred of a match
accursed, and accursed in my living
with them I lived with, cursed in my killing.[27]

The language is no longer the elevated language used by Heracles in the *Trachiniae*, rich in powerful images, exclamations, and enumerations of his own sufferings; instead, we find here a restraint, for instead of exaggerated gesture at a moment of pathos there is a single image (not for mere decoration but a true image of the sense), and instead of underlining of too obvious a kind we find a sort of litotes—a litotes of gestures that are left to convey their own meaning. Similarly it can be seen that in the final narrative, which again has many features in common with the final narrative of the *Trachiniae* (900 ff.), although the pathos is by no means diminished in the *Oedipus*, its significance is now not so much confined to the

pathos itself, as an expression of pain; rather the pathos is filled with
a more general significance, and thus it is able to express the actual
tragic content. I do not mean the kind of gnomic summing-up
which we find everywhere at the conclusion or opening of a speech,
but the universal significance of the whole. It is true that in the
material of the *Trachiniae* everything is already much more limited
and more intimate, but the powerful public and universal significance of the last part of the *Oedipus* does not signify any lack or
shortage of some element present in the *Trachiniae*, but only that its
character as a general moral example outweighs its interest as an
individual case. We no longer have a story with its own beginning,
its own end, its own reversal, presenting an emotional shock in all
its details, as in the *Trachiniae* (900 ff.), no longer a narrated drama
for the second act and continuation of an acted drama, as in the
Antigone (1205 ff.), but the end of what is already visible, forcing its
way out into the gestures and accusations of the blinded man who at
last can see:

138

Second messenger (speaking of Jocasta) 1242 ff.:

> . . . she went
> straight to her marriage bed, tearing her hair
> with both her hands, and crying upon Laius
> long dead—Do you remember, Laius,
> that night long past which bred a child for us
> to send you to your death and leave
> a mother making children with her son?
> And then she groaned and cursed the bed in which
> she brought forth husband by her husband, children
> by her own child . . .

(speaking of Oedipus) 1268 ff.:

> . . . He tore the brooches—
> the gold chased brooches fastening her robe—
> away from her and lifting them up high
> dashed them on his own eyeballs, shrieking out
> such things as: They will never see the crime
> I have committed or had done upon me!
> Dark eyes, now in the days to come look on
> forbidden faces, do not recognize
> those whom you long for . . .

Here the action in itself has already become an image, and the diction too: the image depends on the fact that physical and spiritual sight have been combined—it can hardly be the physical sight of Oedipus now that becomes aware of his past actions. 'Committed' and 'had done upon me' are polar expressions, referring to the whole of existence, and they should not be interpreted as a paraphrase for the marriage unwittingly contracted and his murder of Laius; on the contrary, the phrase signifies that he has 'committed' and 'had crimes done upon' him in a reversal of the normal sense. In the future 'darkness' there will be a 'seeing' and a 'not seeing', as there has been until now in the light: a seeing of things which he should never have seen with his eyes; and a not seeing, a not knowing of people whom he would wish to see: for thus he was driven by his will to discover his origins; in the 'darkness', the physical and spiritual darkness: for it is with this that his real seeing begins, in the form of recognition out of the night of blindness, recognition which is self-recognition. In the same way as Jocasta had left the stage earlier on with a speech in a form resembling a riddle or *griphos* (1249–50), here, too, the *griphos*-like tangle indicates the tangled nature of Oedipus' fate, in which blindness and seeing are confused.[28]

Finally, the last lament shows again, this time in lyrics, how the particular case contains a more general significance, and how the physical fate contains a spiritual one as well: the 'suffering' is 'twofold' (1320). In the rather similar lament in the *Ajax*, 'night' and 'light' stand for the realms of 'life' and 'death' which the sufferer transposes as he pours out a torrent of lament invoking both; here in the *Oedipus* the lament goes beyond its literal meaning, so that 'darkness' means both physical blindness and the threatening darkness of fate and the daimon:

Ajax (394)
> O
> Darkness that is my light,
> Murk of the underworld, my only brightness,
> Oh, take me to yourself to be your dweller.

By contrast, in the *Oedipus Tyrannus* (1313):

Darkness!
Horror of darkness enfolding, resistless, unspeakable visitant
                    sped by an ill wind in haste!
madness and stabbing pain and memory
of evil deeds I have done!

Again, it seems characteristic of the *Ajax* and the *Trachiniae* as opposed to the *Oedipus* that the sinister and threatening region into which the *Oedipus* is continually reaching is not given a name in the two earlier plays, nor does it enter into the situations in them. The Athena who punishes the hero in the *Ajax* is a figure familiar from epic, and as such she takes over and conceals in herself the rôle of the enigmatic and sinister element, the 'cloud' which looms over man's splendour in the *Oedipus*, independent of any character and hardly given a name, not even that of Apollo.

Something which is peculiar to Attic tragedy as a whole, the habit of luxuriating in horror, of investing terror with a kind of voluptuousness, has in this play more than any other extended into the attitude of the tragic hero. Whereas elsewhere the choruses, the words, the poetry, but not the unconscious victims, luxuriated in the delights of pain, here the victim and the one who luxuriates, writhing and pointing to himself, flowering in his torment, speaking and singing out the burden of his obsession, are one and the same. Now there are no biers, no *ekkyklema*, no apparatus: from inside the house the blinded man calls for someone to open the door and lead him to the light.[29] Instead of being brought in, put on show so that men can point him out, the victim is eager to put himself on show, to display the monstrous discovery that he has made in his search for himself: the blinded man that he has been all along . . .[30] And the traditional action of display, such as the exhibition of the blood-stained Heracles, as he throws back his coverings to show the state that he is in (*Trach.* 1078), or of the blood-stained dummy which represents Ajax, sword in breast—for the covers were only thrown over it so that it could be uncovered afterwards (*Ajax* 1003, cf. 915)—this piece of tragic stage-action, with its archaic colouring, in the *Oedipus* becomes for the first time part of the figure of the hero himself; whereas the exhibition of the dead Ajax and the dying Heracles remain merely something which is done to them, here the exhibition is a gesture and action of self-exposure, which cannot be divorced from the character of Oedipus himself.[31]

Everything which had surrounded and supported Oedipus, the whole world around him, ancestors and contemporaries, parents and children, city and people, his own rank and his own royal judgment (1369 ff.), all these expel him: how is he to 'see his children', his 'city' with its 'towers', its 'images of the gods', his people amongst whom he grew up to be regarded as the noblest of all men[32]—expelled as he is from now on both from the realm of the living and from the realm of the dead: even death, as a home-going, as the gathering of a man to his own, would be some sort of belonging; but this, even as a possibility, is totally denied with all the vehemence of tragic unconditionality (1368 ff.):

Chorus
    You would be better dead than blind and living.
Oedipus
    What I have done here was best done—don't tell me
    otherwise, do not give me further counsel.[33]

It is Ajax in reverse, as it were: no longer a man who calls 'death to his aid', who remembers in his last wishes the world of his fate that surrounds him—Zeus and the Erinyes, Salamis and Troy, river and field, Hades and the light—but a man who, if it were only possible, would like nothing better than to destroy his hearing too and thus 'dam up' all the 'sources' by means of which he participates in the world (1388).

And the apostrophes in the finale, which are usually addressed to friends, intimates and relations—in the *Trachiniae* to the hero's own arms, shoulders and bodily strength, in the *Ajax* to the scene of his heroic deeds, in the *Antigone* to the dead of the family—are now addressed to what had been estranged, inimical, false, from the beginning (1391 ff.):

Oedipus
    Cithaeron, why did you receive me? . . .
    O Polybus and Corinth and the house . . .
                        Crossroads,
    and hidden glade . . .

141

> . . . O marriage, marriage!
> you bred me and again when you had bred
> bred children of your child . . .

Now for the first time the apostrophes become in themselves tragic figures of speech, since they are directed against the very man who utters them—an invocation of the life which is turning against itself. And in the end the revelation, with its last requests, becomes in itself a tragic form, because it is self-contradictory, self-destructive, denying itself through its own actions. Oedipus' retraction of his own words and his curse upon them, his fervent request to the others to cover him, kill him or throw him into the sea, to expel him, to do anything to ensure that he shall never again be seen by a single soul—all this is self-contradictory after he himself had cried out to be led into the light. But at the same time this contradiction is part of the very nature of tragic pathos: for it is characteristic of tragic pathos to exult in itself, and in so doing to affirm what in its suffering it denies . . .

A counterpoint to Oedipus and the curses he calls down on himself is provided by the entry of a non-tragic figure: Creon. That same Creon who, when unjustly accused in the *agon* scene, proved that he was in the right, now decides the fate of the polluted outlaw, with down-to-earth sympathy, not even inhumanely or unfeelingly, nor without first consulting the gods. Thus, as the character with no fate, the character alien to fate, Creon serves as the unchanging standard against which all the changes are measured: it is not so long since Oedipus had heartily despised him, yet now, to the fallen hero in his storm of self-abasement, he is the 'best of all' as opposed to the 'basest' Oedipus (1433); and when he does not prevent the monstrous blind man from touching his daughters once again he is regarded as granting a great favour. Thus, for all his sympathy, he seems all too cold in comparison with Oedipus, whose full heart pours forth love from his sufferings. As one who is safe from tragedy, in his combined rôle of companion, opponent and friend, he stands in the same relationship to Oedipus as Odysseus to Ajax. But here again we see how in the *Oedipus* the spirit that moves the play has changed by comparison with the *Ajax*. For not only is there no development in the *Ajax*, there is no reversal in the relationship between the opposing forces either: Odysseus stands in the same

relationship to Ajax at the end of the play as he does in the beginning. Yet the figure of Odysseus in the epic cycle would not have
been resistant to a change in his attitude towards his mortal enemy
during his lifetime and after his death. Thus whereas the *Ajax* is a
stationary drama, the *Oedipus Tyrannus* moves and turns. At the
same time the opposition of the figures in the *Oedipus* is deepened to
the point of impenetrability. There is certainly a difference in greatness, nobility and humanity at the end between Oedipus and Creon,
greater than is shown in any other drama; and yet it is no longer
possible to reduce the contrast to an easy formula, about characterization, for example, or about morality. Opposed to Ajax and his
great, but rigid, heroism, stood the mobility, humanity and insight
of Odysseus, and the vengefulness, conceit, envy and pettiness of
the figures of Menelaus and Agamemnon. In the *Antigone*, self-
sacrifice and youth stood opposed to age and the tyrant's self-
assertion . . .—in opposition to Oedipus there stands no more than
the merely non-tragic.

143

But in this tragic lesson, this *Ecce*, there is one question that has
not been raised—a question which no-one since Sophocles, not
even Euripides, seems to have been able to avoid as soon as they are
confronted with tragedy: where does the guilt lie? Admittedly,
Oedipus speaks of himself in words which are used of a criminal
who is guilty of another's death.[34] But that does not mean that any
question was raised about the guilt (*αἰτία*). Admittedly, the god is
named as the author of the deed, yet this is not so that man may get
the better of the god, or of himself in the eyes of god, nor that he
may wrestle with god, or destroy himself before god for the sake of
his guilt, but only to indicate the correlation between man and god:
for the naming of a god is part of the lesson: it is a manifestation of
god which coincides with a manifestation of man (1329 ff.):

Oedipus
It was Apollo, friends, Apollo,
that brought this bitter bitterness, my sorrows to completion.
But the hand that struck me
was none but my own.[35]

Nor is the language of sacral law, which is certainly heard here,
enough to make any difference to this omission. It is rather that the

language of sacral law is used because it is concerned with the same rules and foundations of life which are here in question. But there is no search for where the 'guilt' lies in the sense of sacral law either. And even if one were to imagine that a court composed of gods or men had acquitted Oedipus of all guilt, like Orestes in Aeschylus, it would still not help him in the least; for what meaning would such an acquittal have in the face of the contradiction between what he has imagined he is, and what he is? Nor would the opposite verdict of 'guilty' add anything to his state. Orestes *can* be acquitted, by himself and by others, but Oedipus *cannot* be released from what he has recognized as the truth about himself. The question of responsibility for what happened, wherever it is raised and in whatever form, whether this responsibility lies with men, with gods or with the laws of nature, and whether the answer is yes or no—this question, without which the greatest tragedies of Euripides and Aeschylus are unthinkable, just does not arise in Sophocles. So there is no decision here about justice and atonement—nothing would be more misguided than to regard Oedipus' blinding as an atonement—or about freedom and necessity.[36] What we have had to consider is illusion and truth as the opposing forces between which man is bound, in which he is entangled, and in whose shackles, as he strives towards the highest he can hope for, he is worn down and destroyed.

V

ELECTRA

Was it impossible to improve on the fate-laden style which had reached the heights of the *Ecce* in the *Oedipus Tyrannus*? Was the *Oedipus* the culmination of a poet's career? When that play and those which led up to it were finished, had the poet said everything that could be said in that form? It is a fact that this style is no longer to be found in those later dramas that have survived.

Of all the plays of Sophocles, it is the *Electra* in which the construction, the experienced controlling hand of the poet, is most clearly in evidence.[1] No new exploration is made here into the extreme areas of human sublimity or danger, to follow those made in the *Oedipus Tyrannus*. Instead, in this play, the dramatist carefully steers, spins, unfolds, and prepares situations in which the spirit can be seen in the richness of its contrasts; he confidently controls a complex game of hearts in love and hate, in powerlessness and resistance, in hope and torment; he allots bitter experiences, removes burdens, intensifies the cries of the heart to a shrill dissonance, which is then resolved in bliss; and instead of invasions from the realm of the daimonic and divine, the outbursts, despair and reversals in this play arise from the struggle of an exiled life to find its connections, the struggle of the soul of a sister for the soil and foothold from which she has been torn by the wickedness of man. Sophocles was clearly not interested in writing a new drama of vengeance in the style of Aeschylus in order to outdo the *Oresteia* or to reinterpret it in Apollo's favour.[2] Rather, he takes the vengeance motif, and uses it as the basis on which to build up his actual drama: a drama of suffering, powerlessness, cruelty, noble immoderation, both in hate and love. Even when vengeance is finally achieved it still has to be justified by suffering. In this play, the fate of isolation and exile is not something which is merely threatened at the beginning and breaks out in a most terrible and bloody form only at the end, as in the dramas of catastrophe from the *Ajax* to the *Oedipus Tyrannus*; the feeling of expulsion is there all the time, spreading out in painful detail through every step and stage of the whole drama, until it is resolved by the divine ordinance. It is clearly no mere chance that this is the form of the three surviving dramas of Sophocles' old age, the *Electra*, the *Philoctetes* and the *Oedipus at Colonus*.

But the *Electra* is even more closely connected with the *Philoctetes* by the fact that each has a framework of intrigue which carries pain and loneliness to their limits before relief comes. It is even possible to narrate the framework of the action of the *Electra* in such a way that it sounds just like the *Philoctetes*, and vice-versa. In both plays, a task is assigned at the beginning in such a way that there is no doubt that it will be performed: it is prophesied, the gods have commanded it. But the person entrusted with the task is faced with the question of how he is to carry it out; a plan is laid, the beginning of a deception is set up before our very eyes[3]—at the expense of a third person, the victim, who at this point is still not known or brought into consideration, yet someone who is close and friendly. . . The plan is held up at one moment, then threatened by a tortured soul who rebels against it, but finally carried out successfully.

This form of intrigue, which begins to dominate the stage more and more from the 420's onwards, is in itself borrowed from the plays of Euripides.[4] But in both the *Electra* and the *Philoctetes* the intrigue sets the stage for the main action, and this main action deals with wider problems than Euripides. In the *Electra* the new outward form even conflicts to a certain extent with the old saga, since the deception spreads beyond all bounds and almost overshadows its own aim, vengeance. But the conflict is not confined to the outward form; the new inner form also clashes with the traditional tale to some extent, for the emphasis placed on the figure of Electra in her suffering is so great that it overshadows the man of action, Orestes, to the same extent that the deception overshadows its aim.

147   All this would be a fault were it not for the fact that the *Electra* is a late variant, superior to its own type, of a dramatic style which had had its day. As a variant of the drama of intrigue, it masks and covers the interaction of rival parties characteristic of the genre with a surge of strong emotion, in relation to which the intrigue is scarcely more than the rolling stone which sets off the avalanche; and as a variant of the drama of revenge and sacrifice, it masks and

covers the fearsomeness characteristic of the genre with the display
of a suffering whose cause is wholly imaginary and unfounded, the
violence of which greatly overshadows the true fearsomeness of the
revenge and the deed to be avenged. Thus this 'tragedy' differs in
two ways from the original form of the story: in taking lightly what
should be taken seriously, and in taking seriously what should be
taken lightly. It is similar to many of Shakespeare's late plays, where
the sense of the framework no longer coincides with the sense of the
actual play.

Since the ending and the beginning, the plan and the deed in this
instance form no more than the framework of the actual play, a kind
of prologue and epilogue, and do not have a tone of voice of their
own, Orestes, and with him Apollo of Delphi, necessarily become
less important. In fact Apollo does appear as instigator, not only of
the deed but also of its manner of execution, the 'trick', but only in
the rôle of supervisor, justifier and guarantor rather than as a figure
who actually participates in the deed and intervenes in the action.
And Orestes is so untragic a character, so unburdened, so cheerful,
so un-Orestes-like, when, at the beginning, he returns home to
perform the command of the god as though it were a heroic deed;
and his joyful eagerness is surpassed only by that of his aged
paedagogus, who delights, as servants do, in outdoing his master.
Yet it is in the same light tone that Orestes alludes to a burden that
weighs surprisingly little on the opening of the play (44 ff.):

Orestes
                        Here is your story.
You are a stranger coming from Phanoteus,
their Phocian friend, the greatest of their allies.
Tell them a sudden accident befell
Orestes, and he's dead. Swear it on oath.
Say in the Pythian games he was rolled
out of his chariot at high speed.
That is your story now.
We shall go first to my father's grave
and crown it, as he bade us, with libations
and with cuttings from my thick, luxuriant hair . . .

For why should it irk me if I die *in word*
but *in deed* come through alive and win my glory?

To my thinking, no word is base when spoken with profit.
Before now I have seen wise men often
dying empty deaths as far as words reported them,
and then, when they have come to their homes again,
they have been honoured more, even to the skies.
So in my case I venture to predict
that I who die according to this rumour
shall, like a blazing star, glare on my foes again.[5]

Thus even the trick which is to have such serious consequences has to lose its serious aspect as far as Orestes is concerned; it cannot be motivated by any perceptible danger or else the play would become a drama of danger; it is enough that Apollo of Delphi has commanded it, and that the announcement that the living Orestes is dead promises success. One has only to look at Aeschylus or Euripides to see how this goes against the grain of the story.

If the figure of Orestes is stripped of tragic weight, Electra, from the moment she appears, carries a proportionately heavier burden: a burning obligation assigned to her, firmly rivetted to her being, an obligation and a passion to keep alive an inescapable, terrible duty in an environment that is partly criminal and partly forgetful. For her part, she does not fulfil any command of Apollo or of any other god—and in this too she differs from Antigone—nor is she merely an avenger or a woman possessed by a daimon;[6] she is not intended, like Euripides' Medea, to show what a mere 'woman' is capable of: on the contrary, she appears in a world of the wicked and the false as the extreme of great-heartedness which enables normal humanity to survive; she is the woman who loves and hates from the depths of her heart; because of her hate and her love, she suffers, is persecuted, and is even alienated from herself, disfigured, and consumed by her own fires. Antigone too had been full of hate and love, but the combination of the two forces is incomparably more extreme and more contradictory in Electra; she is almost torn apart by love and hate. . . This conflict is another indication that this play belongs with the late *Philoctetes* and second *Oedipus* rather than with the works of the early period.

And just as in this late period suffering is no longer brought about by 'fate' or the 'gods' or one's own 'blindness' or the 'daimon' within, but by trickery, cunning and man's inhumanity, so Electra's task, atonement for the murdered victim, becomes almost a symbol of resistance to evil and indifference, meanness and carelessness, man's forgetfulness in general (236 ff.):

Electra
What is the natural measure of my sorrow?
Come, how when the dead are in question,
can it be honourable to forget?
In what human being is this instinctive?
Never may I have honour of such,
nor, if I dwell with any good thing,
may I live at ease, by restraining
the wings of shrill lament to my father's dishonour.
For if he that is dead
is earth and nothing,
poorly lying,
and they shall never in their turn
pay death for death in justice,
then shall all shame be dead
and all men's piety.

At the beginning the brother and sister are worlds apart in nature and emotion. And yet it is at the beginning that they almost come into contact, one coming from outside, enthusiastically bent on victory, the other suffering—this drama of changing tensions between closeness and distance is rich in such 'almosts' (only the *Philoctetes* comes anywhere near it in this respect): Orestes already hears the first sounds of her morning lament, would like to listen, and is already asking: 'Is that not Electra?'—but the eagerness of his old *paedagogus*, in whom the 'urge for victory' of an 'old racehorse' has not stirred in vain, drags him away as he almost recognizes her. . . The climax of the opening scene is a sharp break. It is only by separation and contact that the situation, that is the tension between spirit and event, is created.[7] It is only the unexpected tearing apart at this point which eventually gives the moment when the sister addresses her brother at the end of her monody the sense of an opposition of near and far (110 ff.):

Electra
House of the Death God, house of Persephone,
Hermes of the Underworld, holy Curse,

Furies the Dread Ones, children of the Gods,
all ye who look upon those who die unjustly,
all ye who look upon the theft of a wife's love,
come all and help take vengeance for my father,
for my father's murder!
And send me my brother to my aid.
For alone to bear the burden I am no longer strong enough,
the burden of the grief that weighs against me.

This is no longer a situation where the divinity has its sport with men as in the *Antigone* or the *Oedipus Tyrannus*; this is only the poet having his sport with his creations.

Electra lamenting to the chorus, opposing her sister, then arguing against her mother: that produces, for the first *epeisodia*, two argument scenes of increasing tension. But these are no longer arguments like those in the *Antigone*, let alone those in the *Ajax*: not black against white, like pettiness in borrowed clothing against proven greatness in the *Ajax*, or the 'folly' of wrong behaviour against the 'folly' of self-sacrifice in the *Antigone*; nor do these laments have anything in common with those 'monologues' of archaic style which tell of the suffering caused by fate: in the *Electra* the speeches burst out, 'now at last', after long restraint, or 'now at last in spite of everything', since the opportunity presents itself, and since the burden of the heart must in the end be poured out somehow or other. Aegisthus is away today, Electra is able to move freely, leave the house, leave her usual self, speak to the women. But she is brought to the point of speaking just as much by her mother, and even her sister; everything that has been building up has to come out in reproaches, defence, justification. She overflows with the joy of pouring out her emotions which finds relief in a language which cannot possibly be confused with Sophocles' earlier diction: yet it cannot be regarded as 'rhetorical' and in the Euripidean manner either, except by tone-deaf philologists who have missed the inner impetus which lends movement to the words, and who have studied only the outward scheme, the plan of attack (*epicheirēma*), and have calculated the content by analysing the form.

For example, when the speaker begins by mentioning her reluctance, this is no longer the attitude of defence against the unseemly or against threats from the daimon to which we have become

accustomed; instead, this reluctance now restricts the speech and
dams it in like a river overflowing its banks (254 ff.):

Electra
  Women, I am ashamed if I appear
  to you too much the mourner with constant dirges.
  What I do, I must do. Pardon me . . .

The enclosed, archaic character of the speeches in the earlier plays
has vanished, and instead of the attitude of consciousness of suffering inflicted by fate, instead of the appeals, the *gnomai*, the narratives
of pathos, instead of the solemn introductory phrases such as 'I tell
you', 'know that' and so forth[8]—instead of all this there is an
outpouring which invades and overwhelms the mind of the listener
(266 ff.):

Electra
  What sort of days do you imagine
  I spend, watching Aegisthus sitting
  on my father's throne, watching him wear
  my father's self-same robes, watching him
  at the hearth where he killed him, pouring libations?
                    (And Clytemnestra—)
  No, as though laughing at what was done,
  she has found out the day on which she killed
  my father in her treachery, and on that day
  has set a dancing festival and sacrifices
  sheep, in monthly ritual, 'to the Gods that saved her'.
  So within that house I see, to my wretchedness,
152   the accursed feast named in his honour.
  I see it, moan, and waste away, lament—
  but only to myself. I may not even cry
  as much as my heart would have me . . .

That her sufferings are retailed to attentive ears, and apprehended
by sympathetic hearts, is so essential to the pace, the tone, the beat,
that the idea of pathetic 'narrative' no longer arises. Not only is
there no speech in the whole of Aeschylus with such power to
penetrate the consciousness of another, but there is nothing
approaching it in the *Ajax* or the *Trachiniae* either. Indeed, it is an

innovation more recent than the forcefulness of the speeches in the *Oedipus Tyrannus*. And it is clear that it is not just a question of an exceptional character, not just the special case of the rejected king's daughter, but a new stylistic phase—for the same language appears again in the *Philoctetes*, which was written soon after and displays the same unburdening, the same abundance of forms of speech which reach out, move forward, and touch the spirit. Just as here in the *Electra* we have 'what sort . . . do you imagine', so in the *Philoctetes* (276 ff.):

Philoctetes
  Think, boy, of that awakening when I awoke
  and found them gone; think of the useless tears
  and curses on myself. . . .

Unlike what is found in the earlier narrative form, the content of these words no longer stands as a self-contained entity, like a solid island with 'pathos' lapping at its shores; instead, it is carried along by its flood and outpouring of communication. So important is it that the listeners should understand exactly how the speaker feels that the language becomes imitative—in an unprecedented fashion; not merely in the sense that every speech in a theatre is imitative, but imitative in a way that stems from the inner movement of the words: to make known what she has suffered, Electra must start to imitate the voice she hates (287 ff):

Electra
  For this woman, all nobility in words,
153 abuses me: 'You hateful thing, God-hated,
  are you the only one whose father is dead?
  Is there no one else of human kind in mourning?
  My curse upon you! May the Gods below
  grant you from your present sorrows no release!'
  Such is the tone of her insults . . .

The pathos of the earlier style was certainly more dignified, more elevated in its isolation from the outside world. But to compensate for this loss, this new kind of pathos is more mobile and more active; and instead of accepting the situations given by the invasions of fate, it creates and begets them itself in an ever-changing series, out of its own self and its relationship to the presence of the listener. It is characteristic of the phase to which the *Electra* and the *Philoctetes* belong that in the relationship between one person and another, in hate as well as in love, in the voice of a tender heart as well as of bitterness, both plays succeed in sounding notes which had never been heard before.

Just as Ismene had been contrasted with Antigone, so Chrysothemis is contrasted with her sister, Electra. Again there is a confrontation between the 'unreasonableness' (ἀβουλία, 398) of obstinacy and the 'reason' (φρονεῖν, 394) of compromise, between the refusal to abandon 'loved ones' and the 'yielding' to the power of 'the ruler' (395 f.) But the speeches are now so much more fluid, the contrasts are expressed with so much greater an abundance of words. Instead of the earlier magical effects of reserve, hardness and bitterness, instead of such unheard-of things as the argument between the girls in the *Antigone* about the two kinds of sisterly devotion, we now have for the first time a use of antithesis in such breadth that critics might well be tempted to dismiss it—hastily and mistakenly—as 'Euripidean'. However, Sophocles makes use of this form not in order to set one principle against another—nor one will against another, as in the *Antigone*, either—but to distinguish a whole manner of life (*bios*) that consists in suffering, with its self-assertion, from other possible *bioi* which expose it to danger, disfigurement, attack and opposition. To the same extent that Electra is the exiled, hard, unrelenting character, Chrysothemis is the easy, comfortable figure; she lives like a princess, Electra like a slave, although she need say no more than a word in order to receive the same treatment. It is on account of the manner of life (*bios*) chosen by Electra that the antitheses go so much deeper than those of the *Antigone*. It is the way in which the whole breadth of a person's existence forces its way into the language—though this is not to be confused with the attitude which is found in the *Trachiniae*—which demonstrates how closely the *Electra* is related to the *Philoctetes*.

An achievement cannot be repeated, either in literature or in life. The contrast between Chrysothemis and Electra uses more advanced and more developed means of expression. Every word that Antigone had uttered was so stark, so firm, so self-sufficient! Anything which was not part of her and of her deed was something alien, something disturbing. The fact that even in her sister she came up against nothing but doubts was enough to make her want to have nothing more to do with her (*Ant.* 69). And this was reflected in her language: it separated her from others, raised barriers, it was inimitably noble in its reserve (83, 553, 555):

Antigone
  For me, don't borrow trouble. Clear your fate.

  To save yourself. I shall not envy you.

  You chose to live when I chose death.

So too all her other brief remarks. But observe by contrast to what an extent Electra's accusations in this passage reach out, how they put themselves in the place of the other, compare, expose, and destroy her! She breaks out at the very point where Antigone had fallen silent. And all that she says is packed with expressions that go home to the other (345 ff.):[9]

Electra
  Now you must make your choice, one way or the other,
  either to be a fool
  or sensible—and to forget your friends.
  Here you are saying: 'If I had the strength,
  I would show my hatred of them!' You who, when I
  did everything to take vengeance for my father,
  never did a thing to help—yes, discouraged the doer.
  Is it not this cowardice on top of misery?
  Tell me, or let me tell you, what benefit
  I would achieve by giving up my mourning?
  Do I not live? Yes, I know, badly, but
  for me enough. And I hurt them
  and so give honour to the dead, if there is, there
  in that other world, anything that brings pleasure.
  But you who hate, you tell me, hate in word only
  but in fact live with our father's murderers . . .
  Have your rich table and your abundant life.
  All the food I need is the quiet of my conscience.

But the reply of Chrysothemis, too, strikes home the harder, and

hurts the more, because what Electra finds most monstrous does
not even make an impression on her (372 ff.):

Chrysothemis
  O ladies, I am used to her and her words.
  I never would have mentioned this, had not
  I learned of the greatest of misfortunes coming
  her way. . . .

And, conversely, what is most terrible for Chrysothemis, what
she mentions as an awful warning—imprisonment in a subterranean dungeon—is something which Electra all the more
mockingly asks for and longs for: then just let Aegisthus come, in
that case—*you* will be out of my sight! There are cruel words in the
Antigone, but none saved up and delivered so woundingly. The
relationship in the *Antigone* is one of growing separation; in the
Electra it becomes positively aggressive. The lack of comprehension
is no longer a force which encircles two centres and returns to itself,
but in this new style it turns outward, pours out, clashes in a
friendly or unfriendly fashion. The change that we see in the language is the same that has affected the scenic form.

Now the same thing can be perceived in the 'characters'. Certainly we would be the last to deny that there are such things as
'characters' in Sophocles. Electra is not Antigone, Ismene is not
Chrysothemis. However, if one puts the *Ajax*, the *Antigone* and the
Trachiniae on one side, and the *Electra* and the *Philoctetes* on the
other, there is a noticeable difference in the attitudes and actions of
the characters over and above the difference in characterization. In
the former, earlier group, the individual is concerned only with
himself in his *pathos*. In the last analysis there is no give and take,
either of good or of bad. This is just as true of the language as of the
action. Even the arguments between the characters in the earlier
dramas arise from irritation caused by their own selfishness, nobility or blindness more often than from any desire to wound
each other by means of the penetrating knowledge that they have
of each other, or with an eye for the other's vulnerability. Quite
apart from all the differences in characterization, the different
nature and attitude of the arguments in the *Electra* would make
them impossible in the early plays, as impossible as the extra-

vagances of Electra's blossoming love, her ardour and devotion.

The scenes themselves are no longer the unambiguous reactions
of a *pathos* to unambiguous situations dictated by fate; most of them
have a turning-point in the middle and tend to have a double
theme.[10] The two girls had been torn apart by the fact that Electra
revels in endurance and Chrysothemis is stifled by it, but the first
glimmer of hope—Clytemnestra's terrifying dream—is enough to
bring them together again after the mounting discord. (The reversal
begins at 405). To ease the transition from the dissonance of the first
half of the scene, the second half begins with one character following the lead of the other, and ends with an agreement between the
two sisters on a unanimous decision to sacrifice and pray (435 ff.):

Electra
Throw them to the winds! Or hide them in deep hollowed
earth, somewhere where no particle of them
may ever reach my father where he lies.

The poor but pious gift from a loving heart is to take the place of
the showy offering from the murderess. Whereas in Aeschylus'
Oresteia the procession of the women, the sacrifice and the dream
had been united in a single surging sweep of lyric, Sophocles
constructs two scenes of increasing tension from the sacrifice and
prayer; sacrifice to the dead and conjuration of the dead, which in
the *Oresteia* pervade the stage with the immanent power of incanta-
tion, are transformed in the *Electra* to dialogue, to pleading, to
command, to words that strike home.[11] Instead of Electra being
present for the sake of the conjuration, as she had been in Aeschylus,
here the *thought* of the conjuration is present for the sake of
Electra—in order to reveal her in her poverty, her nobility, her
greatness, her weakness. This change in sense brings with it a
change in tone—everything is now far removed from Aeschylus
(450):

Electra
  . . . Such a small offering
yet all I have! Give him this unanointed
lock of hair, and here, my girdle, unadorned. . . .

The word 'mutilation' (ἐμασχαλίσθη, 445), which in Aeschylus [*Choeph*. 439] is a cry which spurs the conspirators on to revenge, in Sophocles is not even addressed to Orestes, but is added, as one more antithesis, to the pleas from sister to sister. How flat this is in comparison with Aeschylus![12] But the difference between them makes it all the more clear that it is now no longer a question of sacrifice, fate or ruling powers, but of moods, the tones of the heart, and contrasting attitudes of one human being to another.

In the scene which contains the argument between daughter and mother there is again a reversal, of a type which is only to be expected after the *Antigone*.[13] Thus 556:

Clytemnestra
> Of course, you may speak the truth. If you had always begun
> our conversations so, you would not have been
> so painful to listen to.

prepares for the reversal in 622:

Clytemnestra
> O vile and shameless, I and my words and deeds
> give you too much talk.

At the same time the increase in tension is less sudden and the reversal less powerful than in the *Antigone* or the *Oedipus Tyrannus*. Instead, something else now assumes greater significance for the form of the speeches in the argument: in place of that strong rejection, that violent expulsion which was so characteristic of the earlier style, we now have for the first time the force of attraction between enemies. The belligerent words begin to stretch out their tentacles, so to speak. They suck everything into themselves, and leave nothing behind. Even the malicious irony is an aspect of this sucking-in. Much of what is usually called rhetoric here is in fact nothing other than this violent attraction and pulling of one existence into the subjective realm of validity of another; and the weaker its position, the more fiercely this realm of validity defends and entrenches itself: e.g. 526 ff.:

Clytemnestra
> The death he got from me. From me. I know it,
> well. There is no denial in me. Justice,

Justice it was that took him, not I alone.
You would have served the cause of Justice if
you had been right-minded.
For this your father whom you always mourn,
alone of all the Greeks, had the brutality
to sacrifice your sister to the Gods . . .
Tell me, now, why he sacrificed her. Was it
for the sake of the Greeks?
They had no share in my daughter to let them kill her.
Was it for Menelaus' sake, his brother? . . .
Or had the God of Death some longing to feast
on my children rather than hers? Or had
that accursed father lost the love of mine
and felt it still for Menelaus' children?
This was the act of a father thoughtless
or with bad thoughts. That is how I see it
even if you differ with me.

But this malevolent characteristic of getting hold of another is
not confined to the speeches of Clytemnestra. Electra's arguments
come very close to them as far as *form* is concerned: she pulls her
enemy out of her hiding-place, drags her into the light. . . To
answer the question of justice it is the legend that she chooses to use
(563 ff.):

Electra
Ask Artemis the Huntress what made her hold
the many winds in check at Aulis. Or
I'll tell you this. *You* dare not learn from her.
My father, as I hear, when at his sport,
started from his feet a horned dappled stag
within the Goddess' sanctuary.

To interrogate the divinity would be a transgression, οὐ
θέμις . . . But on the human level the question of right becomes
entangled in self-contradiction (582 ff.):

Electra
If we shall kill one in another's requital,
you would be the first to die, if you met with justice.
No. Think if the whole is not a mere excuse.

Please tell me for what cause you now commit
the ugliest of acts . . .

False humanity is now dragged forth, like a reluctant beast from
its den. Never before had a dialogue dug its claws into an alien
creature like this, or pursued it like this to the very last refuge . . .[14]

But this *epeisodion*, too, changes direction, first from the argument between mother and daughter to Clytemnestra's prayer, then
from that to the announcement of the death of Orestes. It is only
after the quarrel has reached its height and Electra has come out
victorious that a transition comes, after the recriminations of
Clytemnestra in her wounded pride—a transition similar to that in
the *Oedipus Tyrannus* from the argument between the brothers-in-
law to the confidences between mother and son (630 ff.):[15]

Clytemnestra
Hold your peace at last. Allow me sacrifice,
since I have permitted you to say all you will.

Electra
I allow you, yes, I bid you, sacrifice.
Do not blame my lips; for I will say no more.

And by this means the scene achieves the same alternation between inward barriers and gestures of approach which first complicated the action in the *Oedipus Tyrannus*.[16] Although the quarrel is
over, it still echoes on, vibrating in the mind, and its waves continue
to overflow into the silent prayer. The silent but all the more
triumphant presence of the victorious Electra—and her triumph is
the greater because she is apparently only obeying her mother,
speaking at her command and falling silent at her command—this
triumph affects the guilty woman's prayer: Clytemnestra, with her
hypocritical heart, that heart which refuses to admit the truth even
to itself, is able to express herself even less freely in the presence of
Electra than she would otherwise have done (637 ff.):

Clytemnestra
Phoebus Protector, hear me, as I am,
although the word I speak is muted. Not among friends
is it spoken, nor may I unfold the whole
to the light while this girl stands beside me,

lest with her chattering tongue, wagging in malice,
she sow in all the city bad reports.

She is thus forced to conceal her true desires in two ways: from herself, and from the threatening presence of the other woman (657 ff.):

Clytemnestra
>   Grant to all of us what we ask.
> For all the rest, although I am silent,
> I know you are a God and know it all.

For if it had not been her deepest desire to conceal from herself the truth about herself, to justify herself in her own eyes, she would not have commanded her daughter to speak first. Thus in her prayer concealment and revelation, fear and hope, appearance and reality, confession and evil intent are all at war with one another; her very attempt at concealment reveals her as a creature who is falsely ambivalent, who hides her own nature from herself, a creature who has become corrupt.

But quite apart from her corrupt character, her concealment no longer takes the form of a monologue as in the *Ajax* and the *Trachiniae*, but is only one part of a whole which is composed of reciprocal kinds of behaviour. A scene like this second *epeisodion* has more than an end and a beginning. As in the revelation scene in the *Oedipus Tyrannus*, where Jocasta's rise to triumph and her downfall ran in counterpoint to Oedipus' downfall and rise to triumph, like the voices of a two-part fugue, so too Electra's rise and triumph and her downfall combine to form a counterpoint to the downfall and rise of Clytemnestra. And even if the momentum for these rises and falls is no longer provided by fate or the gods, even if it only a case of man's deceitful hope and despair being set in a cruelly deceitful confrontation and becoming the victims of a poet's arbitrary whim and direction, nevertheless, because of that very fact, there is here an even greater wealth of nuances of hatred and love, of conflict and of passion: for now all that is left is the sound of the spirit and of the emotions as they vibrate in relation to each other. The play of the two voices at the turning-point of the action creates in the dialogue contrasts and repetitions which are almost symphonic (673 ff.):[17]

161

Paedogogus
Orestes is dead. There it is, in one short word.

Electra
O God, O God! This is the day I die.

Clytemnestra
What is this you say, sir, what? Don't listen to her.

Paedogogus
What I said and say now is 'Orestes is dead'.

Electra
God help me, I am dead—I cannot live now.

Clytemnestra
Leave her to herself. Sir, will you tell me the truth?

The interruption of the prayer by a messenger who enters with news which apparently answers the prayer, as though the gods had granted it, is another feature taken over from the *Oedipus Tyrannus*: it repeats the way in which Jocasta's prayer is apparently granted in that play. But this time the part played by fate and the gods is played by mere intrigue. And this time illusion is no longer a symbol of the human condition, but simply a successful trick. . . . The sharpening of the situation shows an experienced hand, but that is all. It is only in Clytemnestra's prayer that fate and symbolism are still manifested. But these would still have been there even if there were no messenger to bring the fulfilment. And again fulfilment does come, but it comes with the purpose of laying bare the cunning of a soul ensnared in guilt, rather than the deceptiveness and fragility of human existence. What was once significant in itself has now become a means to an end.

Furthermore, the announcement of the death of Orestes, with its great length and its diction that wallows in its own pathos, is little more than a virtuoso display. The 'old racehorse' runs his race only too well. Sophocles has permitted himself in this speech of intrigue a kind of diction which as a tragic writer he had probably long abandoned for serious material. It is as though he were playing a game with his own earlier tragic style. But it is a cruel game. For to prove its power and display its beauty, it must break Electra's heart. Nor, probably, is it a mere matter of chance that this is the longest of all the messenger-speeches in Sophocles—his intention is to pro-

162

long the torment. All the means which are used to express the truth
in, for example, Euripides' account of the fatal ride of Hippolytus,
are used in this speech to embellish the heart-breaking deceptive
fiction which lures evil on to its triumph. Sophocles piles on the
agony in this simulated tragedy (686 ff.):

Paedogogus
   His running was as good as his appearance.
   He won the race and came out covered with honour. . . .
   . . . But when a God sends mischief,
   not even the strong man may escape. Orestes
   when, the next day, at sunset, there was a race
   for chariot teams, entered with many contestants.
   There was one Achaean, one from Sparta, two
   Libyans, masters in driving racing teams.
   Orestes was the fifth among them. He
   had as his team Thessalian mares. The sixth
   was an Aetolian with young sorrel horses.
   The seventh was a Magnesian . . .

   The precise details, the pompous setting of the scene, the skilful
creation of tension, the splendid array of rhetorical devices and
everything that a Greek would have called *peithō*—in all of these the
deception obtrudes so obviously that only someone who was
totally ignorant of style, tone and dramatic art could fail to perceive
it.[18] Another outward indication of Sophocles' ironical use of his
earlier style is that he has transferred the messenger's speech from
its original position at the end of the tragedy to the middle. And yet
even this false Orestes whose death is announced, an Orestes surrounded by an aura of fame, victory and sport, must resemble the
real Orestes to some extent, for both the real and the fictitious
Orestes are equally remote from Electra's suffering and, unmoved by the distress of their sister, think only of fame and
victory.
   The messenger's speech has come to an end, but it does not evoke
a cry of jubilation from the victorious Clytemnestra. Her triumph
has to fight its way through her initial doubts, and develop gradually. There is again a twist, a reversal. And her emotions, the
feelings of a mother for her dead son, and those of a guilty woman
whose anxieties are at last allayed, are at war with each other, until

finally her sense of triumph over Electra, her rival, overwhelms everything else (766 ff.):

Clytemnestra
Zeus, what shall I say? Shall I say 'good luck'
or 'terrible, but for the best'? Indeed,
my state is terrible if I must save
my life by the misfortunes of myself.
. . .
But now, with this one day I am freed from fear
of her and him. She was the greater evil;
she lived with me, constantly draining
the very blood of life. . .

Transition, vacillation, the heart of the matter breaking out from all the layers that surround it—this technique replaces the steady flow of emotion that we find in the earlier plays, and reveals the contradictory nature of the spirit of the character. The *pathos* which had previously been stifled is now let loose, and from this point onwards is felt to be the greater force, both in evil and in good.[19]

This long tempestuous scene ends with an epilogue in which sound and image, diction and stage-craft combine in a way which is seldom achieved even by Sophocles. The door of the house shuts as the triumphant queen admits the messenger. Electra remains on the stage. Her monologue, the language that she uses when she is by herself, with its shifting to and fro, contains yet again enough inner movements to make a drama in itself. (How different from the *Trachiniae* and the *Ajax*!) (807 ff.):

Electra
                . . . No, I tell you,
she parted from us laughing. O my God!
Orestes darling, your death is my death.
By your passing you have torn away from my heart
whatever solitary hope still lingered . . .
But now where should I turn? I am alone,
having lost both you and my father. Back again
to be a slave among those . . .
. . . No, this I will not—

164

live with them any more. Here, at the gate
I will abandon myself to waste away
this life of mine, unloved. If they're displeased,
let someone kill me, someone that lives within.

The scene on the stage becomes the scene of fate, the threshold on
the stage becomes the threshold which separates the lonely, despair-
ing woman and the sounds of a jubilation that is alien to her.

It might be thought that this moment, when Electra is bowed
down with such great grief, would be a good opportunity for the
brother whom she believed to be dead to enter with the urn, and to
bring her lament to an end by revealing himself. Indeed, as far as the
development of the plot is concerned, the lengthy argument between the two sisters which intervenes at this point might just as
well be omitted. But to do that would cut short the poet's ironic
game: deception and truth have to change places once more, Electra
has to argue, convince, and struggle; the force of *peithō* has to be
summoned up once more to fight against feeble halfheartedness;
and, when that fails, Electra is even driven to attempt the impossible, in order to shoulder the burden of the deed by herself; already
she is almost threatening, to our alarm, to turn from suffering to
action—and then the merciful release finally comes. For the poet has
to prolong his sport for just a little longer, to the point where the
drama seems to run the risk of being shattered; this is a consequence
both of the contradictions in the character of Electra and of the
fundamental ironic form which sets everything into motion at this
point: the same fundamental form as in the *Philoctetes*, which is the
sole justification for the *deus ex machina* in that play—for we can
hardly regard the ending of the *Electra* as any different, even if in
the *Electra* it is not the god on the stage but instead the deed commanded by the god which brings about the final resolution.

In structure, this scene again falls into two parts: first comes an
argument about illusion and truth, and then another about the deed.

165   The action again turns from one theme to another. But this time the
change of direction has nothing of the mystery and fatefulness of
the change of direction in the *Oedipus Tyrannus*. It results rather
from the control of a steady hand than from the poet's obedience to
the prompting of an uncanny inspiration.

With the joyful discovery of the offering that Orestes has

brought to the tomb, it seems as if the truth has at last begun to shine through; but at first it is actually denounced as a deception by a deception disguised as truth (879 f.):

Electra
>   Are you mad, poor girl, that you laugh
>   at what are your own troubles as well as mine?

Once Sophocles has created this delicately balanced situation, he extends, draws out and makes full use of its shifts of weight from one side to the other, just as he was to do in the *Philoctetes*. Chrysothemis' joy at her discovery has to be allowed full scope before she is told . . . that Orestes is dead! There is no point in asking why Electra does not tell her immediately, reasonable though it might seem for her to do so; it is the poet's ironic game, just as, whatever might reasonably be expected, it is the poet's game when Orestes allows his sister to mourn him at such length before he reveals himself to her.

But the purpose of all this irony lies in the recognition scene and has done all along. It is this scene that has always been so greatly admired, especially by Goethe,[20] and it is this scene which once and for all made 'recognition' a thing of living speech and movement again, instead of the mere theatrical device which it was increasingly tending to become. But even in the midst of all this touching emotion we should not forget the irony of deception![21] It is no accident that the entrance of Orestes (followed by a servant who bears the urn) is so solemn. He uses his words in such a way that they can be taken in two senses, one deceptive and one truthful: they threaten and promise at the same time, and, strangely veiled, alien and ambiguous, they thrust their way into the world of his sister's sorrow (1098 ff.):[22]

Orestes
>   I wonder, ladies, if we were directed right
>   and have come to the destination that we sought?

166

Chorus
>   What do you seek? And what do you want here?

Orestes
>   I have asked all the way here where Aegisthus lives.

Chorus
    You have arrived and need not blame your guides.
Orestes
    Would some one of you be so kind as to tell
    the household we have come, a welcome company?
Chorus
    This lady, nearest you, will bear the message.

Thus his words are as ambiguous as his presence—a living man carrying his own ashes. And so the greatest of all laments, in which not a chorus but a single forsaken character pours out her heart, misses its target, and in missing it comes to find it (1126 ff.):

Electra
    Oh, all there is for memory of my love,
    my most loved in the world, all that is left
    of live Orestes, oh, how differently
    from how I sent you forth, how differently
    from what I hoped, do I receive you home.
    Now all I hold is nothingness,
    but you were brilliant when I sent you forth.
                        . . .
                        The hands of strangers
    gave you due rites, and so you come again,
    a tiny weight enclosed in tiny vessel.
    Alas for all my nursing of old days,
    so constant—all for nothing—which I gave you;
    my joy was in the trouble of it. For never
    were you your mother's love as much as mine.
                        . . .
    Therefore, receive me to your habitation,
    nothing to nothing, that with you below
    I may dwell from now on. When you were on earth,
    I shared all with you equally. Now I claim
    in death no less to share a grave with you.

The form as well as the content of this lament is new; this can be seen if one compares it with the lament of Teucer for the dead hero in the *Ajax* (992 ff.):

167 *Teucer*
    This sight of all sights that my eyes have seen
    To me is harshest, and no other road,

Of all my feet have taken, so has grieved
My soul as this, dear Ajax, which I took
In haste to seek the truth and trace it home
When first I heard the news of your disaster . . .

The 'road', the 'sight', the 'news', the 'haste', the 'grief' in his 'soul'—these all tell us how the *speaker* is affected; grief springs from the dead man and flows in wave upon wave into the speaker, who unburdens his pain by apostrophizing his own emotions. In the *Electra*, 'all that is left of live Orestes', the 'different' return, the 'nothingness' in her hands, the 'coming', the 'nursing', in short, everything that she calls upon, everything that her words conjure up—all these refer to aspects of the fate of the dead man, and sorrow forces its way *from* her own pain in wave upon wave *towards* the dead man, so that at the end she prays that she may herself share in his death. In both the *Ajax* and the *Trachiniae*, pain, and indeed *pathos* in general, tends to be self-contained and to pour itself out in a monologue of lament that is uninterrupted, self-sufficient and independent of all that is not part of itself. The same is also true of Antigone, who in her lament over her own fate apostrophizes her grave and puts into words what she is doing for her brother. Similarly, in the whole of Teucer's lament the centre of gravity lies in the person who laments: in Ajax's death Teucer laments his own fate, and, together with it, human fate in general. Furthermore, the gnomic element contributes to making the lament self-contained and self-sufficient. But here in the *Electra* the *pathos* now makes its way with tremendous force over to the other person. It is impossible to find a more resounding outburst of a sister's love towards her brother.

Yet even this is not enough. Electra's lament for the dead, in spite of being directed so totally to another, is on the printed page still a monologue, that is, a speech which follows its own course, independent of the presence of other characters, directed away from all else, and self-engrossed—in other words it is apparently another example of the self-contained form of speech characteristic of Sophocles' earlier style; but in fact it is a monologue which differs from all earlier monologues, indeed from all monologues in any literature, by virtue of the fact that, although the speaker is not aware of it, her words storm and surge across to a listener who is the very person to whom they refer, seize him, penetrate and shatter him with such force that it would be impossible for any speech which was openly and consciously directed towards the other to equal its penetrating power. Illusion and reality change places in the action once more, in order to show inner reality, the reality of the spirit—but in this case to show it no longer in its lonely rejection but in a most painful yet most joyful contact.[23]

And with what breadth and abundance this new *pathos* floods forth! The voices of the brother and sister who have at last found each other mingle and echo one another in constantly changing dissonances and transitions, right up to the point where they finally hold and accept each other; their voices sound strange to each other but yet respond as if one were the echo of the other; they sound very near but as the same time are like cries from afar; the tension between distance and nearness continues, grows, intensifies step by step, until at last the soul of Orestes is torn asunder (1174 ff.):

Orestes
Ah!
What shall I say? What words can I use, perplexed?
I am no longer master of my tongue.
Electra
What ails you? What is the meaning of your words?
Orestes
Is *this* the distinguished beauty, Electra?
Electra
                                        Yes.
A miserable enough Electra, truly . . .
Orestes
Form cruelly and godlessly abused!
Electra
None other than myself must be the subject
of your ill-omened words, sir.
Orestes
                                O, alas!
For your life without husband or happiness!
Electra
Why do you look at me so, sir? Why lament?

Orestes
How little then I knew of my own sorrows!

By a constantly changing series of fresh misunderstandings, the *dénouement* is postponed from one moment to the next, and almost at the very moment of complete possession the illusion of complete bereavement has to intrude discordantly before the final resolution (1205 ff.):

Orestes
Give up this urn then, and you shall know all.
Electra
Don't take it from me, stranger—by the Gods!
Orestes
Do what I bid you. You will not be sorry.
Electra
By your beard! Do not rob me of what I love most!
Orestes
I will not let you have it.
Electra
                              O Orestes!
Alas, if I may not even give you burial!

The outward, psychological appearance of truth can no longer stand when confronted with the real truth of the inner situation.[24] This pathos is very different from the pathos in the monologues of the *Ajax* or the *Trachiniae*. And the *dénouement* of the intrigue is also very different from those in the plays of Euripides. If there are two possible senses of *anagnōrismos*, recognition of a person, and recognition of his innermost being, then Sophocles is concerned only with the latter, unlike Euripides, whose dramatic technique concentrated on situations. Moreover, in Sophocles, the former does not become the precondition for the latter; rather, the former is included in the latter, so that recognition of the person becomes symbolic of the discovery of his innermost being. Like all great representations of innermost character in art, this can only partly coincide with what is possible in the psychology of real life. The act of recognition becomes an act of grasping on the part of the soul, and the act of grasping into one's possession becomes a break-through from the image of a person that has been nursed in one's mind to the body of the person actually standing before one's eyes. In the recognition scene in Euripides' *Electra* (570 ff.), out of all this it is only the idea that it is more than could be hoped for that is stressed, and it even forces its way into Electra's exclamation of recognition: 'I hold you as I had never hoped to do' (ἔχω σ' ἀέλπτως) (579). In Euripides' play, recognition begins with the enigma of the stranger standing there, an enigma to be solved, and therefore it unfolds in the reverse direction . . . In Sophocles the pent-up spirit breaks out and surges towards its kindred spirit (1221 ff.).[25]

Electra
　Is he alive then?

Orestes
　　　　　　　Yes, if I am living.

170　*Electra*
　And are you he?

Orestes
　　　　　　　Look at this signet ring
　that was our father's, and know if I speak true.[26]

Electra
　O happiest light!

Orestes
　　　　　　　Happiest I say, too.

Electra
　Voice, have you come?

Orestes
　　　　　　　Hear it from no other voice.

Electra
　Do my arms hold you?

Orestes
　　　　　　　Never again to part.

For just as it requires the constraint of deception to make Electra display the depths of her sisterly qualities, so too Orestes, developing only under the same constraint, must change from being the eager hero bent upon victory into one who painfully experiences and shares her suffering, so that this contact with a kindred spirit may kindle his own brotherly feelings. And just as the play was almost dislocated before, now it threatens to disintegrate completely as a result of the torrent of feeling and immoderate joy which can only find full expression in the more emotional style of lyric; the intrigue, the plan, all are in danger of disappearing from view—if it were not that the drama is finally forced back on to its original tracks (1288 ff.) Now it is Orestes who takes the lead and gives the orders, while Electra, who had only recently been on the point of taking action herself, willingly submits to his orders, imparting her ardour to him, yet happy to be once more within the bounds of her femininity. Her sisterly voice rises once more in sustained diction, then the outward action on the stage continues the play of inner forces only in so far as it forms a frame for it. When the faithful *paedagogus* steps forward, after watching behind the doors so long in case some traitor might overhear the flood of revelations, the deed which serves only to bring the play to a close acquires a welcome colouring of courage and resolution. Otherwise there is not much to say about the end, except that it is the end. The discordant, repellent aspect of the matricide is muted,[27] the two murders are shown as revenge for the death of Agamemnon, as a liberation from slavery, as the execution of divine justice rather than as the personal responsibility of the murderers, but the inner life of the characters does not emerge again; action and language have done their duty simply by meeting the stylistic requirements which had been expected of them ever since Aeschylus. Even the *ekkyklema*, the platform on wheels which goes with this style, is brought into use,[28] when Aegisthus unveils the body of Clytemnestra which lies covered on a bier, thinking that it is the body of Orestes, while the avengers stand around him, and Electra flatters him. . . All this is certainly not without effect, but it has no significance in itself: it is theatrical rather than poetic tragedy. If we want to see stage effects of this sort, we can easily find them in the works of playwrights other than Sophocles.

But the ancient saga and all that goes with it has only one part to play here: to provide the text for a new, previously unheard melody.[29]

171

VI

PHILOCTETES

In one of his speeches [*Or.* 52], Dio of Prusa made a comparison between the three treatments of the Philoctetes theme by the three tragic dramatists. He saw the noble moderation of Sophocles' version as the mean between two extremes, the archaic strength of Aeschylus' version and the rhetorical colour and diversity of that of Euripides. Regarded chronologically, however, Sophocles' version comes last—its date, 409, is known; the poet was in his eighties; the *Electra* must be dated not much earlier, though before 413 as it is earlier than Euripides' *Electra*.[1] Euripides, though the younger poet, had written his *Philoctetes* much earlier, in 431, at the same time as the *Medea*. Stylistically, moreover, the *Philoctetes* of Sophocles, to judge by the surviving fragments of the other two plays, takes its place not between them, but as the most advanced of the three.

In the *Philoctetes* of Aeschylus, Odysseus and the resentful, suffering Philoctetes stood face to face in isolation; in the *epeisodia* the prevailing form was tragic narrative; Philoctetes made his accusations in the presence of a chorus of Lemnians; Odysseus, whom Philoctetes did not recognize, told lies about disgraceful deeds which he said that he had committed. . . Euripides retained the chorus of Lemnians, but the simple confrontation was replaced by a complicated intrigue: the long-abandoned, sick hero suddenly finds himself sought out and caught up in a net of intrigue, as two parties—an assembly from Troy, and Odysseus, with the assistance of Palamedes—each struggle to bring him over to their side. . . Sophocles is the first to make Lemnos into a completely deserted island, to make his chorus into a ship's crew, to intensify the solitude of Philoctetes and, by adding the character of Neoptolemus, to increase the number of characters from two, which had permitted only straight confrontations, to three, which gave an opportunity for new links between the characters and movement that revolves. It is only when there are three characters that the interchange of a continually turning play of forces permits variety, and intrigue becomes the bond and the fate of the souls entwined in it.

173   Thus the *Philoctetes* became the most exquisite and profound Attic play of intrigue, the poetic justification for the whole genre. This intrigue is equally remote from the political action which it becomes in Euripides, and from the exciting adventure, the strange event, which is another form in which it appears in Euripides. In Sophocles' *Philoctetes* it is based purely and simply on human necessity, it stirs up human wishes, doubts and sufferings; it isolates, shatters, divides, seizes—and not merely because of the unusual nature of the circumstances. It is only here that 'low cunning', devious means, appears as a necessary constituent of success and victory.[2] In so far as Neoptolemus, as his father's heir, is intent on victory, he must somehow and at some time come to terms with the crooked element without which it is apparently impossible to scale the heights of this world. Because of this, his relationship to the intrigue becomes an essential theme of the play; it cannot be considered an incidental relationship like that of Orestes in the *Electra*. It would be even less justifiable to consider the nature and the fate of Philoctetes, the unyielding sufferer, without reference to the 'trickery' that plans to make use of him without any regard for his status as a human being. Like the 'recognition scene' in the *Electra*, the 'intrigue' in the *Philoctetes* is no longer a mere theatrical cliché: Sophocles has restored it to the realm of art.

The 'prologue', that is, the first scene up to the *parodos* (the entry of the chorus), resembles an overture in that it introduces the themes which are later to set the action in motion, but which at this stage are still undeveloped and lead to a temporary resolution which is the reverse of the final outcome. The contrast between Philoctetes, the lonely sufferer, and Odysseus, the calculating opportunist, is already apparent, although as yet the only indications of the sufferer are the things that he has left behind, his hut and his belongings. So too with the conversation between Odysseus, the prudent leader, and Neoptolemus, the still almost boyish, docile seeker: it is more than mere characterization in dialogue—we can already sense a disharmony in their words and a conflict in their attitudes (26 ff.):

Neoptolemus
What you speak of is near at hand, Odysseus.
I think I see such a cave . . .

Odysseus
See if he is housed within, asleep.

Neoptolemus
I see an empty hut, with no one there.

Odysseus
And nothing to keep house with?

174 *Neoptolemus*
A pallet bed, stuffed with leaves, to sleep on, for someone.

Odysseus
And nothing else? Nothing inside the house?

Neoptolemus
A cup, made of a single block, a poor
workman's contrivance. And some kindling, too.

Odysseus
It is his treasure house that you describe.

Neoptolemus
And look, some rags are drying in the sun
full of the oozing matter from a sore.

Odysseus
Yes, certainly he lives here, even now
is somewhere not far off. He cannot go far,
sick as he is, lame cripple for so long.

In this prologue Odysseus is already smoothly adaptable, and
even his instructions to Neoptolemus stem from his knowledge of
the other's character. If we compare them with Creon's instructions
to his son in the *Antigone*, which are equally fatherly in intention, we
see that in the case of Creon each phrase was conditioned by the
character of the speaker; he uttered no maxims which he did not
believe in himself, whatever turns his argument took. . . But here,
in the character of Odysseus, we meet, by contrast, an adaptability
almost like that of an adult speaking to a child. Even Odysseus'
promise of a future full of honesty—as if decency and shabbiness
had anything to do with time—means nothing to the speaker
himself. . . At the same time he makes no effort to gloss over the
shabbiness of the plan he proposes. And the cunning Odysseus is

himself quite undissembling, to the point of irony. But this means that there is a strange relationship between the fatherly tone and the content of his speech (52 ff.):

Odysseus
>   If you should hear
> some strange new thing, unlike what you have heard
> before, still serve us; it was to serve you came here.[3]

Neoptolemus
> What would you have me do?

Odysseus
>   Ensnare
> the soul of Philoctetes with your words. . .
>   . . .
> If, when he sees me, Philoctetes
> still has his bow, there is an end of me,
> and you too, for my company would damn you.
> For this you must sharpen your wits, to become a thief
> of the arms no man has conquered.
> I know, young man, it is not your natural bent
> to say such things nor to contrive such mischief.
> But the prize of victory is pleasant to win.
> Bear up: another time we shall prove honest.
> For one brief shameless portion of a day
> give me yourself, and then for all the rest
> you may be called most scrupulous of men.

75

Even an abrupt transition such as 'I know, young man . . .' (79) is something that does not occur in the earlier plays. Taken in conjunction with similar features and such things as Electra's mimicking of her enemy's voice, there is, quite apart from all the differences in characterization, a marked difference in the language as a whole. Earlier, in the *Ajax* and the *Trachiniae*, even low cunning was presented in a disguised form; it appeared as the speaker's *pathos*, as his driving force, as the manifestation of his daimon, that did not reach out to involve a second person.

In the *Philoctetes*, however, we find something quite different: the reaction of one human being upon another. Odysseus is a man who has so adapted himself to circumstances, and is so much a mirror of chance fortunes, that his heroic qualities become questionable; by contrast Neoptolemus is a man who chafes so hard against the bit of circumstances that in the end what becomes questionable is whether he is the right man to do the job. His perception fails him, he is continually making mistakes, his honesty makes him become more dishonest than his dishonest friend, until in the end he believes that he is capable of cutting the knot himself. . . He believes himself to be so independent, yet in reality he is so pliable and excitable, merely youthful material that can be manipulated first by Odysseus, then by Philoctetes.

And here in the prologue we can already hear, muted though it is, the sound of the conflict that is to come. The youthful dignity with which Neoptolemus begins (86 f.):

Neoptolemus
Son of Laertes, what I dislike to hear
I hate to put in execution.

is all too soon converted and transformed into obedient silence. He has almost given in, when he renews his opposition. The speeches run once more through the circle of arguments, not so much to break right out of it as to make sure that nothing has been omitted (116, 119):

176

Neoptolemus
They must be my quarry then, if this is so . . .
Odysseus
You shall be called a wise man, and a good.

The boy stands between the two older men who are firmly set in their beliefs, and he has to fight out their disagreement within himself. He has something in common with both sides: he shares his situation, his task and outward pressures with one of them, his nature and his inclination with the other. Thus he is the character who links and echoes the fate of all three, and in doing so binds them together. But although he has to fight out his battle within himself, it is not the sort of conflict found in German drama, a conflict between moral principles, views of justice or ideas. His own task, his own heroism, his reputation, his inheritance, his own future into which he has to grow, and above all his own self, drive him to do battle with his own nature, not such things as reasons of state, duty, natural law or abstract principle. Odysseus is right: since this is the way that the gods manage affairs in this world, such noble ends are unattainable without the use of crooked means.

As far as the main principles are concerned, the conflict between honesty and deceit, justice and glory, is soon settled, for Odysseus and Neoptolemus still know nothing of Philoctetes, a human being like themselves: the victim has not yet appeared. This destitute man, whose true qualities are revealed by his destitution; this courageous man, who is unbalanced in his greatness; this man of suffering and sorrow; this man who is a spectacle the like of which the young Neoptolemus has never encountered before and who is more than a mere spectacle to him since he actually affects him with the enchantment of his soul—it is not until his entry that the real conflict starts and the inner battle is raised to the level of fateful significance.

But so far the prologue has been moving freely and lightly, like the prologue of the *Electra*. It ends with the all too easy victory of 'cleverness' over 'justice', and it is at just this point that the one element that had not been taken into account, the other human being, first enters, bringing with him a new turmoil both of spirit and of language: for from his very first syllable his tone of voice vibrates in contact with the other, and revels in the long-denied pleasure of conversation (223 ff.) (There is nothing comparable except in the *Electra*):

77

Philoctetes

Greeks, indeed, you seem
in fashion of your clothing, dear to me.
May I hear your voice? Do not be afraid
or shrink from such as I am, grown a savage.
I have been alone and very wretched,
without friend or comrade, suffering a great deal.
Take pity on me; speak to me; speak,
speak if you come as friends.
       No—answer me.
If this is all
that we can have from one another, speech,
this, at least, we should have.

Such a flood of words from the lonely sufferer, sweeping across to this visitor that he has at last been granted—in the face of this the rôle which has been forced upon Neoptolemus becomes meaningless. Now he is an embarrassed listener, and he has to make his excuses when he picks out no more than the actual question from Philoctetes' torrent of words (232 ff.):

Neoptolemus
　Sir, for your questions, since you wish to know,
　know we are Greeks.
Philoctetes
　　　　　　　Friendliest of tongues!
　That I should hear it spoken once again. . . .

But the greater the inadequacy and doubt that the young man feels in the presence of Philoctetes, the greater the compulsion with which the words of the older man take hold of his innermost being. This is a basic situation which remains constant throughout, however much the action moves to and fro; it is a situation which is unknown in the earlier plays, and appears for the first time in the *Electra*: two people, each straining intensely to reach out towards the other, yet failing to make contact, and the more intensely each strains towards the other the less he makes contact. The more the one dissembles, masks, falsifies, with growing amazement, the more the other lays bare his heart, full of boundless love and boundless hate, a heart deceived in its devotion. It is only because of this deception and the alienation that it creates that Philoctetes can unleash his emotions, just as in the second part it is only because at the end Philoctetes fails to understand Neoptolemus that the latter in his turn is able to reveal his true nature. At the same time there is an abundance of nuances in the language, which is direct, without metaphors, and receives its impetus solely from the surge of its movement; yet it is incomparably superior to Sophocles' earlier style, which had achieved its pathos either by the use of *gnōmai* or by the richness of its imagery (260 ff.):

Philoctetes
　　　　　　My boy,
　you are Achilles' son. I that stand here
　am one you may have heard of, as the master
　of Heracles' arms. I am Philoctetes
　the son of Poias.

This qualifying 'may have' (261) adds a further touch to the picture of himself that Philoctetes has built up: the conflict of pride and renunciation characteristic of this heroic figure, forgotten by the world, expelled from it, although he is its only true surviving hero. The deep tones of truth and sincerity in his voice are such that the discordant replies of Neoptolemus, who forswears himself in such artificial, counterfeit tones, appear in even sharper contrast (324 ff.):

Neoptolemus
> Give me the chance to gratify my anger
> with my hand some day!
> Then will Mycenae know and Sparta know
> that Scyrus, too, breeds soldiers.

Neoptolemus begins his deceitful tale with a false note—μόλις (329), 'with difficulty', here used in a double sense—but he has scarcely begun before he is interrupted. The death of Achilles, which for Neoptolemus is only the starting point for a longer account (331):

Neoptolemus
> When fatefully Achilles came to die . . .

affects his listener so profoundly that for a moment the illusion is shattered:

Philoctetes
> O stop! tell me no more. Let me understand
> this first. Is he dead, Achilles, dead? . . .[4]

Neoptolemus
> God help you, I would think that your own sufferings
> were quite enough without mourning for those of others.

But after the interruption we are plunged even deeper into the tones of deceit—the note of truth has hardly sounded before it is again superseded by that of falsehood.[5] But what is falsified is not so much the general situation in which the heroes find themselves as the manner in which Neoptolemus depicts himself as a member of the heroic community: the young man who is only too adaptable

and sacrifices his honesty only too readily appears as a paragon of
heroic defiance, apparently intent on surpassing the anger of Achilles.
As in the *Electra*, the more blatant the deception becomes, the
more heavily the false narrative is overloaded with an abundance of
emotional detail—note the frequent use of direct speech. Even
gnōmai are pressed into the service of the deceitful performance.[6]
The speaker himself enters actively into his own deceit, and his urge
to equal his father combines with his feigned role so that as he acts it
out it suits him to an astonishing degree (367):

Neoptolemus
 I burst into tears, jumped up, enraged,
 cried out in my pain, 'You scoundrels, did you dare . . .?'

 They needed brazen faces for their answer

The intrigue is developed to such an extent that the chorus,
breaking in with a song as Neoptolemus' speech of deceit dies
away, confirms his deception with a most solemn invocation of the
Phrygian Mother-Goddess; just as earlier, in the *Electra*, not only
the content of the messenger's speech but the whole genre of
emotionally charged messenger's speeches was turned into a play
within the play, so here the traditional form, the pathos of tragic
misfortune together with the support given to it by the entry of the
chorus, is deprived of its original meaning and brought instead into
the interplay of illusion and reality (391 ff.):

180 *Chorus*
  Earth, Mountain Mother, in whom we find sustenance,
  Mother of Zeus himself,
  Dweller in great golden Pactolus,
  Mother that I dread:
  on that other day, too, I called on thee . . .

The divine attributes, their position and their meaning, the mention
of the dwelling-place of the goddess, the reminder of the former
occasion on which the goddess had given proof of her power,[7]
make this chorus a perfect example of the traditional style of Greek
prayer. But it continues (396 ff.):

Chorus
   . . . I called on thee, Thou Blessed One,
   Thou that rides on the Bull-killing Lions,
   When all the insolence of the Atridae assaulted our prince,
   When they gave his arms, that wonder of the world,
                to the son of Laertes.

    The precedent referred to in accordance with solemn custom by the person praying (or calling the goddess to witness, which in this case amounts to the same thing) is an undisguised falsehood, and the falsely pathetic invocation 'Thou Blessed One' that is inserted is a repetition of the false pathos of Neoptolemus' narrative (363): 'They needed brazen faces for their answer.'
    Here, as in the *Electra*, commentators anxious to suppress the abnormal have formulated a rule for Sophocles, that he blindly surrenders to the *pathos* of each moment, without expecting his audience to consider the past or the future. Yet it is obvious that he is playing a game with the situation: this is clearly reflected in the way in which the harmony of the solemn formula is disturbed—for there is no longer anything sacred or pious in the intention that would correspond with the sacred nature of the invocation.[8] What should be most holy has become a means of betrayal! The antistrophe, which is separated from the strophe by the dialogue, goes even further: all this business of play-acting—pleading, hesitating, convincing and conceding—which has been used so often with tragic effect, now becomes a deceitful illusion.[9] It is in the name of Zeus the protector of suppliants that Philoctetes has made his plea to Neoptolemus (484); the chorus urges him to grant the request 'and so escape the nemesis of the gods'. The betrayal of all that is inviolable in human life does not hesitate to take cover under the religion of inviolability (507 ff.). Even though the spirit of the time, the spirit of the last third of the Peloponnesian War, is not evident in tendentious remarks as it is in Euripides, the heroic community in Sophocles is nevertheless imbued with that spirit; deceit holds sway, and Odysseus is not the only deceiver.[10]
    But now truth and falsehood start to become intertwined. What the exiled Philoctetes learns about the fates of the heroes from whom he has been separated, is true. That Ajax is dead, but Diomedes is alive, that Patroclus had to die, but not Thersites, that

181

the cunning and mean remain under the protection of the gods, while death snatches away the good and the just, that Odysseus is now celebrated as the great man, that the leaders of the expedition set the tone—all this is true. The dismal parade of heroes in this conversation is much more than a mere repetition of the archaic forms of narrative retaining many features of epic, of the kind that Sophocles was still using to recapitulate past events in the *Trachiniae* and which characterized so many scenes in that play. What is revealed by this dialogue is as much a part and an expression of the existence of the outcast as the barren rock and the open sea; that is what the world of the community of heroes looks like from the shore where the lonely hero lives, a world which is set at a distance from the scene of his sorrows and which serves as a background and a frame to them. As the existence of the outcast is described, how he sleeps and how he hunts, how he keeps warm and how he shivers, how nature is both friend and foe to him, in short, as his whole *bios* is described, with a wealth of detail such as is found elsewhere only in the *Electra*, the limits of this life of his are defined by contrast with the world which has rejected him. The detailed description of the environment in both the *Electra* and the *Philoctetes* is essentially different from the short fate-laden passages which combine to form the general picture of fate in the *Trachiniae*. Only a modern critic could make the mistake of imagining that these short passages merely present the *milieu* or environment. Details such as Aegisthus seated on Agamemnon's throne in Agamemnon's clothes, or Clytemnestra's ceremonial sacrifices, or the princess-like way of life that Chrysothemis enjoys, have in fact the same relevance to Electra's sufferings as the painful, degrading background has to the sufferings of Philoctetes. As the defiant sufferer, Philoctetes stands in the same relationship to the world to which he originally belonged, and which is now triumphant over him, as Electra does to her world. And just as she hears the distant celebrations, the shouting and the sounds of happiness, he hears the distant sound of praise bestowed upon fortunate but unworthy men, those who feel themselves at home in the confusion that prevails in that distant world. In the *Philoctetes* the milieu is wider, and embraces near and far, friend and foe, and the whole heroic world, whereas in the *Electra* the surroundings are confined to the circle of her nearest blood relations, her house and courtyard, and the narrow cult.

However, this is due to differences in the material, not in the nature of the tensions involved.

But the deceitful game which baseness has been playing with truth is carried still further when Philoctetes, the victim of deception, makes a request which is followed by thanks of an almost unprecedentedly touching and effusive nature. Neoptolemus seems to be turning to go (here again, as in the *Electra*, it is characteristic of the lengthy *epeisodia* that they set off in a new direction half way through); then we hear language of an almost unprecedented clarity, that has been liberated by the deceit.

What is new in this tone of voice, and how much more rapid, unadorned and therefore more appropriate and suited to the situation this language is, can perhaps be seen most clearly if it is compared with an equally urgent plea from an early play, Tecmessa's speech in the *Ajax* (485 ff.). There, the suppliant is so filled with the *pathos* of her own plea, the fatefulness of her request, that one might almost say that she would be recognizable as a suppliant even if there were no-one to listen to her; she begins gnomically, keeping to the style of a tragic narrative; the object of her request becomes an example of a universal truth about fate; at this early stage of Sophocles' development, even her request takes the form of tragic exposition. Her starting-point is not the person to whom she is speaking; the impetus of her words does not come from the other person: on the contrary, she sets off in wide circles centred on herself, and goes a long way round to reach her goal, and herself, again; in resounding parallel phrases she lists those in whose name she makes her appeal, and the division of these into three (506–13) provides the inner frame of her plea; and just as the whole speech begins gnomically, rises, and strides on its way, so each sentence rises, reaches its height, and sinks to its conclusion.

183   In the *Philoctetes*, on the other hand, instead of making a structured speech heavy with sound and significance, the speaker advances by fits and starts; he constantly returns to the attack; instead of the long way round he takes the direct path to the heart, both in the whole speech and in each sentence. There is no longer any division into sections; the vehicle and impetus for the request are provided by the urgent desire of Philoctetes to rouse Neoptolemus into a state of mind like his own: his words are given their impetus not by the speaker but by the listener; even the *gnōmē* which

supports his plea moves in this direction and is determined in sense and tone by the *ēthos* of the other (466 ff.):

Philoctetes
>   Boy, are you going,
> going now? . . .
> My dear—I beg you in your father's name,
> and in your mother's, in the name of all
> that you have loved at home, do not leave me here
> alone, living in sufferings you have seen
> and others I have told you of.
> I am not your main concern; give me a passing thought.
> I know that there is horrible discomfort
> in having me on board. Put up with it.
> To such as you and your nobility,
> meanness is shameful, decency honourable.
>   . . .
> Come! One day, hardly one whole day's space
> that I shall trouble you. Endure this much.
> Take me and put me where you will,
> in the hold, in the prow or poop, anywhere
> where I shall least offend those that I sail with.
> By Zeus himself, God of the Suppliants,
> I beg you, boy, say 'Yes', say you will do it.
> Here I am on my knees to you, poor cripple,
> for all my lameness. Do not cast me away
> so utterly alone, where no one even walks by. . .

There is a corresponding distribution of weight between the speaker and the listener, so that the more emphasis is placed on the listener, proportionately less importance is given to the speaker, who is conscious of, and resigned to, his loss of dignity (488 ff.):

184 *Philoctetes*
> Either take me and set me safe in your own home,
> or take me to Chalcedon in Euboea.
> From there it will be no great journey for me
> to Oeta or to ridgy Trachis or
> to quick-flowing Spercheius,
> and so you show me to my loving father.
> For many a day I have feared that he is dead. . .

Again, the tone of this gentler kind of tragic poetry is something quite unknown in the earlier plays. Nor did they know anything of this vacillation between pride and the humility of suffering, or of an attachment like that which Philoctetes feels towards the scene of his suffering; for this scene has been his dwelling and his world, and has become so inseparable from the sufferer that he cannot drag himself away from it without a sense of awe.

But what is the consequence of his plea? Philoctetes had been trapped physically: now he is trapped psychologically. Now it is not merely a case of a distrustful man being deceived with false stories; now it is an impetuous heart, a spirit that gives itself entirely to the illusion presented to him by one who is very like himself. A lie told by a good person is always much worse than one told by a habitual liar. The response to the command 'Nerve yourself' (475) is a pretence of hesitation, the simulation of rivalry in noble intentions (522–5), a victory over oneself, as if it were a question of no more than that. . . And when at the end (528) Neoptolemus concludes with one of those ambiguities which are familiar to us from Orestes in the *Electra*, how much more complex and intricate the situation has become in the *Philoctetes*!:

Neoptolemus
May the gods give us a safe clearance from this land
and a safe journey where we choose to go.

Then the messenger from Odysseus arrives, disguised as a merchant on his way home from Troy. With this, a piece of that heroic world which is flaunting itself over there comes onto the stage as a conspiracy and threat. We see again that in this play intrigue is not so much an isolated venture as the general state of the world. Although his message—that two ships are on their way, one to capture Neoptolemus, the other Philoctetes—is again untrue in detail, the general background against which these particulars are set is authentic enough. How little is left of the heroic world of Homer! Reputation and action, formerly so inseparable that one might stand for the other, have begun to fall apart. Ostentation, boasting, bluster and promises precede the action, or rather the 'heroic enterprise' which it already boasts of being. We hear that the triumphant Odysseus has captured the prophet Helenus on a night

raid, and is parading him before the Achaeans in chains, as a 'splendid prize' (609); and when the prophet foretells that Troy will not be
conquered without Philoctetes, Odysseus immediately promises to
fetch him and *display* him to the people, and if he does not come
willingly he will be brought by force! If he fails in this, he says, then
anyone may chop his head off. What heroism! And the victim of
these threats, listening to all this, believing it, and begging for
rescue from the schemes of his persecutor, is running unawares into
his trap! The reality of the deed to which Neoptolemus devotes his
honest heart—is it not much worse than the illusion and deceit from
which the unknowing victim hastens away, full of loathing? This is
the extent of the twisting and complication imposed in this late
work upon the situation, a situation once so simple and straightforward in its *pathos* (633 ff.):

Philoctetes
> But he can say anything, he can dare anything.
> Now I know that he will come here.
> Boy, let us go, that a great sea may sever
> us from Odysseus' ship.[11]

Neoptolemus is to rescue Philoctetes from the menacing intrigue, Neoptolemus is different from the world out there—and
this same Neoptolemus, because he is different, is to carry out and
fulfil the betrayal.[12]

But again the *epeisodion* takes a new turn at the end. The number
of changes of direction might almost be taken as an indication of the
date of the play. The change starts (637 ff.) when Neoptolemus, the
traitor, who a moment ago had been so eager to leave, begins to
hesitate, to consider, to waver—'And is the wind favourable?'—
'Well then . . .'—'Is there nothing else to fetch?' . . . and out of the
atmosphere of falseness there rises a concord of hearts, the first
notes of friendship. . . Cunning is drowned by the sound of harmony, in the union of pride and respect for the heir of a higher
heroic ideal, for the memory and the promise linked to the weapon,
the bow once carried by Heracles (656 ff.):

Neoptolemus
>   May I see it closer,
> touch and adore it like a god?

Philoctetes
                You may have it
and anything else of mine that is for your good.

Thus the first act closes on a note of unresolved tension: truth and falsehood have driven each other to such a point—a point so far beyond their conflict in the *Electra*—that they are so opposed to each other that the final break can be no longer postponed. But, as in the *Electra*, the conflict between the inner and the external situation, between the inner self and the events that occur, is played out further and further, for Sophocles takes pleasure in prolonging the moment of precarious balance which links the two dramas from the point of view of form, if not of content. For it is only the continuing violence of the situation, a situation fraught with conflict, that enables him to reveal the inner self in its pain and its entirety.

It is true that what follows, as the next *epeisodion*, is a relatively short act, which seems to revert rather to the earlier style: it is entirely devoted to the pathos-laden outpourings of a suffering being, while a listener accompanies the unfolding of the melody of pain with sympathy but without offering any advice. Thus the same type of scene with which we are familiar from the end of the *Trachiniae* seems to recur here: Neoptolemus seems to stand in the same relationship to Philoctetes here as Heracles did to Hyllus in the *Trachiniae*. The resemblance of content extends even to individual phrases, such as the wish to die and so forth. Yet the similarity is superficial, and does not extend to the inner life of the characters: in form and style the two scenes differ as greatly as Sophocles' later manner does from his earlier.

In the earlier play (the *Trachiniae*) the dramatic presentation of physical suffering serves only to show the contrast between the good sense of the hero and the senselessness of what is happening to him; the life of a conqueror, his innate character, his physical strength, his victories are invoked; the invincible hero has to 'weep like a girl'; he who faced every monster has been vanquished by a false woman. . . Thus alienation from himself must precede recognition of his daimon. Just as, despite the conflicts involved and despite the presence of Hyllus, the situation remains basically one in which the speaker's fate is expressed by means of a monologue, so the language also moves within the bounds of a self-portrait descriptive of the speaker's fate. Every sentence, in the final analysis, is a different form of invocation of his own daimon. Characteristic of this language, as of this fate, are the rolling rhythms, the pathos-laden epithets, the abundance of mythical images: pain as a rapacious monster, death as a winged daimon, Hades as the brother of Zeus, and a brother no less powerful than he . . . (*Trach.* 1024 ff.):

Heracles
   My son, my son! where are you? Help me, here,
   here, lift me up. Oh! Oh! My fate!
   It lunges, lunges again, the vile thing
   is destroying me—
   savage, unapproachable sickness.

   O Pallas! It is torturing me again. O my son,
   pity me who begot you, draw the sword—no one
   will blame you—strike me in the breast, heal the pain
   with which your godless mother has made me rage . . .
   Sweet Hades, kinsman, brother of Zeus, lull me to sleep,
   to sleep; with quick death end my agony.

Philoctetes' sufferings, on the other hand, no longer signify that a man who finds himself in a monstrous, an altogether alien situation has to recognize that it is relevant to him and is his own. If this suffering is fate, it is fate of a different kind, as is all the *pathos* in this play, whatever form it takes, friendship, victory or what you will. Its basis lies in its relationship to the other person, or rather to the whole situation, instead of in its relationship to a man's own daimon. But just as the tension between the sufferer and the listener, and the tension between the sensation of pain and its expression, make a dramatic situation of incomparably greater richness—for Philoctetes' pain is shot through with anxiety that his sufferings may alienate his young friend, whereas in fact it is only this suffering which has brought him over to his side—so too the language in this outburst of pain is incomparably freer, more like dialogue, directed to a greater degree to his companion, poorer in decoration and imagery, with fewer descriptive passages, but all the more intimate for that (for intimacy can exist only by contrast with the remoteness of another), richer in rapid movement, new starts, new thrusts, with more nuances, more directness; and whereas heroic pathos was characteristic of the earlier style which Sophocles used to express fate, this style makes use of silence, quietness, gentle hope, lack of self-restraint, unbridled curses, collapse . . . (730 ff.):[13]

Neoptolemus
  Come if you will, then. Why have you nothing to say?
  Why do you stand, in silence transfixed?

Philoctetes
  Oh! Oh! . . .

Neoptolemus
  Is it the pain of your inveterate sickness?

Philoctetes
  No, no, indeed not. Just now I think I feel better.
  O Gods!
                              . . .

  I am lost, boy.
  I will not be able to hide it from you longer.
  Oh! Oh!
  It goes through me, right through me!
  Miserable, miserable!
  I am lost, boy. I am being eaten up. Oh!
  By God, if you have a sword, ready to hand, use it!
  Strike the end of my foot. Strike it off, I tell you, now.
  Do not spare my life. Quick, boy, quick.

189   And on top of this comes the sad misunderstanding, when Philoctetes believes that Neoptolemus cannot overcome his disgust and is only hesitating because of that (807 f.):

Philoctetes
  No, boy, keep up your heart. She is quick in coming
  and quick to go.

The new subject-matter with which this play is concerned cannot be expressed in the language of the *Trachiniae*, any more than the language of the *Philoctetes* would be capable of expressing fate as seen in the *Trachiniae*; whereas there is nothing in the *Ajax* for which the language of the *Trachiniae* would be unsuitable. At the same time, the portrayal of pain in the *Philoctetes* is more graduated, more developed in both its inner and outward aspects, it changes and evolves—it is already a 'drama' in itself; at the same time it is also divided, vacillating between the cares of this world and the otherworldly ecstasy of pain. . . There can be no doubt that the wandering glance, the desire to escape, no matter where, the feverish thoughts, the eyes grown dim—that none of these developments are to be seen in the figure of the suffering Heracles in the *Trachiniae*. But here we find (814 ff.):

Philoctetes
Now—take me away there, there—

Neoptolemus
What do you mean?

Philoctetes
Up, up.

Neoptolemus
What madness is upon you? Why do you look on the sky above us?

Philoctetes
Let me go, let me go.

Neoptolemus
Where?

Philoctetes
Oh, let me go.

Those critics who follow a purely pragmatic method of interpretation have deduced from this passage that Neoptolemus has made a mistake, and that Philoctetes simply wants to go back to his cave. This is not supported by the text.[14] The repeated 'away there, there' (ἐκεῖσε) is enough to show that the place that he desires to go to is not of this world. Then, too, his anxiety about the bow, his frightened request, the clasping of the hand, the sudden delirium —Neoptolemus embraces him firmly, then lets him slip to the ground . . .: all this has quite enough significance as action, without any additional external function. Moreover, if it were just a mistake by Neoptolemus, it would not lead anywhere. The desire to soar, the glance towards heaven, stands in contrast with the collapse to the ground (819): 'Earth, take my body, dying as I am.'

190

There can be no doubt that this technique of detaching dramatic details and giving them an independent life is a feature of Sophocles' late and last works, the end of a development which had begun with the *Trachiniae*. At the same time, it is not so much a question of whether Sophocles when he wrote the *Electra* and the *Philoctetes* was no longer free to return to the form that he had used earlier; it is rather a question of whether at the time when he was writing the *Trachiniae* and the *Ajax* he would have been capable of writing a drama like the *Philoctetes*—a drama of inner tensions which alternately link characters and isolate them—with such mastery of all the means at his disposal. What matters is always the new achievement, not the possibility of occasional retrogressions, though the latter should not be regarded as impossible, even though we know of no actual examples.

The second part of this scene is linked to the first by the gentle so-called 'lullaby' which, however, despite its quiet appeal to Hypnos, is in fact anything but a lullaby, but rather a song of gentle enticement to deceit, all the more forceful for its gentleness (*Phil.* 827 ff.):

Chorus
   Sleep that knows not pain nor suffering
   kindly upon us, Lord,
   kindly, kindly come.
   Spread your enveloping radiance,
   as now, over his eyes.
   Come, come, Lord Healer.
   Boy, look to your standing,
   look to your going. . . etc.

The voice of temptation is all the more fascinating for murmuring so quietly. It is by no means to Neoptolemus' moral credit that he does not succumb to it. The lines between *strophe* and *antistrophe* in which he replies to it, in hexameters, in other words in the metre used for oracles, show him to be perplexed, certainly, but not perplexed about the voice in his own heart, only about the command of the gods: what good would the bow be without the hero, according to their oracle? He has not yet reached the point at which he can break through the deceit.

191

It is here, in the song which brings the act to an end, that the chorus is most closely connected with the intrigue. It is not until the lyric intermezzo that the ironic contrast between the completely different but completely intertwined anxieties of the two characters reaches its peak. It is only temptation, in contrast with the gratitude and relief of the awakening hero, that makes it intolerable to continue the deceit (867 ff.):

Philoctetes
Blessed the light that comes after my sleep,
blessed the watching of friends.
I never would have hoped this,
that you would have the pity of heart to support
my afflictions, that you should stand by me and help.
The Atridae, those brave generals, were not so,
they could not so easily put up with me. . .

The chorus has a dual function here: to add resonance to the intrigue it has to give its support to Neoptolemus' lies; for its voice to accompany Philoctetes' sufferings it has to dwell on them with sympathy. This dual role can be seen at the very beginning (150 ff.) The first *stasimon* is sung in lyrical sympathy with Philoctetes (676 ff.), although previously the same chorus had joined wholeheartedly in the deception. . . Thus its function is both to echo and to contradict, to harmonize at one moment, and to conflict melodramatically at another. One has no more right to require that it should always sustain the same rôle than to criticize an orchestral accompaniment for changing its style according to the nature of the drama.

The drama has passed the halfway point, but so far the tension, unchanging amidst all the changes, has only increased, step by step; then comes the discovery, and with it the sudden break. It is only to be expected from the stylistic phase to which the *Philoctetes* belongs that the reversal from one *pathos* to another now constitutes the peak of the development of an *epeisodion*. As in the *Electra*, an intrigue of increasing misunderstandings is necessary to delay the breakthrough of the truth to the very last moment, misunderstandings which may be compared with discords before the final resolution. But, even more than in the *Electra*, this intrigue now creates a

192

tension between a genuine and a deformed type of humanity, between alienation and sympathy (899 ff.):

Neoptolemus
　　I do not know what to say. I am at a loss.
Philoctetes
　　Is it disgust at my sickness? Is it this
　　that makes you shrink from taking me?
Neoptolemus
　　All is disgust when one leaves his own nature
　　and does things that misfit it.
　　　　　　. . .
Philoctetes
　　Unless I am wrong, here is a man who will
　　betray me, leave me—so it seems—and sail away.

But what immediately follows the discovery brings not a solution but even deeper confusion. For the action moves from one misunderstanding between hearts to another. And scarcely has the first stumbling-block, the deception, been removed, than there emerges from behind it the second, the truly insuperable stumbling-block: the wounding and numbing of a soul that has been too deeply hurt. It now becomes clear that Philoctetes regards his friend's genuine, honest concern for his healing and victory as much worse than treachery! The more honest and courageous Neoptolemus is seen to be, and the more his concern is seen to be only for his friend, the more disconcerted, uncontrolled and confused becomes the resentment of the other. What was true of the contrast of voices in the *Oedipus Tyrannus* and the *Electra* is also true of the *Philoctetes*. The great middle act in particular, with its changes of emphasis and its inner twists, allows the new style, which is given full scope for the first time here in the *Philoctetes*, to unfold in its full splendour. Such a passage as the speech of Philoctetes that begins at line 927 not only corresponds with his speech on awakening like an antistrophe to a strophe, but is also in itself and by itself a drama in its own right, with its abundance of changes of direction, with its alternation of tones of voice and with its abrupt transitions, to a greater degree than any comparable speech: the most bitter curses alternate abruptly with the most fervent pleas, he beseeches

Neoptolemus, then abruptly beseeches himself, then just as abruptly beseeches Nature . . . and this sequence is repeated, and recurs almost strophically, until it is brought full circle with a torrent of the same curses with which it began. A change in the *pathos* within a speech can already be found in the *Electra* (cf. Clytemnestra's speech of victory, *El.* 773 ff., and Electra's monologue, 804 ff.), but here it is a great deal more extreme (927 ff.):

Philoctetes
You fire, you every horror, most hateful engine
of ruthless mischief, what have you done to me,
what treachery! Have you no shame to see me
that kneeled to you, entreated you, hard of heart?
You robbed me of my livelihood, taking my bow.
Give it back, I beg you, give it back, I pray, my boy!
By your father's Gods, do not take my livelihood.
He does not say a word,
but turns away his eyes. He will not give it up.
Caverns and headlands, dens of wild creatures,
you jutting broken crags, to you I raise my cry—
there is no one else that I can speak to—
let me tell you what he has done to me, this boy,
Achilles' son . . .etc.

Such a change of *pathos* within one and the same speech is the continuation and final result of the reversals and changes which have transformed the style of the *epeisodia* more and more from the *Oedipus Tyrannus* onwards. The prime example of this type of scene is the middle act of the *Philoctetes* as a whole: the change from deception to truth is not enough. Neoptolemus is already wavering, hesitating, he is already hardly able to resist the plea, everything seems to be hanging in the balance—then once more before the end the whole play undergoes a violent change of direction.

The change of direction is caused by the arrival of the third character, Odysseus. He steps out so suddenly from his hiding-place that his first words cut across both the beginning of the line (974) and the beginning of the newly forged friendship. The sense of 'almost' which, as we have already seen in the *Electra*, is characteristic of this type of drama, here becomes the bridge between the two halves of an unusually constructed act. What was divided

between different *epeisodia* in the *Electra*, the reversal of the direction
of the play just before the end—in that play, before the appearance
of Orestes—is here packed into one and the same act together with
the breakthrough of two hearts to each other.

As Neoptolemus now sinks into a deeper and deeper silence—and his silence means not a weakening but a strengthening of
his presence[15]—so Odysseus climbs to the peak of his claims and his
power. His victory in this scene is all the more incontestable, the
further he is fated to climb down from his peak, step by step, in the
next. He rises above himself just once more, before the reversal
makes him fall short of himself. But here we perceive all the more
clearly that his words have that special ring which is the guarantee
of success; and when he appeals to Zeus, he is certainly not made to
do so in order that the situation shall form an ironic contradiction to
his appeal (989 f.):

Odysseus
    It is Zeus, I would have you know, Zeus this land's ruler,
    who has determined. I am only his servant.

If anyone demands that the basis of tragedy should be the conflict
of two equally justified principles, he can find this demand more
fully satisfied in this play than in the *Antigone*, which is so often
misinterpreted in that way; for here we certainly have a confrontation, equally weighted at least on the surface, between Odysseus the
ambitious opportunist and Philoctetes the voice of betrayed and
wounded humanity, and both are justified. It is true that when
Philoctetes threatens to kill himself he is prevented by force, and the
captive's physical weakness certainly provides a moving contrast
with his mental rebellion, but when Odysseus, who has only just
seized him, releases him again, his gesture seems all the nobler as a
result (1052 ff.):

195   *Odysseus*
    What I seek in everything is to win
    except in your regard: I willingly yield to you now.
    Let him go, men. Do not lay a finger on him.
    Let him stay here. We have these arms of yours
    and do not need you, Philoctetes.

For once Philoctetes has been released, he stands bound by his own resentment and resistance to a greater degree than he had ever been bound by any physical restraint. As a sufferer, Philoctetes may well be in the right; he may also be in the right when, in tones which anticipate the *Oedipus at Colonus*, he blames the inner contradiction which lies in the false semblance of humanity, the distortion of the human countenance whereby base profit gives itself the semblance of human feelings (1029 ff.; cf. *Oed. Col.* 433 ff.):

Philoctetes
   But now why are you taking me? For what?
   I am nothing now. To you all I have long been dead.
   God-hated wretch, how is it that now I am not
   lame and foul-smelling? How can you burn your sacrifice
   to God if I sail with you? Pour your libations?
   This was your excuse for casting me away.

But he is as much wrong in his actions as he is in the right in his sufferings. He is not merely an innocent victim. In his actions he is blinded by bitterness (1035 ff.):

Philoctetes
   May death in ugly form come on you! It will so come
   for you have wronged me, if the Gods care for justice.
   And I know that they do care for it, for at present
   you never would have sailed here for my sake
   and my happiness, had not the goad of God,
   a need of me, compelled you.

   In his passionate hatred he erects a world-order for himself which is far from being the true one.[16] Indeed, his obstinacy even justifies the way in which Odysseus, as opposed to Neoptolemus, behaves towards him. Thus he is not spared the sight of his newly-won friend leaving him, following Odysseus and carrying the stolen bow. They are no doubt both counting on a quick change of mind on the part of the man they have abandoned and forsaken.
   The extent to which he has been forsaken is shown by the song between the acts, which takes the form of lyric dialogue between the chorus and the forsaken Philoctetes. We may take this as the ebb and calm of despair after the storm of pain, as the lull before the

196

beginning of the last part of the action; it is comparable with the scene in the *Electra* where Electra sinks down at the entrance of the palace and the triumphant Clytamnestra forsakes her (*El.* 804 ff.)[17] But here the despair of the forsaken person goes much further than in the *Electra*, and becomes a drama in its own right. It begins as a *kommos*, superficially no different from the *kommos* of the *Antigone*. Philoctetes laments, while the chorus in antiphony tells him of his own guilt: you yourself, your own god-sent fate did that to you, not my cunning, says the chorus (1095 ff.). . . It is up to you to cast off your misfortune (1166) . . . and so forth. But now everything becomes more profuse, freer, richer in language. Individual components begin to separate and to become independent. The lament of Philoctetes is also influenced by the general change which affected lyric poetry at that period, so that the language itself has lost its singing quality and no longer contains its own music; instead, it provides motifs for singing and begins to be treated as a text to be sung (1081 ff.):

Philoctetes
  Hollow in the rock, hollow cave, sun-warmed, ice-cold,
  I was not destined, after all, ever to leave you.
  Still with me, you shall be witness to my dying etc.

But soon the traditional *kommos* form is broken wide open. A conflict now develops in the lyric dialogue: a conflict not between two different people, but between one man and his own nature —for there are no longer two voices alternating with each other, but a single voice which, against the unchanging background of the chorus, changes from pleading to aversion, from submission to resistance, and so creates its own antiphony and its own reversal. The following lines will give some idea of it (1177 ff.):

Philoctetes
  Leave me now . . .
Chorus
  I am right willing to obey you.
  Let us go now to the ship . . .
Philoctetes
  No, by the God that listens to curses, do not go,
  I beseech you.

Chorus
>   Be calm!

Philoctetes
>   Friends, stay!
I beg you to stay.

Chorus
>   Why do you call on us?

Philoctetes
O daimon, daimon! . . .
My foot, what shall I do with this foot of mine
in the life I shall live hereafter?
Friends, come to me again . . .

Although Philoctetes still invokes his own daimon, as Ajax, Deianira, Creon and Oedipus had done in the earlier tragedies of fate, his daimon is no longer the god-ordained doom that hangs over him, as it had been for them. It is simply the deliberate turning away and the erection of a barrier that has been his own choice: simply his own being, separated from the encroachment of the world-order. The invocation of the daimon is no longer, as in the earlier plays, the fulfilment of the command γνῶθι σαυτόν, but its reverse. And once again the same fluctuating action runs in circles around itself and comes to an end, as in a finale where the beats become increasingly more rapid and more insistent, with the desperate man's request for a weapon, sword, axe or spear, to kill himself. . . Dialogue and lyric are both in the grip of the same stylistic change. The new form had already gained control of the two genres in the *Electra*.

At the moment when desolation is at its extreme, liberation is at hand. At least, that is what happened in the *Electra*, and it seems to be happening in the *Philoctetes*. Engaged in an extremely violent exchange of words, Neoptolemus, followed by Odysseus, hurries back to the cave. The inner tumult of the rueful Neoptolemus, in whom 'righteousness' has triumphed over 'cleverness' (1246), the astonishment and increasing consternation of Odysseus who until that moment has been the leader, means that the arguments are flung out line by line and interrupted before they have been completed. In the course of a rapid development, first their words, then their actions correspond, like two archers aiming their arrows at

198

each other. But then Odysseus draws back. The suffering Philoctetes is called out of his cave. He no longer believes that there can
be any change. After the lie by which he has been deceived it takes a
great effort on the part of Neoptolemus to convince him that he is
sincere. Philoctetes can scarcely believe his eyes: his bow is put into
his hand, his honour, his power, his fate, his freedom of choice and
his friends—suddenly all are restored to him. The usual change of
direction, and everything that we know or can deduce from the
Philoctetes of Aeschylus and of Euripides, would lead us to expect
the reversal and reconciliation at this point, and nothing more. But
Sophocles has no intention of following the obvious course! The
first thing that Philoctetes does when he has been freed is to use his
new freedom to aim his bow at his enemy. It is only thanks to
Neoptolemus that Odysseus, who has suddenly appeared on the
stage for the last time, escapes disaster. 'See how cowardly they are!'
Philoctetes mocks. And when Neoptolemus promises him, with
every possible guarantee, that he will be healed—and what carries
the narrative along here is no longer a tragic report in Sophocles'
earlier style but affirmation and assurance—Philoctetes feels driven
to a deeper despair than ever before (1348 ff.):

Philoctetes
    Hateful life, why should I still be alive and seeing?
    Why not be gone to the dark?
    What shall I do? How can I distrust
    his words? . . .

All representations are in vain; it is in vain that this human
conduct is held up before him as it were in a mirror; and in all this
we hear the voice, not so much of the youthful Neoptolemus, as of
the poet himself, who alone has the skill to depict it (1316 ff.):[18]

Neoptolemus
    The fortunes that the Gods give to us men
    we must bear under necessity.
    But men that cling wilfully to their sufferings
    as you do, no one may forgive nor pity.

199   In these lines the difference between this and the tragedy of fate of
the first four plays (*Ajax, Trachiniae, Antigone, Oedipus Tyrannus*) is

given almost formal expression. Now the old Greek problem of the 'voluntary' fate, controlled by man himself, is carried to its absurd human conclusion.[19] For Philoctetes is not deceived by his false hopes, as Aegisthus is when he moves towards his destruction in spite of divine warning, according to Homer (*Odyssey* i 35 ff.), and as short-sighted mortals without divine directive are deceived, according to Solon (Diehl fr. 1). On the contrary, he sees on the one hand the certainty of sickness, on the other his rescue and the divine order of things, and yet he is not able to adapt himself to his own salvation. He is so firmly embedded in his own world that he even believes that he can give Neoptolemus some advice (1362 ff.):

Philoctetes
　I must indeed wonder at yourself in this.
　You should not yourself be going to Troy
　but rather hold me back. They have done you wrong
　and robbed you of your father's arms. Will you go and help them
　fight and compel me to the like?
　No, boy, no; take me home as you promised.
　Remain in Scyrus yourself; let these bad men
　die in their own bad fashion.

Neoptolemus does not even trouble to correct his mistake. When patience is exhausted, what is the use of explaining the rest of the lies? Philoctetes and Neoptolemus would travel home, leaving Troy to look after itself; even the most terrible consequences would not disturb them; the mind of men would write it all off and forget it: that, if it depended on mortals only, would be the end of the *Philoctetes*. And as though we were indeed intended to lose our patience, this senseless ending is spun out, and even twisted one way and another—until the god appears.

Regarded from a purely external, formal point of view, the appearance of a god at the end of the play is an imitation of the stage technique of Euripides, which for some time now had become no more than a convention. But this device, which by this time had already become lifeless, is given new significance by the spirit which now takes possession of it.[20] The *deus ex machina* does not cut the knot of a plot which is otherwise insoluble. The god—it is Heracles, the very god whose primal presence has been felt throughout the play—appears as the visible standard against which man is measured; his words indicate the divine mission which has been rejected by a will that despite its greatness and nobility has become insanely self-engrossed and at odds with the world (1413 ff.):

Heracles
    . . . It is to serve you I come and leave my home among the dead.
    I come
    to tell you of the plans of Zeus for you,
    to turn you back from the road you go upon.[21]
    Hearken to my words.
    Let me reveal to you my own story first,
    let me show the tasks and sufferings that were mine,
    and, at the last, the winning of deathless merit.

None of the injustice that has been done to Philoctetes is retracted, nor anything of the contemptible character of the commanders—Neoptolemus does not put in a single word on behalf of the Atridae at the end, easy though it would have been if their malice had only been a pretence—the world is really just as Philoctetes sees it. And yet his actions remain inadequate, for he sees the world only from his own angle, participates only in his own view, his ἴδιος κόσμος (private world), to use Heraclitus' phrase, and not in the whole. As a motto at the head of this drama might well stand the words of the Heraclitean author of the treatise *On diet* [Diels–Kranz[6] 22 C 1], ch. 11: 'What men have ordained, whether rightly or wrongly, never remains fixed; but what gods have ordained, both right and wrong, remains eternally right: so great is the difference.' The end of the *Philoctetes* also demonstrates a truth: not the truth that the coincidence of the will of men with the will of the gods is shattering, as in the *Oedipus Tyrannus*, but the truth that separation from the course of the world is absurd. The conflict between divine truth and human illusion, *alētheia* and *doxa*, to use the philosophical and Parmenidean expressions, which pervaded the *Oedipus Tyrannus*, gives way in the *Philoctetes* to the painful relationship between the 'part' and the 'whole', in the Heraclitean sense. For unlike Euripides and Shakespeare, the poet does not stand on the side of the one who frees himself but remains on the side of the gods who rule the world.

201

The announcement of what will happen afterwards, of the healing and the victory soon to come, in a manner very close to that of Euripides, is no more than the external completion and rounding-off of the tale.

VII

OEDIPUS AT COLONUS

The *Oedipus at Colonus* was produced as a posthumous work in 401. The poet had died four years previously, at the age of eighty-nine. Between his death and the production of the play came the fall of Athens.

Because of the position of this work in the poet's whole world—final in more senses than one—it has been compared, no doubt with good reason, with Shakespeare's *Tempest*; and it is personal to the point of self-portrayal, as in, for example, the chorus of the old men of Colonus in which they speak about the sadness of old age (1211 ff.). Like the poet, the grey-haired Oedipus of this drama stands on the threshold which leads from one realm to another, as Shakespeare's magician stands between the world of men and the world of spirits. However, the divine voice which calls to Oedipus is very different from the voice of the spirits which the magician summons around him. Shakespeare's magician makes the voices subservient to him, raises them, conjures them, dismisses them . . . The divine voice which speaks to Oedipus demands absolute obedience. Shakespeare's magician undoes his magic and goes home, in order to depart from the world. Sophocles' aged hero finds shelter with the divine powers of the locality and is carried away to the guardian spirits of the land.

Heroization and metamorphosis were certainly not unusual as conclusions for tragedies on the Attic stage—such conclusions become more common with the dramatization of sacral material of local interest, of 'aetiological legends'—but this is the only work in which the transformation is not merely prophesied or tacked on to an eventful drama as a miraculous fantasy-ending or new perspective, as in Euripides: this is the only work in which the miracle by which the main character is carried away becomes the purpose and the main significance of the whole action. As a consequence, the action on the stage, again for the last time in this last play, becomes an enactment of a cult-legend: the visible testimony and perception of a mystery presented as a narrative, celebrated in song and dance, and still potent.

Thus, in a sense, with the second Oedipus drama Attic tragedy returns to its original significance as mime in the context of cult. And yet between this reversion and the original form there lies not only the whole history of the liberation of all its artistic forms, and of all its human content, but also the whole individual career and especially the last years of a poet who was at the same time a priest. If the end can be said to turn back to the beginning, it is with a markedly spiral curve. Indeed, if this last work can be interpreted as a reversion, it might equally well be interpreted as a final development and final phase. For it is so very much *nature* itself, that there is nothing romantic or 'artistic' in this reversion, nothing in the way of a literary slogan, not even any sense of there being a return. Although Euripides also returns to cult for the material for his last drama, the *Bacchae*, the similarity to Sophocles is only superficial. The second Oedipus play remains simply and solely the expression of this one man who at the end of his life had come so very near to the subterranean region.

Thus this play has two peaks: with one it reaches into the realm of spirits and heroes, with the other into the buffetings of fate that beset a life that is unique and plagued by suffering. Parts of it resemble the form of a 'sacred action', other parts are filled with the emotional outpourings of an uncanny old man who is immoderate both in hate and in love. He has all the 'malice of strength in old age, the fate of ancient greatness'.[1] And in so far as the anecdote that Sophocles strenuously defended himself in a lawsuit brought against him to have him declared incapable reflects something of the strangeness of this old age, one is inclined to believe it.

But this first contrast is linked with another: that between the quiet grove dedicated to supernatural powers and the world with its business, machinations, blindnesses and injustices. Oedipus comes in from that world, exiled and uprooted from it, to find a place where he can put down new roots. But the action is not a steady progress from the profane to the sacred. Holiness—the holy place

with its trees, birds, bowls and altars—is close at the beginning, and it is close at the end as Oedipus is carried away; but between the beginning and the fulfilment there is a violent setback: he is already close to completing the course assigned to him when he is once more thrown back and dragged into the confusion of the blows of fate which he has suffered earlier in his life; sombre conflicts spring up, rival parties force their way to him, and suddenly he intervenes in their affairs. Thus, of the whole play, it is the opening or 'prologue' that comes closest to the ending, whereas the middle part moves further and further away from both beginning and end. It would be possible to make the end follow straight on from the beginning so as to form one unbroken ceremony—though certainly not a drama. For in Sophocles drama comes more and more to mean the riddle of a man's inner conflict. Thus the opposing parties are, on the one side, the individual human life, narrow and limited, uncommonly self-centred in its affirmations and denials, and on the other side its involvement with the fate of the locality, the power to bless or curse for all time, the obligation to guard and protect. From this clash springs the play of forces by which the figure of the hero as well as the action is carried along, and without which the death of Oedipus would hardly serve as material for a Sophoclean tragedy. Because of this very clash, this work has been taken to be a work of old age, left unfinished, its material insufficiently controlled, a series of single scenes written at different times; and this theory has been used to explain away the difficult join at the end where malevolent curses and saint-like demise, implacable anger and transparent spirituality are brought into juxtaposition with each other.[2] But this transition is only the final, most abrupt climax of a series of such transitions throughout the whole drama, and sudden changes of tone are not usually signs of weakness in composition in Sophocles.

But its uniqueness does not mean that this work should not be classified, like any other, as an example of a particular genre. Which genre? The second *Oedipus*, like the *Electra*, belongs with those dramas in which there is a certain contrast between the literary form and the inner form. In terms of genre, it does not belong within the development of sacred mime—there was no such genre—but to a form of drama known only to the Attic theatre, of which the surviving examples range from the *Suppliant Women* of Aeschylus to the *Suppliant Women* and the *Heraclidae* of Euripides. The stage as refuge and sanctuary; the persecuted and the threatened coming to seek asylum; injustice and attack in the world outside; help, reception and restoration from the just king of the land; vacillation between fear and hope, alternation of menacing violence and gratitude for rescue; struggle and resistance off-stage: these are more or less the motifs which are appropriate to this genre and which these plays have in common with each other and with the *Oedipus at Colonus*.[3] But even in Aeschylus this genre had already outgrown its original character of a pathos-filled danced cult-mime, which was all that his *Suppliant Women* had been, and had taken for its content national legend—in his lost plays, his *Heraclidae* and *Eleusinians*—and Euripides had developed it even further, making it into a vehicle for patriotic sentiment and action and a reflection of the politics of his day. The two plays of this genre which Euripides wrote, both during the Archidamian war—the *Heraclidae* about 430, the *Suppliant Women* perhaps 421—are scarcely more than patriotic *pièces d'occasion* with touchingly emotional *epeisodia*.[4] Moreover, they owe their survival not to deliberate selection, but to a chance in the transmission of the text. It is not the older form but this newer form, especially that of the younger poet, which Sophocles fills with new force, bursts open and overwhelms, just as the new content of his *Electra* and his *Philoctetes* had burst open the genre of the Euripidean drama of intrigue.[5]

The relationship of this particular play to the genre is brought out clearly when it is compared and contrasted with the *Heraclidae*. What in Sophocles' prologue is a mysterious discovery to which Oedipus is led by a god is 'exposition' in Euripides: we are in Marathon and sit in supplication before the altar of Zeus . . . (32 ff.) The entrance-song of the chorus takes the same form in both plays, the form of questions: Where do you come from? From what land? What is your desire? (*Heracl.* 73 ff.: *Oed. Col.* 203 ff.) And in both plays the replies follow in such profusion that the name of the person who is being questioned is only revealed after a long exchange. But in Euripides this takes place without any painful revelations: the *parodos* of the *Heraclidae* is dramatic only in externals, whereas in the *Oedipus at Colonus* there is also an inner conflict. The reception and safe-conduct home in the *Heraclidae* (250 ff., 873 ff.) corresponds to the promise of safe-conduct back to the city and reception for the suppliant in the *Oedipus* (636). The suppliants are invited into the house of the king of the land, and are unwilling to leave sacred ground, both in the *Oedipus* (643 ff.) and in the *Heraclidae* (340 ff.), but the scene in the latter play lacks the passionate and mysterious overtones of that in the former. Similarly the gratitude of Argos towards Athens, the praise of the great-hearted son of Theseus, the 'saviour', in the *Heraclidae* (309 ff.) is a counterpart to the praise of Athens in the *Oedipus*, and to Oedipus's gratitude towards Theseus (1125 ff.). But here the *Heraclidae* lacks the greatness in humility that we find in the *Oedipus*. Iolaus' warning to Argos not to march against Athens in the future (*Heracl.* 313 ff.) is placed, in Euripides' shorter play, at the point that corresponds with Oedipus' prophecy concerning the fragility of mortal bonds and the breach of the friendship between Thebes and Athens (607 ff.); but the *Heraclidae* does not have the power of voice that enables the *Oedipus* to speak across the ages . . . Indeed, at the end of the *Heraclidae* there is even the prediction of a future heroization, and, what is more, there is the promise of a future protection as well: the hero's bones buried in front of the temple of Athena Pallenis, in the Attic deme of Pallene, will ward off enemy attack. The difference is that in the *Heraclidae* the person who makes this prediction belongs to a single episode and is not a prophetic character; and the way in which Eurystheus, the bitter enemy and the persecutor in the saga, is turned into the future guardian of the land (*Heracl.* 1026 ff.) is too superficial. And although Eurystheus goes on to mention a cult of his grave, the play does not in fact have any cult content. Forms and motifs which come up in Sophocles more than twenty years later are juxtaposed here but do not cohere, spring to life or draw breath.

The *Oedipus at Colonus* can only be comprehended as a work of old age if it is approached from the point of view of its genre and its relationship with Euripides: it is not until Sophocles that this traditional genre of play acquires religious solemnity, enlargement of its dimensions, expansion of its content, deepening and intensification of its relationships; it is only in this play that we find, instead of mere patriotism, that roots are sent down deep into the soil and that there is an identification with it; it is only now that the motif of asylum turns into living landscape, that the traditional 'praise' of Athens becomes the cult of the local district, and that the hero seeking protection becomes an unforgettable figure.[6]

The prelude, the prologue, describes in small arcs the same curve which will be repeated on a larger scale by the drama as a whole. In this aspect, its relationship to the whole play, it may be compared

207

with the prologue of the *Philoctetes*. The *Oedipus* too begins with a revelation, but one that is much more measured in its pace, much more solemn—with the gradual revelation not of a fate but of a local mystery, or rather of a fate only in so far as the fate of an individual is determined by the local mystery:

Oedipus
    My daughter—daughter of the blind old man—
    Where, I wonder, have we come to now?
    What place is this, Antigone? What people?
    Who will be kind to Oedipus this evening
    And give the wanderer charity?
    Though he ask little and receive still less,
    It is sufficient: suffering and time,
    Vast time, have been instructors in contentment,
    Which kingliness teaches too. But now, child,
    If you can see a place where we might rest,
    Some public place or consecrated park,
    Let me stop and sit down there.
    And then let us inquire where we may be.
    As foreigners and strangers we must learn
    From the local people, and do as they direct.

Antigone
                                    . . . the towers
    That crown the city still seem far away;
    As for this place, it is clearly a holy one,
    Shady with vines and olive trees and laurel;
    Snug in their wings within, the nightingales
    Make a sweet music . . .

Oedipus
    And now have you any idea where we are?

Antigone
    This place I do not know; the city is Athens.

Oedipus
    Yes, everyone we met has told us that.

208 *Antigone*
    Then shall I go and ask?

So the inner restlessness of the seeker grows, until, at the entry of the local inhabitant, there follows the revelation, with one of those

dissonances before the final resolution that are familiar to us from the *Electra*. But here the dissonance becomes an expression of the significance of the place (33 ff.):

Oedipus
    Friend, my daughter's eyes serve for my own.
    She tells me we are fortunate enough to meet you,
    And no doubt you will inform us –

Stranger
                  Do not go on;
    First move from where you sit; the place is holy;
    It is forbidden to walk upon that ground.

Oedipus
    What ground is this? What god is honoured here?

Stranger
    It is not to be touched, no one may live upon it;
    Most dreadful are its divinities, most feared,
    Daughters of darkness and mysterious earth.

Oedipus
    Under what solemn name shall I invoke them?

Stranger
    The people here prefer to address them as Gentle
    All-seeing Ones; elsewhere there are other names.

Oedipus
    Then may they be gentle to the suppliant.
    For I shall never leave this resting-place.

Stranger
    What is the meaning of this?

Oedipus
                It was ordained.

Here we have practically the whole drama in miniature. Similarly, the chorus of old men of Colonus repeats more intensely what the single man from Colonus has said, just as the later struggle for possession of the holy place repeats the first dispute, though in an incomparably richer and more developed way.

The prologue ends (after the local cults have been mentioned and we have been prepared for the king of the land) with a prelude to the end of the whole drama, a prayer which stands in the same relationship to the last act as request to answer. Again, just as at the beginning of the *Trachiniae* Deianira knows of Heracles' approaching death, Oedipus knows of his own death from an oracle. But the oracle no longer sticks out as an awkward, clumsy element, undigested, still in the form of a narrative and a history of events before the beginning of the action, as does the oracle at the beginning of the *Trachiniae* (47 and 156 ff.); it no longer serves as a lever to the action, but is now no more than one wave in the great surge of a spirit prepared for its end, near to death, turned towards the gods. Even without it, the feeling of premonition, of comprehension, of mystery, would still be the same (84 ff.):

Oedipus
　　　　　　　Ladies whose eyes
　Are terrible: Spirits: upon your sacred ground
　I have first bent my knees in this new land;
　Therefore be mindful of me and of Apollo,
　For when he gave me oracles of evil,
　He also spoke of this: a resting place,
　After long years . . .

In the early work, the oracle was so far from being part of the movement of the apprehensive spirit that we are told how it was kept safe in the house 'written on a little tablet'. What a difference there is between the early and the late Sophocles![7]

The entry song of the chorus is another complete play in itself, in melic dialogue which to some extent repeats the motifs of the prologue, with an abundance of variations, transitions and contrasts. The pursuit and search for the transgressor as he hides in the sacred grove, the words 'Here I am' as the awesome figure of the blind man emerges from his hiding-place, the frightened steps of that frail figure, the anxiety of the girl who supports and guides him, the cries of 'Go on, go on', 'Stop', 'Go back', the short rest, the questions, and the movement which surges forward again almost as soon as it has stopped, the revelation in the face of painful resistance, the intensification of the chorus' horror when they hear the name of Oedipus, the renewed threats and conjurations, leading to the girl's breathless prayer of intercession: such an abundance of opposing movements is much more than is usually found in earlier choruses;[8]

it is an example in the *parodos* of the same late style which is displayed in the *kommos*, or lament of the chorus, that almost resembles an intermezzo, in its great melic dialogue with the forsaken Philoctetes.[9] Such characteristics reveal not merely—as has been suggested—the influence of the baroque forms of the new music of the time, since the parts of Euripides in which music was involved, which were affected by the same influences, are totally different; they also reveal one final change of form which stems from within the dramatist himself: for the struggle to create dramas within the drama itself, as it were, is not restricted to the musical parts of the play in Sophocles, but affects the dialogues and choruses just as much.

The beginning of the first *epeisodion* is a continuation of the *parodos*. The praise of the hospitality and piety of Athens is an age-old feature of the species of drama to which this play belongs (line 260 is, as it were, an indication of the genre). But the voice which here calls upon the ancient fame of Athens is that of a man who is not only being persecuted, like all the suppliants in this type of drama, but a man between whose nature and whose actions and fate there yawns a gap as wide as that between the aching edges of a wound. So great is the discord which has replaced the unity of the *Oedipus Tyrannus*. And what a difference in the way that the pain is now veiled in the language! (270 ff.):

Oedipus
    And yet, how was I evil in myself?
    I had been wronged, I retaliated; even had I
    Known what I was doing, was that evil?
    Then, knowing nothing, I went on. Went on.

The clash between the heart and the frame of a man's destiny, the inward innocence of a man who is outwardly guilty, the higher purity of the pollutor, and the hidden holiness of the marked man—this clash rises up and fills the supplication with ever-increasing movement (285 ff.):

Oedipus
    Give me, too, sanctuary; though my face
    Be dreadful in its look, yet honour me!

For I come here as one endowed with grace
By those who are over Nature; and I bring
Advantage to this race . . .

But even the first *epeisodion* contains that change of direction which has characterized the style of the scenes in Sophocles ever since the *Electra*. *Epeisodia* devoted to a single theme give way to *epeisodia* with two or more themes. In this case, the scene had begun at first to move towards the approval of Oedipus' presence and the expected approach of Theseus. But from another direction, as unexpected as its unexpected bearer, comes the reflection of that other, outside world—after the lines in which expectation, mingled with feelings of unworthiness, apprehensiveness and timid hesitation, has made a short scene within the scene on its own. Will he come? . . . And on my account? . . . Do not fear! . . . [10] If this had been an early play, it would have been impossible for the person expected not to have appeared. But the person who comes instead, wearing a traveller's hat, riding a mule, and first seen in the distance by Antigone, is—Ismene; and this results in another little scene within the scene (315 ff.):

Antigone
  I don't know!
  Is it or isn't it? Or am I dreaming?
  I think so; yes!—No. I can't be sure.
  Ah, poor child,
  It is no one else but she! And she is smiling
  Now as she comes! It is my dear Ismene!

While Ismene is dismounting from the mule, a whole recognition scene in miniature is enacted, culminating in the name of the person recognized, as the identification becomes certain after initial doubt. This scene is certainly not without life, but it is scarcely of any importance for the main action. Nothing depends on it. External, peripheral and subordinate matters are presented at length, loaded with detail, and dealt with in a way previously reserved for central matters. This seems to be a general tendency in these works of Sophocles' old age; it is just as apparent here in the new strict style of the second *Oedipus* as the in the freer, looser style of the *Philoctetes*. Similarly in the touching reunion between Oedipus and his second

212 daughter (327 ff.), in which the duet-form of rediscovery is repeated from the great scene of reunion in *Electra*:

Oedipus
Child, you have come?
Ismene
                    Father, how old you seem!
Oedipus
My children . . . and sisters.
Ismene
                    Oh, unhappy people!
Oedipus
Child, are you here?
Ismene
                    And such a time I had!
Oedipus
Touch me, little one!
Ismene
                    I shall hold you both!
Oedipus
She and I?
Ismene
                    And I with you, unhappy.

But the old man's tearful joy turns to an old man's anger. Ismene brings secret knowledge, fulfilling, as a messenger of revelation, a function similar to that of the messenger in the *Trachiniae*; both, by entering, unmask imminent deception. It is true that Ismene herself is no longer of much importance, and serves merely to bring the message, but her message differs from the archaic form of messenger's speech in that what she announces—the outbreak of discord between the brothers, and the secret plan of the two conflicting parties to ensure that Oedipus is on their side as a talisman—is important only in its effect: for as the news is gradually revealed by questions it transforms the Oedipus who is dedicated and prepared for death, through successive stages of suspended amazement and angry comprehension, into the furious Oedipus with his terrible curses.[11] Thus the questions now build up (393 ff.):

Oedipus
    Am I only of use when I am nothing?
        . . .
    Age cannot restore what was ruined young.
        . . .
    What good will be my grave outside their gates?
        . . .
    Then they shall never hold me in their power!
        . . .
213 And will they cover me with Theban dust?
        . . .
    And it is I that Phoebus says this of?
        . . .
    Has either of my sons had word of this?
        . . .
    The scoundrels! So they knew all this, and yet
    Would not give up the throne to have me back?

until they reach a climax in the speech in which the storm breaks
(421 ff.):

Oedipus
    Gods!
    Put not their fires of ambition out!
    Let the last word be mine upon this battle
    They are about to join, with the spears lifting!

His speech is full of angry wrangling, protesting and settling of
accounts with his sons. This Oedipus is no longer merely the
cursing figure of the saga; his reproach is not merely that his sons
have not honoured their father, but that, in their conduct, action has
parted company with meaning, and the appearance of justice with
its reality. It is the protest of a man with an overflowing, sensitive,
violent, aching heart against a race of men and a world which
neither shares it nor senses it in another.

In this revolt against a prevailing attitude which, in its concern
with appearances, makes a mockery of genuine humanity, the
second *Oedipus* reveals its kinship with the *Philoctetes*. For in the
second *Oedipus*, too, it is not only the sons who are like this, any
more than in the *Philoctetes* it is only Odysseus; it is also Creon and
all Thebes (427 ff.):

Oedipus
These were the two
Who saw me in disgrace and banishment
And never lifted a hand for me. They heard me
Howled from the country, heard the thing proclaimed!
And will they say I wanted exile then,
An appropriate clemency, granted by the state?
That is all false! The truth is that at first
My mind was a boiling cauldron; nothing so sweet
As death, death by stoning, could have been given me;
Yet no one there would grant me that desire.
It was only later, when my madness cooled,
And I had begun to think my rage excessive,
My punishment too great for what I had done;
Then it was that the city—in its good time!—
Decided to be harsh, and drove me out.
They could have helped me then; they could have
Helped him who begot them! Would they do it?
For lack of a little word from that fine pair
Out I went, like a beggar, to wander for ever! . . .

With these words Oedipus reproaches a whole attitude, and his reproach recurs more sharply act after act and is directed against the treacherous Creon as much as against the penitent son. The sense of these lines constantly recurs in intensified form, just as the same action retraces the same course in ever-decreasing circles: see lines 591, 765 ff.; 1354 ff.

But, before it ends, the same *epeisodion* takes yet another new turn: already in this scene curse and blessing, angry defence and sacred action have followed each other antithetically (475 ff.), so as to create the same contrast that is brought out in a more intense form at the end of the whole drama; for at the end, instead of the narrated message and the cursing of an absent person that we get in this scene, father and son stand face to face; and instead of initiation into the cult of the Eumenides, we have the answer to the prayer by the lightning flash from Zeus. To understand the play it is essential to realize that this ending is already present in this beginning. Thus already in this scene the cursing is followed by initiation into the cult, which is given a significance of its own as a sacred action within the action as a whole; there is scarcely any other text which

expresses so purely the nature of a sacrifice performed in the spirit
and with the gestures of the classical age (466 ff.):

Chorus
  Make expiation to these divinities
  Whose ground you violated when you came.

Oedipus
  In what way shall I do so? Tell me, friends.

215 Chorus
  First you must bring libations from the spring
  That runs for ever; and bring them with clean hands.

Oedipus
  And when I have that holy water, then?

Chorus
  There are some bowls there, by a skilful potter;
  Put chaplets round the brims, over the handles.

Oedipus
  Of myrtle sprigs, or woollen stuff, or what?

Chorus
  Take the fleeces cropped from a young lamb.

Oedipus
  Just so; then how must I perform the rite?

Chorus
  Facing the quarter of the morning light,
  Pour your libations out.

Oedipus
  Am I to pour them from the bowls you speak of?

Chorus
  In three streams, yes; the last one, empty it.

Oedipus
  With what should it be filled? Tell me this, too.

Chorus
  With water and honey; but with no wine added.

Oedipus
  And when the leaf-dark earth receives it?

Chorus
  Lay thee times nine young shoots of olive on it
  With both your hands; meanwhile repeat this prayer:

Oedipus
This I am eager to hear: it has great power.

Chorus
That as we call them Eumenides,
Which means the gentle of heart,
May they accept with gentleness
The suppliant and his wish.
So you, or he who prays for you, address them;
But do not speak aloud or raise a cry;
Then come away, and do not turn again . . .

Even the first *epeisodion* rises and falls in exactly the same rhythm as the whole.

The chorus which follows, another *kommos* in free question-and-answer form, no longer serves to bring the first act to a close, but to introduce the second, by a contrast similar to the contrast in the *Philoctetes* between the 'sleep song' and the scene of awakening.[12] Oedipus has to be torn back into his torments once more before Theseus can free him.[13] But his torments no longer appear to be inflicted by the gods. Where the first *Oedipus* play would lead us to expect the name of Apollo and the Delphic oracle, we now find the 'city' (525 and 541), and, instead of tragically accepting his daimon and the will of the gods, the sufferer twists and turns in painful denial of his guilt. Just as in the *Electra* and the *Philoctetes*, so too in the second *Oedipus* the causes of suffering are entirely human. And more and more, as the human takes the place of the divine in the causation of suffering, so the divine becomes something which stoops down to man from above, at the last moment, to guide and to reconcile.

As the genre requires, the king of the country now comes out to meet the man who is seeking refuge. If we examine this scene again from the standpoint of its traditional features, we soon see to what extent Sophocles lifts the genre above its own limitations. Traditionally there should now follow cries of supplication, laments, refusal . . . In the *Heraclidae* of Euripides the supplication required long, skilful speeches, leading up to the king's decision (*Heracl.* 236); the mothers of the seven heroes in the *Suppliant Women* have to circle around Aethra, and Adrastus has to clasp Theseus' knee in supplication (Eur. *Suppl.* 163), and in Aeschylus the Danaids even have to go as far as to threaten suicide in order to gain a hearing from the king (Aesch. *Suppl.* 465). Sophocles' Theseus does not allow things to go so far (556). That a human being, who is aware of the human condition, and senses what is to come, should rescue another from his situation and so enable him to avoid his suffering, and that this should be felt with such sensitivity, such gratitude; that from such mutual recognition and mutual liberation, in giving and taking, there should arise a scene such as this, without pomp or passion—nothing like this had even been seen before on the Athenian stage, despite its rich diversity. Even if the figure of Theseus appears less strongly drawn than Oedipus, there can be no doubt that for Sophocles Theseus represents the purest essence of humanity which he had ever attempted to create: *his* Theseus, the hero of *his* Athens; Theseus embodies the great security, peace and warmth above all the fears and storms that have beset the man singled out by the forces of fate.

But it is not only its tone of deep sincerity which makes this scene different from the usual run of scenes in which the king receives the suppliant: Oedipus brings a gift; he only hints at its nature, but in such a tone of voice that there can be no doubt of its meaning: his gift is his death and his grave. For just as in other cases death signifies a return of the individual to the universal, a return to the basic substance of the world, so here, in a sense that is not entirely dissimilar, death signifies a return to the spirits of the place, a return to the eternal source from which in the course of time, when his people are in danger, his powers of defence will flow. Thus in the middle of this *epeisodion* the course of the action is interrupted by the loftier matter of Oedipus' consecration, just as the end of the previous *epeisodion* had been interrupted by the instructions for the sacrifice: the interruption here takes the form of the prophecy of a future in which the fate of the country will be linked with the fate of Oedipus (607 ff.):

Oedipus
                The immortal
Gods alone have neither age nor death!
All other things almighty Time disquiets.
Earth wastes away; the body wastes away;
Faith dies; distrust is born.

And imperceptibly the spirit changes
Between a man and his friend, or between two cities.
For some men soon, for others in later time,
Their pleasure sickens; or love comes again.
And so with you and Thebes: the sweet season
Holds between you now;[14] but time goes on,
Unmeasured Time, fathering numberless
Nights, unnumbered days: and on one day
They'll break apart with spears this harmony—
All for a trivial word.
And then my sleeping and long-hidden corpse,
Cold in the earth, will drink hot blood of theirs,
If Zeus endures; if his son's word is true . . .
However: there's no felicity in speaking
Of hidden things . . .

Here the real meaning of the prophecy is neither the ancient
Greek belief in the magical powers of heroes in its primitive form,
nor the actual contemporary state of affairs; rather, the belief in
heroes is made into the support and vehicle for the real meaning—the mystic union (if I may be permitted this phrase) of this
most tragic of figures with his spiritual heritage, the gods of Athens.
And even if the legend, or an oracle, did mention at some time or
other a defeat of the Thebans at the grave of Oedipus, nevertheless
what Oedipus envisages here is something that goes far beyond the
events and occasions implied by such traditions.[15] Sophocles uses
the traditional legend as an outer shell to convey the hidden meaning, just as he uses the belief in the powers of heroes and the dead.
The protection of the city by the hero's grave predicted in
Euripides' *Heraclidae* can be dated to a precise year, and has a
particular significance which applies only to the one, passing situation. In the *Oedipus* the date of the situation foretold by the
prophecy is a puzzle to the historian, for the fate that is prophesied
lies outside history as we know it.

The longest scene of the play, which now follows, taking up the
whole of its central part, is also the swiftest in movement, the
richest in action on the stage, and at the same time the most
traditional in construction. The antagonist, Creon of Thebes, enters
with a large number of armed followers; Oedipus and his daughters, who have been left behind by Theseus, are threatened, first

with words and then physically; the armed men take action and the defenceless girls are dragged away; then there comes rescue in the hour of their most urgent need; and finally might is overcome by right, thanks to the decision of the righteous king of the country—all this is unfolded in scenes which in externals do not differ in any way from the other scenes of supplication known to us, even those of Aeschylus. The poet is positively archaising when Theseus is called to the rescue by the entreaties and invocations of the chorus (884 ff.)—we are not intended to wonder how far away he may be, any more than in the corresponding situation in the *Suppliant Women* of Aeschylus at lines 872 ff.[16] But the hand of Sophocles can be more clearly seen in the breadth and scope of his treatment of emotion, with its climax and gradations; first the forceful abduction of the girl from the arms of her blind and helpless father, with the mocking epilogue addressed to him by Creon, when the scene already seems to be coming to an end (848 ff.); then the unexpected outbreak of rage from the oppressor at the protest voiced by the leader of the chorus; and finally the blind fury of the two old men as they attack each other—while the parallelism of the two parts of the scene is further emphasized by the parallel lyric strophes that punctuate it. But this too should perhaps be regarded as merely part of the dramatic craftsmanship. What is uniquely Sophoclean is the way in which this scene of attack is transformed into a scene of *revelation*. Sophocles had always been an unrivalled master of dramatic revelation. But what is now dragged out of its disguise into the light is not some tragic entanglement, as in the earlier plays, but the primeval threat to humanity: cold utility in the guise of justice and sincerity, the primeval enemy against whom the primeval Theseus of Sophocles' Athens raises his hand in protection. There is already an element of the ideal in this conception of Theseus, who stands in the same relationship to Sophocles' other characters as Plato's primeval Athens is related to his other historical states: he serves as the standard by which to judge what Athens should and should not be. Similarly, it is no mere accident that his antagonist, the sly, senescent Creon, is the most obnoxious figure, the figure drawn with the greatest exasperation, in the whole range of Sophocles' work. Creon the tyrant in the *Antigone* was a twisted human being, but at least one could say that he rushed blindly to his fate. The Creon of the *Oedipus Tyrannus* remained without a fault and without a fate. But the Creon of this play is so repulsively hypocritical that by comparison Odysseus, the liar in the *Philoctetes*, seems positively decent, and Clytemnestra warmly humane.

At the moment of his entry his disguise is complete. And if this first speech of Creon were all of the second *Oedipus* that had survived, if it were the only fragment, not even the best of critics would fail to be edified by its *ēthos* (733 ff.):

Creon
   . . . I am old, and know this city has
   Power, if any city in Hellas has.
   But for this man here: I, despite my age,
   Am sent to bring him to the land of Thebes . . .
   So, now, poor Oedipus, come home.
   You have heard my message. The people of the city
   Are right in summoning you—I most of all,
   For most of all, unless I am worst of men,
   I grieve for your unhappiness, old man.
   I see you ravaged as you are, a stranger
   Everywhere, never at rest . . .
   Is not this a disgrace? I weep to see it!
   Disgrace for you, for me, for all our people! . . .

220   This speech has everything that demands the highest respect and the deepest attachment: blood relationship, justice, the homeland as 'nurse' . . . Everything which in Theseus is genuine in Creon appears as part of his disguise. The moment of revelation tears off the false appearance that masks the human face. (What was true of the way in which the arguments in the *Electra* reach out towards and grasp each other is true here also, except that here the tone is more elevated and the symbol more universally valid: 761 ff.):

Oedipus
   You brazen rascal! Playing your rascal's tricks
   In righteous speeches as you always would! . . .

And even if the unmasking is caused by the irritability of a self-engrossed nature, nonetheless it drags a man's entire public life

and conduct into the light: the inhuman in the guise of the humane.
What has happened to Oedipus becomes a symbol of any injury
inflicted on any human being (776 ff.):

Oedipus
  Suppose that when you wanted something terribly
  A man should neither grant it you nor give
  Sympathy even; but later when you were glutted
  With all your heart's desire, should give it then,
  When charity was no charity at all?

Such a relationship, or rather such a twisting of a human relationship as we encounter here, is evidence of a concept of humanity
different from that which we have encountered in the earlier plays.
In those plays there was indeed black and white, hate, love, deceit,
even indeed greatness in *hybris*, sincerity in madness, nobility in
wildness . . . but as yet no example of humanity so tormentingly
wounded by the *illusion* of humanity. Again it is the *Philoctetes*
which comes nearest to it. But the *Oedipus* goes further in its
branding of falsehood. And when the wily Creon, in order to fool
Theseus, goes so far as to pretend to be acting in the best interests of
Athens, and says that he is only seeking to protect Athens, the most
god-fearing of cities, and its sacred Areopagus from pollution by a
man guilty of parricide and incest, then out of the tormented heart
of Oedipus, and out of his indignity and shame, flinging off the veils
which cover it—and with an inner momentum which makes this
too almost a drama in itself—there breaks forth with the power of
an eternal reckoning the annihilating comparison of the tragic and
the anti-tragic, of the marked man and the so-called 'righteous'
man. Never again has the rank of a man who bears a burden that fate
has imposed on him been raised so abruptly above the kind of man
who only makes use of the fate of others; never again has such a
clear-cut line been drawn between a speaker who carries such a
burden and a listener who carries none (980 ff.):

Oedipus
  But I shall speak, I'll not be silent now
  After you've let your foul talk go so far!
  Yes, she gave me birth—incredible fate!—

But neither of us knew the truth; and she
Bore my children also—and then her shame.
But one thing I do know: you are content
To slander her as well as me for that;
While I would not have married her willingly
Nor willingly would I ever speak of it. . . .[17]

But it is not only Oedipus who generates so much material that the traditional form is filled almost to bursting point; there is just as much danger of the material concerning Theseus overflowing its limits. The Theseus of Sophocles is not the ideal patriot that he always is in Euripides. He does not trot out political maxims, nor does he feel that he has to give his country's enemy a piece of his mind (lines 1143–4 of his speech sound as if they are directed against over-patriotic speechifying). He himself stands outside the opposing positions. Anger is not for him. (One should not forget that Sophocles had known Pericles very well, and we can read anecdotes in Plutarch's life of Pericles about the gentlemanly way in which he treated his opponents.) He sets in order what is out of place, and measures each thing by its own measure, allotting to each its own rights. In so far as the traditional form permits, his actions are regulated by this aim. The punishment for the wrongdoer will be simply that he himself must make good the wrong that he had done (905 ff.). One almost wishes that this Theseus had more to worry about than the abduction of Oedipus' daughters; the girls bring with them almost too much theatrical sentimentality. But the more the traditional form and the action keep within their limits, the more the speeches must carry us outside these limits. Theseus indeed takes the *measure* of Creon but does not punish him according to his guilt; he is measured against the true *Thebes*, whose nature he has falsified; the law is sacred—not only the law of Athens but that of the other city and of every other city—and the territory of every city is inviolable; here we have a confrontation between the height of respect and total lack of respect—and all this is what makes Theseus different, even in his tone of voice and his gestures, both from the baser politics of Creon and from the stormy forces by which Oedipus is controlled. This means that each of these three, Creon, Theseus and Oedipus, stands in his own sphere, and has no contact with the others (911 ff.):

Theseus
> . . . your behaviour is an affront to me,
> A shame to your own people and your nation . . .
> I doubt that Thebes is responsible for you:
> She has no propensity for breeding rascals . . .

At the same time we should remember that this must have been written at a time when Thebes was the bitterest of all Athens' enemies. It was in compliance with the demand of Thebes that Athens was compelled to demolish her walls in 404. Would the enemy have been praised like this at such a time? Is this a 'compliment' for 'political' purposes in a play which otherwise is careful to avoid all political allusions? Some critics have come to this conclusion, and by so doing have given the claim of Theseus a significance, an upper limit, a level of meaning which is out of keeping with the speech and the character. What was it that made Theseus so outstanding? Is it possible that Theseus, who so outshines his opponent Creon, that specialist in compliments, should himself become the vehicle for a 'compliment' paid to the neighbour of Athens in connection with one particular situation? [18]

Thus the question of justice, which was originally linked with the type of drama exemplified by the *Suppliants* of Aeschylus, is now finally given due honour again, though in a different sense. Just as the ageing Sophocles has come to regard suffering more and more as the result of human action, so too he has come to regard 'the unwritten law' more and more as a corresponding concept of justice. Without being forced to do so by the plot, he abandons the limited sphere of sacral and particular justice to which the *Suppliants* is confined, and proclaims in its place a universal form of justice, not divine, but human—not indeed in the manner of Euripides as an abstract idea imposed upon the world, but a concept which is demonstrated all the more impressively by being displayed as part of the nature of an exemplary man, a noble justice that transcends everyday justice, an Attic justice that transcends un-Attic justice. [19]

After the chorus which brings the act to a close—and which, since it is on the theme of battle and victory, also takes the place of a narrative of the fighting, since such a narrative would no longer have any point now that the traditional form of the genre has been broken open[20]—we expect the contents of the next *epeisodion*, in accordance with the genre, to be gratitude and praise for the rescuer. But the major key of the opening darkens into tragedy, for the lightning requires a menacing bank of cloud from which it can flash down as a sign of the departure of Oedipus into another existence. Without the scene between Oedipus and his son, the expression of gratitude by Oedipus would be followed immediately by the drama of his heroization, which would consequently begin without any feeling of dread; and the brightness of the other world would not be able to stand out in contrast with a world clouded by blindness and obstinacy. Outwardly the next *epeisodion* is merely a link, but as such it is the most extreme example, apart from the prologue of the *Electra*, of the way in which the ageing Sophocles makes a break into a support, into a clamp which joins together a scene composed of two parts, and which contains a reversal of emotion—a father's curse and a father's affection, each equally excessive, break forth from the same mysterious source. At the same time the first half is again so heavily charged with emotion, with the clash between gratitude and shame, that at first gratitude builds up into a stormy torrent, even to the extent of Oedipus wishing to embrace Theseus and shower kisses on his friend's head, only to break off all the more suddenly and humble itself to such a degree that Oedipus merely utters a timid greeting from a respectful distance (1132). Only a moment ago he was pitting his pride in his innocence against Creon's so-called 'righteousness'; now faced with Theseus' purity he remembers his own pollution, and shows himself as immoderate in self-abasement as he had been in anger. Tensions and breaks of this kind within one and the same speech do not occur in the earlier plays and are not found before the *Electra* in a form comparable with that which they take in the second *Oedipus*.

224

But the main break in the middle of this scene is caused by the intrusion of an external factor—the mention in passing of an unknown suppliant (1150 ff.). At this point the first shadows fall upon the joyful splendour of love and gratitude, and become increasingly dark and menacing the more tightly the net is drawn round the unknown person, until from the riddling obscurity there emerges the name of Oedipus's son; once again, Sophocles shows himself to be the master of gradual revelation.[21] But here the action and the tragic figure do not coincide as they had done in the *Oedipus Tyrannus*. The discovery which plunges the scene into darkness is like a musical figure, a cadence, which also affects lesser matters, helps the play of opposites, and is an effect that can be repeated.

Up to this point, the fundamental situation of the play has remained the same; sometimes it has been varied, but never completely interrupted (see line 1208). But now, as a result of this chance occurrence, it is reversed: the man on trial now has to be the judge; the man who a moment ago was a suppliant himself is now faced with a suppliant, guilty, it is true, yet repentant—his own son; but it is here that Oedipus' immoderate spirit, shackled by its own self-regard, reaches its limits. Again, as at the beginning, it is Antigone who has to intercede, but this time *against* Oedipus, and she does not hold back the bitter truth (1189 ff.):

Antigone
    . . . Even had he wronged you, father,
    And wronged you impiously, still you could not
    Rightfully wrong him in return! . . .

One cannot speak of Sophocles' 'justifying' this retaliation, this ἀντιδρᾶν, here any more than in the earlier passage (953)[22], or in the *Electra* (577). But then the second *Oedipus* clearly resembles the *Philoctetes* in as much as they both show that it is the tragically violent man, the man who suffers, who, in the final analysis, is the one who is limited and confined. What Oedipus has to hear from his daughter is set at the same point in the play as a whole as the truth about himself that Philoctetes has to hear from Neoptolemus. It is the poet himself who is speaking, in the *Philoctetes* through the mouth of Neoptolemus[23], here through the mouth of Antigone. Despite the closeness of the relationship which he has achieved, Sophocles finally moves away from his hero, almost as far away as Goethe moves from his at the end of the Second Part of *Faust*. But whereas Philoctetes, full of complaints and suffering, retreats from the world of deceit into his familiar hiding-place, Oedipus surges forward with uncanny eagerness into the affairs of the world with his enigmatic, abundant and violent curses, and what is released by his daimon stands revealed in its human limitation.[24] The elemental forces do not break or dissolve into a final gentle calm. Only the lightning of Zeus can wrench the secret future meaning from the destiny of the mortal—just as the visible manifestation of the god does at the end of the *Philoctetes*.

Clearly the purpose of the Polynices scene is not merely to present the second of the two 'parties' fighting for the support of Oedipus, to balance the first. Rather, it serves as a bridge-passage which carries the tensions of the Creon scene over into the tonality of the scene that follows. The *Oedipus* is a tragic drama of which we can say 'here beginneth the tragedy' only when the final part begins. Similarly, from the point of view of its type, the Polynices scene is not a revelation scene but a scene of separation and decision.[25] It opens with one character severely shaken, the other malevolently silent. The father's silence causes the son's speech to falter (1271). Antigone has to act as mediator between the two, to encourage the son to speak up and break the father's silence. Again, the suppliant's speech is no longer a narrative like the tragic 'pathetic' narratives of the dramas of the earlier style: Polynices discourses, enlarges on his theme, attempts persuasion but gets lost in the situation, explains himself, loses himself in the details of the plan of campaign, of the bitter injustice he has suffered, of the successes he hopes to gain— while all the time the silence of Oedipus, becoming deeper and deeper, more and more oppressive from sentence to sentence, undermines his speech and leaves it hanging in mid-air. And as it ends, on a foolish note of high expectation, the same silence into which it had been forcing itself closes behind it—until the tension is broken by the curse. There are pauses in this speech, not imposed arbitrarily by critics, as in the 'speech of deception' in the *Ajax*, but audible in the words: Polynices (1271): 'Why are you silent? Speak to me, father! . . .'; chorus (1346): 'For the sake of the one who sent him, Oedipus, speak to this man. . . .' The silence of Oedipus is penetrating and destructive; the silence of Ajax towards Tecmessa was self-contained. So was that of Deianira, when she heard the results of her action; so was that of Iole. The same is true of the famous silences in Aeschylus, of Prometheus, Niobe, Achilles . . .[26] This silence of Oedipus is closer to that of Electra during Clytemnestra's prayer. All the others belong to the style of scene which is in the form of a monologue, self-contained and full of the *pathos* of self-revelation, whereas the two latter examples belong rather to the connecting, linking, penetrating style of the dramas of Sophocles' old age.

226

The scene with Polynices differs from the scene with Creon in its form, and correspondingly in its significance. The Polynices who tries to gain possession of Oedipus is not the embodiment of heartless, soulless politics, as Creon is, but of limitation and blindness. Hence the futility, vanity and deception, as if the son's ambition and plan for revenge could possibly concern a father such as his; hence his blind illusion of community with his father as if they were bound together by one and the same fate, as if *his*, Polynices' exile, were comparable with that of Oedipus, and as if it were possible to imagine Oedipus entering Thebes, with his son at his side wearing a victor's crown.[27] And throughout the whole of the heroic part of his speech, even during the catalogue of the seven champions, we hear the note of delusion. If the unforgiving Oedipus is subject to human limitations, how much more so is Polynices! It is true that he is gripped by violent feelings of repentance, when he is hard pressed by his own fate and realizes what he has done to his father; but that does not mean that it is any easier for him to free himself from his all too human limitations. This then is the beginning of a *Thebaid*, but it is not a fulfilment of a daimon in the form of a curse upon a dying race, or of a supreme law, divine intention or fate of a higher order.[28] At the end, despite the pleas of Antigone, Polynices is no longer able to turn from the course on which he has started, and although he can see what lies ahead, he rushes all the more blindly to his doom, dragging his 'companions', his blind victims, down with him. In this, there is a type of fatefulness which no longer bears any resemblance to that of Eteocles in Aeschylus' *Seven Against Thebes*. In Aeschylus the hero suffers a *god*-given fate, but Polynices succumbs to the confusion and complexity of *human* errors, limitations and mistakes, and is dragged away in their clutches.[29] In his downfall he does not invoke his daimon, as always happens in earlier tragedies of downfall, both those of Sophocles and even earlier in Aeschylus' *Seven* (653 ff.); instead he invokes the 'path' which leads from such a beginning to such a destination (1399 ff.):

227

Polynices
   Ah, what a journey! what a failure!
   My poor companions! See the finish now
   Of all we marched from Argos for! See me . . .
   For I can neither speak of this to anyone
   Among my friends, nor lead them back again . . .

For here he perceives nothing of the significance of his downfall, only its inevitability. Nowhere else is the Delphic command so flagrantly disregarded. However, Oedipus is equally incapable of rising above the sinister prohibition; as Oedipus of Thebes his roots go back into the past, his shadow falls across the future, and both are equally oppressive. For all the violence of his appeals to the spirits of the curse and the forces of destruction, the source of his power of cursing is no longer that from which he can draw in Aeschylus. He curses not so much as a human vessel of omnipotent forces, as by the power of his own bitter, injured heart. But although this injury of his weighs so heavily upon him, although the holy and venerable aspect of the man has been so deeply seared by events, this is no excuse for the savagery of his curses. There is no doubt about the righteousness of the powers upon which he calls, but this does not mitigate in any way the terrible harshness, in human terms, of his curse (1360 ff.):

Oedipus
    Weeping is no good now. However long
    My life may last, I have to see it through;
    But I regard you as a murderer! . . .

        . . .

228   Now go! For I abominate and disown you!
    You utter scoundrel! Go with the malediction
    I here pronounce for you . . .

Thus at one and the same time he is a mortal whose behaviour is inexcusably savage by human standards, and a being whose power is so great that he stands beyond human judgment; and as we approach the end of the play, his fluctuations between mortal and daimon become more enigmatic, and no sooner have we grasped him in one aspect than he eludes our grasp by slipping into the other.[30]

The end of the tragedy from the human point of view merges into the beginning of another tragedy—a tragedy of an impulse, conditioned by its human form, pursued by a daimon to a downfall in which it is abandoned by the gods. But this ending, this drama of the 'Seven' in which the sons of Oedipus are shown as the victims of a single doom, forms the *background*, the horizon overcast with dark clouds, *against* which is enacted, in the bright light of the divine, the passing of Oedipus into another existence.[31] The sign from the gods for which we have been waiting since the beginning comes at the point at which human fate and divine intention seem to have moved as far apart from each other as possible. The path taken by the mortal, driven in his blindness by none other than himself, leads as far away from the gods at the end of the *Oedipus at Colonus* as at the end of the *Philoctetes*. Indeed, the dissonance between curse and blessing, fate and transfiguration, becomes increasingly apparent as the unseen harmony, as Heraclitus calls it, becomes increasingly concealed.

Thus the thunderbolt of Zeus is not a mere theatrical thunder-clap, any more than the god in the *Philoctetes* is a mere *deus ex machina*. Several times the chorus interrupts the dialogue and echoes the tumult of forces which suddenly press in and occupy all the space. In the turmoil of the elements, uncanny forces appear to break forth from the blind man's head, uncertain where to discharge their load. The daimon takes the form of lightning which flashes down as if to scorch mother Earth, and it is dangerous to be so close to those around whom the forces of fate and nature are gathering.[32] Theseus is brought to the scene by the cries of the chorus, and Oedipus, who, on the point of death, is still waiting for him to receive as a last commission the secret which Oedipus has been carrying from the beginning. But he is forbidden to speak of it in the presence of others. And we, the audience, must be content with being classed among the 'citizens' of whom he says 'I cannot disclose it to any of these'. . . (1528). All that we learn is that it must be passed on with great solemnity on each occasion from the best person to the best. What kind of secret can this be? Certainly if there had not been such secrets in Greek hero-cult (and there is in fact evidence that there were), Sophocles would not have been able to make use of this particular form for his testament. (It has been pointed out that none of the Thebans except their highest magistrate knew where Dirce was buried, according to Plutarch, *de genio Socratis*, 578 B: 'The retiring magistrate takes his successor there at night, and after performing certain rites, without fire, they clear away all traces and leave by different paths under cover of darkness.') But it does not follow that the end of this tragedy can be dismissed as merely a matter for the history of religion.[33] It is clear that the sacral *aition* is

the external form rather than the essence of the bequest of Oedipus
(1526 ff.):

Oedipus
    These things are mysteries, not to be explained;
    But you will understand when you come there
    Alone . . .
                        But you
    Keep it secret always, and when you come
    To the end of life, then you must hand it on
    To your most cherished son, and he in turn
    Must teach it to his heir, and so for ever.
    That way you shall for ever hold this city
    Safe from the men of Thebes, the dragon's sons.
    For every nation that lives peaceably,
    There will be many others to grow hard
    And push their arrogance to extremes . . .

The Greek belief in heroes is here raised from its primitive,
magical significance to a higher, spiritual and ethical significance.
Magical power has become spiritual protection. The tomb of
Oedipus and its secret will protect Athens from *hybris*, in the face of
the devastation of countless other cities. If it should ever come to
pass that Athens were laid waste by the dragon's seed, that would be
a result of her 'wrongdoing'. But how is it that the secret has this
power? What can it be, that it is capable of so much? Let us not be
tempted to try to solve the mystery; it can be understood better
from the significance of the work as a whole than from any single
detail, let alone any external source. And whatever it may be, part of
it at any rate is the knowledge of the powerful sufferer, the hero
who blesses and curses, and his assimilation into an Athenian context through the cult. So the most tragic figure ever created by
Sophocles rests in the soil of his country, bequeathed by Theseus as
a legacy to Athens, his bones bearing witness from the world
below.
    Through the words of the hero as he moves towards his grave,
seeing with blind eyes, Sophocles sends a final greeting to his people
(1547 ff.):

Oedipus
    This way, O come! The angel of the dead,

Hermes, and veiled Persephone lead me on!
O sunlight of no light! Once you were mine!
This is the last my flesh will feel of you;
For now I go to shade my ending day
In the dark underworld. Most cherished friend!
I pray that you and this your land and all
Your people may be blessed: remember me,
Be mindful of my death, and be
Fortunate in all the time to come!

After his death, in addition to the older cult of Amynos, the 'defender', Athens dedicated to her tragedian the cult of the hero Dexion, the 'gracious' or 'hospitable' one, thereby perhaps revealing, from the point of view of the beneficiaries, something of the spirit in which this work and its secret legacy were bequeathed.

The departure of Oedipus is followed by a song—a gentle song of supplication and magic to banish the terror of Hades, which stands in the same relationship to the narrative of the passing of Oedipus as does a prayer to its unexpected fulfilment. With the laments of the bereaved daughters the drama comes to an end. But by means of the contrast between human sorrow and divine miracle, between admonitions in this world and transfiguration in the world beyond, the coda up to the final *thrēnos* is removed from the world of the torrents of emotion which marked the style which Sophocles had used for the catastrophes of his earlier plays. In the multiplicity of conflicting currents, in the to and fro of the questions and answers, and in the alternation between present anxiety about the future and remembrance of the past, between grief and comfort, the final chorus serves once more as a piece of music to frame the play, on the same scale and in the same style as the *parodos*.[34] And if the lament for the dead at the end of this tragedy no longer has the piercing tone of the laments in Sophocles' earlier plays, it is because this is a drama of a different kind, a drama whose effect is no longer pity and fear, but instruction and intimation.

The last messenger's speech is also in keeping with this attitude. In spite of its form, the narrative of the passing of Oedipus becomes a kind of action, continuing the play of transitions between the two spheres which converge upon the blind man: it describes how he is standing on the threshold, in the mysterious sanctuary of the grove, when the world above opens upon the world below; but how at the same time he is on the threshold of existence, between the calls of this world and of the world beyond, between the last loving embraces, embraces overflowing with love, and the departure to the other world . . . Thus the last scenes force a way in, are intertwined and interrupt each other, even in the messenger's speech: the bathing, then the lament of the girls, then the stillness, which is broken by the voice from the other world, a last moment of concern for the daughters, a speedy release, and at the end Theseus is left alone, shading his eyes with his hand, praying to heaven and to earth . . .

In the language of religion, the messenger's speech can be termed an account of a miracle, and regarded simply from that point of view it is true that it repeats motifs which are also to be found elsewhere. But what is unique and peculiar to the style of Sophocles' old age is the way in which the dissonance between god and man is finally resolved in harmony (1621 ff.):

Messenger
> . . . when they finally stopped,
> And no more sobs were heard, then there was
> Silence, and in the silence suddenly
> A voice cried out to him—of such a kind
> It made our hair stand up in panic fear:
> Again and again the call came from the god:
> 'Oedipus! Oedipus! Why are we waiting?
> You delay too long; you delay too long to go!'

The 'we' (which implies the joint nature of what is happening) with its terrifying yet tender kind of intimacy, partly involving Oedipus yet somehow at the same time mysteriously outside him, has no parallel in the entire range of divine voices of all ages and all religions which those who have been favoured by the gods have heard descending from heaven at the moment of their death. Here there is nothing of the majesty of the visions of the Old Testament, no clash between the forces of heaven and earth, no cosmic drama of an ascension, no transcendental glories floating down from on high, no transfigured sight—the god comes beside Oedipus, addresses him in the first person plural, invites him—he waits, but soon grows impatient . . . This is to some degree the verbal equivalent of

232

the spirit that suffuses the Orpheus and Eurydice relief in Naples. Despite the fact that the death of Oedipus is presented as highly individual and personal, it is still portrayed in the purest and most classical of forms—the carrying away of a mortal to another world.

In the early *Trachiniae*, the legendary death of Heracles on the pyre might well have provided an opportunity for attempting a drama of a type similar to this. But in that play both the hero's cares and the poetry itself are entirely concerned with this world. Death, even when it takes the form of victory over the suffering of the last hours, is only an end (παῦλα κακῶν, τελευτὴ ὑστάτη), not a transition. The otherworldly element is lacking, and therefore there is no mysterious interaction between spheres such as that which turns the death of Oedipus into a truly dramatic event. Death had been presented in the *Ajax* and the *Antigone* as the experience of being torn away, voluntarily but painfully, in the former case from heroism and fame, in the latter from youth and family. But that now lies in the past. At each successive stage, death has been given by Sophocles a form that corresponds with the stage of maturity that he himself had attained.

VIII

FRAGMENTS

The surviving tragedies have now been arranged in a relative chronology, and although this does not present us with the entire life-story of Sophocles, it does at least allow us to differentiate between various phases—early, mature, final perfection of form, and development of a late style. It remains to identify the same phases in the mass of fragments. But here we continually come up against the stumbling-block that the fragments preserved by quotation indicate far too little of the situation, which is what gives words their dramatic quality. However, the order that we shall suggest is confirmed at least to the extent that the chronological indications given by other data do not contradict the conclusions which we have drawn from the linguistic form and, in so far as any of it is still recoverable, the dramatic form. Let us at least demonstrate this with a few examples.[1]

The fragments most closely related to the *Trachiniae* and the *Ajax* are those of the *Eurypylus*, known since the papyrus discovery of 1912 [Carden, pp. 1 ff. = Pearson i, pp. 146 ff.]. From the tattered opening lines it is still just possible to read the warning sign which betrays the genre of the tragedy: for here the sign takes the form of the croaking of ravens, an ominous portent which is disregarded in the heat of excited argument. Longer passages survive from the messenger's speech which follows, dealing with the duel in which Eurypylus, the young son of Telephus and nephew of Priam, Troy's last hope, was killed by Neoptolemus, the young son of Achilles. One has the feeling that this speech is almost the climax of the whole play. To heighten this climax, the speech is interrupted by a lyrical section in anticipation, as it were, of a *kommos*. The content is consistent with such an assumption. Just as Ajax and Hector were killed by the same weapons which they had once exchanged with each other, according to the *Ajax* (see above, p. 31), Neoptolemus here kills the son of Telephus with the same spear with which Achilles had once healed Telephus. And just as this encounter shows the form of fate in which the play unfolds, so Astyoche, the mother of the slain hero, accuses her own folly (ἀβουλία) and guilt in the same way that Deianira accuses her daimon: for it was she who had been bribed by her brother Priam to send her son out to fight. It is indicated that here, too, pride will lead to a fall (P. Oxy. 1175 fr. 94). Similarly, the chorus is still in the old style, simply a sounding-board, and in it we can still hear an echo of the familar early form, as for example the *kommos* of Aeschylus' *Persians*. There is still no trace of a dialogue between three characters, or of a changing situation. And once again it is clear how inevitably the linguistic form matches the scenic form. For here the language in the particular form it takes is still the vehicle of the pathos in a way which is completely different from the later interplay of shifting relationships. As in the *Ajax* and the *Trachiniae*, here too there is an abundance of emotive similes. And the most splendid of them still appears in the narrative [fr. 5, col. iii 70–7]:

Messenger
 And so, prostrate about his wounded body,
 though not his father, yet with a father's words
 Priam bewailed the kinsman of his sons,
 calling him 'boy', 'young man' and 'counsellor';
 not as a Mysian, nor child of Telephus,
 but as his own son he called upon him:
 'Alas my child, I have betrayed you! although
 in you I'd found the last and most secure
 protection for my hopes for Phrygia . . .'

The *Women of Colchis* [Pearson ii, pp. 15 ff.], too, must belong to a relatively early period, since Euripides' *Medea*—performed in 431—follows its version of the story in that the dismemberment of Apsyrtus is made to occur in the house of the king of Colchis and not during the flight. Medea, who is in love with Jason, betrays to him the secrets of the tasks which he has to carry out in order to steal the golden fleece, and makes him swear gratitude to her. For protection against the dragon's fiery breath she gives him the healing ointment of Prometheus, and this leads to a long account of Prometheus' fate. Jason's victory over the dragon's seed was reported to the king by a messenger. To judge by the fragments, the language was heavy, compact, ornate, rich in metaphors, almost—as befits the distant world of marvels—Aeschylean. It would be easy to guess that this play did not belong to the late period, even if we were not certain of the *terminus ante quem*.

The *Thamyris* [Pearson i, pp. 176 ff.] seems to belong to an even earlier period. The hero was a Thracian king, singer and cithara-player, who boasted that he had surpassed the Muses in his playing. The Muses blinded him and took away his gift of song. That is how Polygnotus painted him in his picture of the underworld at Delphi—blind, with unkempt hair and beard, bowed down, the lyre at his feet, with broken bridge and snapped strings. The most famous scene of Sophocles' tragedy showed him in the same pathetic situation. The play must have belonged to the same genre of tragedies of destruction as the *Ajax* and the *Niobe* of Aeschylus. But in this play there must have been even more lyrics. Something of its shattering effect can still be sensed in the vibrancy of the surviving quotations. Since the poet became famous for his cithara-playing at its performance, this play must also belong to the early period.

Another example of an early form of play is the *Nausicaa* [Pearson ii, pp. 92 ff.] or *Plyntriae* ('The Girls Washing Clothes'). Again, the game of ball, in which the poet appeared in the main rôle, was long remembered. The few fragments that survive are enough to show how closely it followed the *Odyssey*; in its first part at least it may not have been so very different from Goethe's sketch. However, whether this was enough to make it a 'tragedy' conforming to the usual rules is more than doubtful; it was probably only a graceful piece, the product of the sheer pleasure that Sophocles took in presentation, mime and dance. It is possible, even probable, that a whole genre of lighter plays, lesser works than the tragedies, may have been lost to us except for a few unrecognizable fragments: graceful plays, pleasant dramatizations of myths, lacking, and not even laying claim to, the power and greatness of the surviving dramas. For amongst all the plays of an author such as Sophocles there must have been rapidly composed pieces as well as dramas that had ripened over many years.

We must therefore consider ourselves all the more fortunate that we are able to catch a glimpse of the playful, early Sophocles from the discovery on papyrus of the satyr-play the *Ichneutae* [Pearson i, pp. 224 ff. = Page, *Gk. Lit. Pap.* pp. 26 ff.]. 'The Hounds on the Trail' (*Spürhunde*), as Wilamowitz translated this title,[2] refers to the main piece of miming performed by the dancing chorus. And how full of dancing the whole of this play is! Previously our only knowledge of this genre was derived from Euripides' *Cyclops*. But in the *Cyclops* we find that Euripides has done little more than repeat situations and predicaments familiar to us from his other plays, albeit in a charmingly light-hearted tone. It is only since the discovery of the *Ichneutae* that we have had an example of the satyr-plays of a tragic poet for whom the gods have not yet become a human institution. And we discover how much more relaxed Sophocles is in playing with his gods than Euripides in playing with his heroes; the deeper his belief in them, the greater his freedom to make fun of them.

In the prologue of a tragedy we can expect to see the entry of a god in all his splendour, to punish and to judge; here too Apollo, the omniscient god of prophecy, enters—but in what a predicament! This time he has to turn to others, and what a crew they are! He is reduced to characters such as peasants, herdsmen, charcoal-burners, spirits of the mountain. For he has been robbed and does not know who the culprit is. The god offers a reward (i. 1 ff.):

Apollo
   A proclamation I, Apollo, make
   to every man and every god: . . .
   Stolen! my milking-cows and all my calves
   and herds of heifers—all of them have gone
   without a trace! . . .
               I never would have thought
   that any god or any mortal man
   would have the nerve to do a deed like this! . . .
               Stricken with alarm
   I search, I hunt, and make my proclamation
   to gods and men, that all may know . . .

So he sets out across the country as his own herald. Just as in the *Triptolemus* Demeter recounts the journey in store for her hero, or as Dionysus in Euripides' *Bacchae* recounts the places that he has come through, so Apollo enumerates the places where he has searched in vain: Thessaly, Boeotia (for he is coming from the north), the Doric lands, all the way to the inaccessible mountains of

Cyllene. But then Silenus comes hastening in answer to the 'loud
herald's cry'—Silenus, leading his chorus, eager out of the kindness
of his heart to act as Phoebus' 'dear benefactor', and to 'hunt out this
thing for him'. The business side must, however, be seen to. But
there is no difficulty about that when dealing with Phoebus.

The dance begins: jumping, hopping, bending, squatting,
finger-snapping—we can still deduce the movements from the
words. In the behaviour of these half-animal creatures there is an
indescribable combination of something of nature, something elemental, and something of the boisterousness of Attic youth: we
could not ask for a finer commentary on the satyrs depicted on
Greek vases. When the god has left, Silenus begins his work with an
almost Aeschylean prayer of supplication: 'Goddess Tyche and
guiding daimon!' When his repetition of Apollo's invocation to the
gods—he obviously feels that he is only a lower court of appeal and
that he is obliged to refer the matter to them—produces no more
results than before, he tries to put the satyrs onto the trail. They
advance in columns towards the ravine [94 ff. Pearson = 66 ff.
Page]:

A
 A god, a god, a god, a god! aha! aha!
 I think we've found them! Stop where you are! No further now!
B
 Yes, these must be the footprints of the cattle here!
A
 Be quiet! there is a god in charge of this adventure! . . .
B
 Quick, run! . . .
 whether or not the sound of lowing's reached your ears . . .

But it is only now that the real difficulty of the task becomes
clear. The cunning of the thief, who has confused the tracks, as we
know from the Homeric hymn to Hermes, gives rise to a dance-
figure: suddenly there is perplexity and embarrassment:

Chorus
 What can it be? What sort of system's this?—
 the front feet shifted to the back, and some
 criss-crossed with each other, going two ways at once!
 Some strange confusion must have struck their driver!

238   But the searchers seem to be just as confused as the tracks. Silenus
himself has never seen such postures: what kind of manners are
these? Lying there like hedgehogs in a bush! Sticking their behinds
out like monkeys who. . . What has got into them? But the only
reply he gets is a horrified 'Hoo hoo hoo hoo!' The lyre of the hidden
god begins to sound softly. Silenus mocks them: they are seeing
ghosts! 'Do you want a beating?'—'Hush! Just Listen!'—'How can
I listen if I can't hear a voice?'—'Just listen a moment! No mortal
has ever heard anything like that before!' But Silenus still hears
nothing: he harangues them, and contrasts their cowardice with the
heroism of his bygone youth, which they are disgracing just
because some practical joker of a herdsman is frightening them off
with a blast on his goathorn . . . Yet another different dance
number: training as hounds. The old man tests them: one after
another the young ones run up, encouraged by whistles and calls,
but every time they push past their goal. At last Silenus too hears the
unheard-of sound—and takes to his heels. The chorus summons up
its courage, and tries jumping and stamping in an attempt to force
the thief from his hiding-place in the ground out into the light of
day—and then there rises before them, like an earth-goddess
ascending from the depths, the nymph of the mountains, Cyllene
[215 Pearson = 168 Page]:

Cyllene
   Wild creatures, why have you attacked with so much noise
   this green and wooded hill wherein the wild beasts dwell?
   What tricks are these? And why this change of tasks from those
   that once you used to undertake to please your master?—
   that master who always used to wear the hide of a fawn
   and carry the thyrsus lightly in his hands as he sang
   the holy song amidst the attendants of the god
   with the nymphs his offspring and a company of youths.
   But now I do not know what's going on, or where
   these new mad whirlings whirl you. Strange indeed: I heard
   a cry like the call of hunters when they find themselves
   close to the brood of some wild creature in its lair . . .

   The speech, with its elevated tone, soars up with as much dignity
as the figure of the goddess in the midst of the wild group. But they
have hardly been quietened before she is already divulging her

secret to the crowd: that she is the nurse of a divine child . . . At the same time she poses a riddle: they must guess what instrument the sounds come from. But then it suddenly dawns upon the chorus: the child is the thief! Cyllene is scarcely able to maintain her dignity and reserve: what a suggestion! This child! With an ancestry like his! Does Zeus steal? Does Maia, his mother, steal? Do they not live in most honourable circumstances? Does anyone go hungry in *this* house? But then the stolen cattle announce their presence! Dung does not lie—and the secret can no longer be kept . . .

Even though the rest is missing, together with the reconciliation between the two gods, and the exchange of the lyre for the stolen herd, the play as a whole is still, in genre, a play of revelation. And as in the case of the tragedies of revelation of which Sophocles is the master, here too there is no lack of stumbling-blocks, tensions and surprises. It is true that the truth is not brought to light by means of the gods' sport with men, but by means of the poet's sport with the gods. But all the same, as masters of such sport, the gods are also the creators of their own form of sport; they are therefore also the creators of the reversal which it brings. For instead of leading to a tragic recognition the discovery leads to a divine miracle: by means of the theft, Apollo becomes master of the lyre, and the instrument which Hermes and Apollo exchange, the instrument which joins in and accompanies the beginning of the play, must have been played beautifully enough by the god's hand at the end, as a symbol of the lighter spirit which is glorified in this play. We ought to remember that something like this may have followed the *Oedipus Tyrannus* as satyr-play! That *this* Apollo, whom Silenus comes to help, could have taken over from the figure of the god who appeared to the blinded man: 'It was Apollo, friends' . . . ! If he is to write the most tragic of all poetry, a man's spirit must be able to make such sport.

NOTES

NOTES to INTRODUCTION

242   1. This was written fourteen years ago. Since then, two monographs have
appeared which, although very different, have in common the fact that
they approach the author from the standpoint of definite theories: H.
Weinstock, *Sophokles*, 1931 (and since then a 2nd abridged ed.), and A. von
Blumenthal, *Sophokles*, 1938; the former heavily influenced by the philosophy of Heidegger (although the second edition omits part of the
methodology), the latter true to its origin in the circle of Stefan George.
There is also W. Schadewaldt, *Sophokles und Athen*, Leipzig inaugural,
1935 (publ. Klostermann, *Wissenschaft und Gegenwart*, xi), which deals with
the biographical problem in the deepest sense, with Sophocles as a
'national classic' (Goethe). We should also mention, among assessments of
all three tragic writers, first: Max Pohlenz, *Die griechische Tragödie*, 1930
[2nd ed. 1954], with a volume of notes, extremely helpful for philological
aspects; E. Howald, *Die griechische Tragödie*, 1930, original, analytical, with
strong emphasis on the historical, psychological and social circumstances
of tragedy and the limits of the genre; and P. Friedländer, *Die Antike* i,
1925, 295 ff. [= *Studien zur antiken Literatur und Kunst*, 1969, 107 ff.].
In what follows, as in the first edition, the last three works will be
referred to by the name of the author only.

There are also: from Italy: Enrico Turolla, *Saggio sulla poesia di Sophocle*,
Bari 1934, very enthusiastic; from England: T. B. L. Webster, *Introduction
to Sophocles*, 1936 [2nd ed. 1969], sober and factual. For other secondary
literature see Bursian's *Jahresbericht*, 1938, 67 ff., by A. von Blumenthal.

E. Wolff, *Neue Jahrbücher für Wissenschaft und Jugendbildung*, 1931, 393 ff.
should also be mentioned.

There have been several recent examinations of the problem of the
chronology, on which see my notes to the *Trachiniae* (p. 239 ff. below).

[Since 1947 the literature about Sophocles has enormously increased. In
1962 H. Friis Johansen published in *Lustrum* vii, 1962, a very useful report
on the Sophoclean literature that appeared between 1939 and 1959, written
in English. Much bibliographical material is contained in the successive
reports on Greek Tragedy in the *Anzeiger für die Altertumswissenschaft* since

1948, many of them by Albin Lesky. The same scholar's indispensable handbook *Die Tragische Dichtung der Hellenen* (3rd ed., 1972) gives useful bibliographical material in its section about Sophocles (169 ff.); and the volume *Sophokles* in the series *Wege der Forschung* (no. xcv) has a useful supplement to Friis Johansen's *Lustrum* report covering the period between 1960 and its own appearance in 1967.

For new material in papyri see Richard Carden, *The Papyrus Fragments of Sophocles*, Berlin, 1974. —H. Ll.–J.]

2. Friedländer, 303, draws attention to the loneliness that surrounds Sophocles' tragic heroes.

243   3. O. Regenbogen, 'Schmerz und Tod in den Tragödien Senecas', *Vorträge der Bibliothek Warburg*, 1930 [= *Kleine Schriften*, Munich, 1961, 409 ff.].

4. Hence 'monologue form' here does not mean 'self-expression' either, as it does in W. Schadewaldt, *Monolog und Selbstgespräch, Neue Philologische Untersuchungen*, 1926, 'occurring wherever a person becomes the sentient bearer of a powerful fate which rules his actions' (36); rather the monologue quality arises from the balance of forces within a scene. Pathos-filled 'self-expression', for example, and report are theoretically, psychologically and stylistically different forms, but they overlap in practice. What is peculiar to both is the fact that they are not 'dialogue', i.e. from the standpoint of the action they have no reference to the other person. Even when a person is present to hear the report, this does not mean that the scene is shaped by the fact that he hears it. On the other hand it can rise to a highly pathetic form of 'self-expression', as in the recognition scenes in the *Oedipus* and the *Electra*, self-expression, however, which is not in monologue form but, from the point of view of the action, definitely dialogue, since the tension between two characters dominates the scene, even at the point where there is a lengthy speech, heavily charged with emotion, which remains, from a psychological standpoint, 'self-expression'. Similarly, a scene which is apparently in dialogue form can really be 'monologue', when there is a single content divided among several speakers and the speeches stand side by side, not in opposition to each other like two magnetic poles. Again, speeches which appear merely to follow on, psychologically for example, can equally well be regarded from the point of view of the action as standing in tense opposition, and so forth.

NOTES to CHAPTER I (AJAX)

1. 'No-one can find what we call dramatic action in this play unless he

knows before he starts that he has to find it' (Tycho von Wilamowitz-Moellendorff, 51).

2. E.g. Pohlenz, 186, and *Erläuterungen*, note to p. 174.

3. On the question of the date: *Ajax* 1295, where Teucer taunts Menelaus with his mother's adultery, cannot be used for dating purposes. It is a very Peloponnesian story: a disgraceful love-affair between Aërope and a slave, before she becomes the mother of Agamemnon and Menelaus. It is re-told *in extenso* in Euripides' *Cretan Women*, produced in the year 438. The discrepancy between the genealogies in Euripides and Sophocles —one mentions Pleisthenes, the other omits him—has been pointed out by Pohlenz, *Erläuterungen*, 51. It is true that Wilamowitz [in *Lyrische und dramatische Fragmente* ed. W. Schubart & U. von Wilamowitz-Moellendorff], Berliner Klassikertexte, v, 2 (1907), 71, believed that Sophocles was alluding to Euripides' play at this point. But if we are looking for an allusion to a tragedy, we should not forget that Sophocles himself wrote an *Atreus* and no less than two plays called *Thyestes*, into which these events may well have been introduced in passing. The νόθος problem appears elsewhere in his works, e.g. *Aleadae*, frr. 83 and 84.

The opening passage of Euripides' *Telephus* (fr. 723 Nauck² [the fragments of the *Telephus* have now been edited by E. Handley and J. Rea, *Bulletin of the Institute of Classical Studies* Suppl. v (1957)—H. Ll.-J.]), the quarrel of the two kings in Argos before the expedition to Troy, was well-known and often quoted:

Agam.: Σπάρτην ἔλαχες, κείνην κόσμει,

τὰς δὲ Μυκήνας ἡμεῖς ἰδίᾳ.

But I see no reason why this line of Euripides should be the model, and Sophocles' *Ajax* 1102 the imitation. The equivalent in the *Ajax* runs:

Σπάρτης ἀνάσσων ἦλθες, οὐχ ἡμῶν κρατῶν.

Teucer therefore speaks as an Athenian. Σύμμαχος means 'ally'. So the *Ajax* cannot be derived from Euripides at this point. Hence too the wealth of vocabulary referring to the power of command in these lines of the *Ajax*: ἀρχῆς θεσμός, ἀνάσσειν, κολάζειν . . . and again κοσμεῖν. The manner in which the noblest royal family of Sparta is reprimanded for arrogance by Teucer, the illegitimate Salaminian, verges on the political. Sparta ought not to have opinions about what is not her concern. The sovereignty of Ajax of Salamis is not inferior to that of the Spartan king. Before 446 the unity of the Athenian empire was threatened by Sparta; Sparta indeed interfered. By the terms of the Peace of 446 there was an agreement on spheres of influence, and towards the end of the Peace it was not Athens who was driven to complain of the arbitrary behaviour of Sparta, but vice versa. Besides, to date the *Ajax* as late as the Peloponnesian war is impossible on stylistic grounds.

245   Similarly, the contemporary references in the chorus beginning at 1185, the condemnation of all wars, the contrast between the joys of peace at Athens, the garlands, cups, flutes, nights of love, Eros (the joys of the Attic aristocrat) and the desolation of the rainy camps of war, and the final expression of a longing to catch sight of Sunium on the journey home from distant parts—all this is more comprehensible at a date when it corresponded with the circumstances than during the long peace after the forties.

W. Buchwald, *Studien zur Chronologie der attischen Tragödie*, Diss. Konigsberg, 1939, 49, attempts to adduce new proof that Euripides' *Telephus* of 438 is a *terminus post quem* for the *Ajax*. He argues that there can be no doubt that Sophocles' *agon*, the quarrel between the Atridae and Teucer, which almost reaches the limits of the tolerable, was inspired by Euripides' *Telephus*. We may admit that poets are easily inspired to write the intolerable, but we must remember that the quarrel in the *Telephus* took place between the two commanders of the army. In the *Ajax* the Atridae are in agreement. And if the dispute in which Teucer argues against the Atridae on behalf of the dead Ajax was based on anything, it was based on the epic tradition. Even if the structure of the drama did not allow the quarrel to precede the suicide, as in the epic, nevertheless the enmity of the Atridae is referred to throughout the whole play, so that we are prepared for the conflict. There is nothing of this in the *Telephus*. Nor is there anything in the *Ajax* comparable to the political quarrel in Euripides. In Sophocles there is no discussion of war or peace: in other words, the central topic of the argument in Euripides is simply not there. And are we to suppose that Sophocles would have been unable to write the *Ajax* without the inspiration of the *Telephus*?

4. There has been lively discussion concerning the identity of the speaker, especially since this affects the emendations to some extent. The extant lines were regarded as a speech of Niobe by the first editor, Vitelli, and most recently by A. Lesky, *Wiener Studien,* lii, 1934, 1 ff.; as a dialogue between a confidante of Niobe and the leader of the chorus by, among others, W. Schadewaldt, 'Die Niobe des Aischylos', *Sitzungsberichte der Heidelberger Akademie*, 1934, Abh. 3 (with detailed commentary). The reasons for my own view that Leto is speaking are given in the first edition

246   and, in more detail, in *Hermes*, lxix, 1934, 233 ff. A. Körte, who in *Hermes*, lxviii, 1933, 252 ff., suggested Niobe as the speaker, supported my view in *Archiv für Papyrusforschung*, ix, 1935, 249. The most recent discussions are:

Karl-Ernst Fritsch, Diss. Hamburg, 1936, and A. von Blumenthal's report on Sophocles in Bursian's *Jahresbericht*, 1938, 134.

[The early date of the *Ajax* is now generally accepted; but few scholars think the *Niobe* fragment so important for dating it as Reinhardt believed. For a text and discussion of the *Niobe* fragment, see my appendix to the Loeb edition of Aeschylus, ii, 556 ff. A vase published by A. D. Trendall, *Revue Archéologique,* ii, 1972, 309 ff. favours the suggestion that the speaker of the passage from the *Niobe* is not Leto, but a nurse; cf. O. P. Taplin, *Harvard Studies in Classical Philology,* lxxvi, 1972, 60 ff. (Reinhardt's attempt to gain further support for his dating from the supposed relevance to the contemporary situation of *Ajax,* 1185 ff. seems to me mis-judged.)—H. Ll.-J.]

On κόμιστρα in line 11 (see Lesky, 12), it may be remarked that the entire action of this drama will in fact have consisted of the fruitless attempts to fetch Niobe away from the tomb of her children, on which she pines away and eventually turns into stone. One cannot see why the children should be fetched home.

5. Sophocles seems to have been the first to deviate from the epic tradition by turning the madness into a ruse of Ajax's patron goddess. In the epic, Athena was able to direct Ajax's madness, which had already broken out, against the cattle. But in Sophocles the madness only begins with that veiling of the senses by which the goddess protects the Greeks (51). Ajax's actual plan of revenge is not madness, and he feels no repentance for it. This innovation too is clearly intended to cast more blame on the hero.

6. Σοὶ δ' ἐφίεμαι: normally verbs such as γουνοῦμαι, λίσσομαι, were used in a prayer. This shows the same attitude—κόμπος—as 774.

7. On the prehistory of the representation of Ajax as the giant, son of the 'giant' Telamon, see Von der Mühll, 'Der grosse Aias', *Basler Rektorats-programm,* 1932.

8. The late Sophoclean *parodoi* of the *Philoctetes* and the *Oedipus at Colonus* are quite different: there are two voices, each with its individual rhythmic movement. Thus in the *Philoctetes,* where the relationship between Neoptolemus and his followers might appear to be similar to that in the *Ajax,* we find an alternation between a desire for knowledge and explanation, between lament and enlightenment, and between astonishment and prophecy. At the end, as the finale of the *parodos,* there is a great increase in pace, and the alternating pattern of the stanzas is interrupted when the approaching footsteps of Philoctetes are heard, while at the same time there is a reversal of rôles: for now Neoptolemus asks the questions and the chorus gives the answers. There is nothing like this in the early *Ajax.*

9. This, too, is Homeric; cf. the cry of Athena when Achilles hastens to the ditch. [It is in fact Achilles whose voice is compared to the trumpet, not

Athena (*Iliad* xviii 219 ff.)]—That the *Ajax* is also linguistically closer to epic than any other of Sophocles' plays is demonstrated by Jebb's commentary, lii; on this see Pohlenz, *Erläuterungen*, 50.—The comparison of the trusty old *paidagogos* with an old racehorse in *El.* 25 is not to be confused with *pathetic* similes: this is reminiscent of the aristocratic type of expression, familiar to us from Plato's *Symposium*, Aristophanes etc.

10. Ever since antiquity the commentators have noted the similarity and sometimes even something of the difference between the two passages, and attribute the latter to the fact that Tecmessa is the slave and Andromache the legal wife. But how can that possibly be a sufficient explanation? As if it were impossible for Ajax to have a sympathetic understanding with a slave whom he loves!

11. He has already called for him from his closed tent; this is therefore not a result of Tecmessa's plea.

12. Here too it is characteristic of Ajax that he speaks of his son's future *fate* as a hero; the comparison between youth and age, 554 ff., is similar to *Trachiniae*, 144 ff. in its gnomic style.

13. On the 'speech of deception' see Wolfgang Schadewaldt, *Neue Wege zur Antike*, viii, 1929, 70 ff.; Wilamowitz, *Hermes*, lix, 1924, 249 ff. [= *Kleine Schriften*, iv, 343 ff.]; Welcker, *Kleine Schriften*, ii, 264; and the commentaries.

14. The ends of the two speeches are also similar, *Ajax*, 684 ff. and *Trach.* 467 ff. *Ajax*: 'But these things will be taken care of.' (This refers to his future friendships and enmities.) 'But you go in and pray to the gods that they may grant fulfilment of my heart's desire.' Similarly *Trach.* 467 ff.: 'But let all that drift away on a favourable wind. To you I say: tell lies to others if you like, but tell the truth to me.' In both passages the similarity does not lie only on the surface; the wish which appears to be benevolent really carries a sinister meaning: my friendships and enmities will be well taken care of when I am dead. Similarly in the other case: 'But let all that drift away on a favourable wind'; Deianira seems to accept the new liaison so calmly, but in fact she herself invites the danger which it implies. (I translate: 'with a favourable wind'; Radermacher's interpretation seems to me untenable. The accompanying wind is also 'favourable' in Aeschylus' *Septem*, 690: favourable, that is, for the downfall, since that is the direction in which Apollo is forcing the house of Laius.)

15. The comments of Wilamowitz, *Hermes*, lix, 1924, 249 ff. [= *Kleine Schriften*, iv, 343 ff.], on this passage are very odd. Ajax's comparisons with the world of nature mean nothing to him; he ignores the tragic element in the tone of the speech; and he analyses it as follows: first, Ajax intended to apply 'a universal law', but suddenly, after a 'new reason had occurred' to him in the form of the *gnomē* of Bias on friendship, 'he could no longer

pronounce the lie that he was giving in, but had to take refuge in an ambiguous expression . . .' 'He loathes having to deceive', so that he 'soon gives up deception' and so forth. A complete reversal, then, according to Wilamowitz. Just imagine the actor, suddenly called on to express loathing of deception, and then inability to continue the deception! How is he to express this loathing? There is nothing about it in the text, so presumably he has to stop to insert a mimed interlude and no doubt other nuances so as to show his disgust. . . .

Moreover, imagine someone on the brink of suicide who is 'disgusted' by having to tell the 'lie' that he is going for a walk!

On the comparisons see also W. Schadewaldt, *Monolog und Selbstgespräch*, 1926, 87.

16. Wilamowitz, *Hermes*, lix, 1924, 250 [= *Kleine Schriften*, iv, 344], in order to explain Ajax's behaviour, refers to Pollux, viii, 120: 'The suicide weapon bears the guilt, and we may therefore compare Athenian lawsuits brought against ἄψυχα; it is buried, just as the latter were cast outside the frontiers of the country by the *phylobasileis*.' So too Radermacher's commentary. But we would be failing to respond to the tragic tone of the passage if we were to take it as no more than a description of an effective magic ritual, as a plausible reason for Ajax to leave the stage. Ritual magic is accommodated to the tragic framework only in the sense that it draws attention to Ajax, in that it no longer appears as magic but as an action, that is, an act of dissimulation. Similarly, washing off the stain is the 'proof' which is 'to be found' so that he may demonstrate that he is a worthy son of his father, 472.

17. It is usually assumed that the stage remains empty for a while, and that Ajax then enters from the side through the *parodos* or behind a hitherto unnoticed bush, buries his sword in the earth in silence, and when he has done this stands in front of it and speaks. Not to mention the impossibility of conveying the effect of great distance in this way, or the problems raised by the miming, this arrangement would also entail that the main scene, where Sophocles says 'Behold, the man', is thrust to one side of the stage instead of occupying the centre. This would have an extremely strange effect on the end of the play. No lamenting retinue, no funeral procession leaves the stage. The chorus exits in groups to either side; Teucer and the boy remain alone by the body and lift it up. This is the end. But how is the stage to be cleared? How will the group around the dead man leave the scene? Are the bushes to suffice for that too? He would have to be carried out eventually. But he could only be dragged along—by Teucer and the boy! And no curtain falls to hide them. The *ekkyklema* resolves all the difficulties. The width of this apparatus would allow its wings, its scenery, and the necessary properties to be pushed out together from the rear

249

wall. Ajax's speech to his sword could begin at the same moment as the new scene was being pushed forward. Since its function was to reveal what cannot be seen on the stage, the *ekkyklema* could probably represent not only an interior but also a distant scene if necessary.

E. Bethe, *Rheinisches Museum*, lxxxiii, 1934, 21 ff., tries to prove that the *ekkyklema* was never used. But there are too many arguments for its existence, not only from the comic poets, but also from indications in the texts themselves. The subject requires investigation in a monograph. [It remains controversial.—H. Ll.-J.]

18. Cf. Radermacher's commentary, where the evidence is given.

NOTES to CHAPTER II (TRACHINIAE)

1. See Wilamowitz, *Griechische Tragödien*, iv, 357: 'This Heracles can boast of his victories over dragons and centaurs; he belongs to the same fairy-tale world as they, rather than with the woman whom Sophocles took from contemporary life. There was many a wife like that in the Athens of his day' etc. This would cause the *Trachiniae* to fall into two completely heterogeneous parts. Since Heracles and Deianira are incompatible, they must have different origins: Deianira in the contemporary surroundings of the dramatist, Heracles in the world of saga. 'He retained the heroic stylization (in the first part), so that the dissonance in the second part is not obvious after all; but he is following the same path as Euripides, whose influence is strong throughout this play, for Deianira is an Athenian woman.' Athenian women were not in the habit of being courted by river-gods and carried off by centaurs, and of deceiving heralds, but. . . . But what? Wilamowitz thinks that they had recourse to love potions: 'We even know of another case, in which the neglected woman unwittingly caused poisoned wine to be served to her husband.' But the love potion in Sophocles comes straight from the world of fairy-tale! How can we make a distinction like this?

An early date for the *Trachiniae* has met with opposition: cf. Schadewaldt, *Deutsche Literaturzeitung*, 1937, col. 999. Meanwhile Johanna Heinz, *Hermes*, lxxii, 1937, 270 ff., reverts to a date between the *Alcestis* and the *Medea*, i.e. between 438 and 431. On this cf. n.19 below.

Webster, *Introduction to Sophocles*, 145 ff. and *Hermes*, lxxi, 1936, 268, after some linguistic comments, divides Sophocles' work into periods on the grounds of poetic vocabulary: 'Sophocles' plays can be divided stylistically into two groups, an early group comprising the *Ajax*, *Antigone* and *Trachiniae*, and a later group comprising the *Electra*, *Philoctetes* and *Coloneus*, with the *Tyrannus* between the two. The early style is smooth and highly coloured; many words are borrowed from Aeschylus and Homer; compound adjectives, privatives, agents and variations of form are commoner than in the later plays.' On the whole that view is in agreement with the collections of examples of Sophocles' poetic vocabulary on which my judgement is based; cf. pp. 7 f., 18, 50, 59, 142, 157–158, 168, 173 of this book. Comparison of the different forms of dialogue and staging led to the same result. I should never have thought of writing a book about Sophocles that was not an enquiry. But since the style never fails to lead to the work, I could not stop at style in the strictly formal sense. Linguistic style is linked to dramatic style. . . I have repeatedly been informed that conclusions drawn from the form of the dialogue and the staging are not valid, but, as far as I can see, no reasons for this assumption have been offered.

251   The division into periods which resulted from my studies differs from Webster's only in that the *Ajax* and the *Trachiniae* came out as definitely early, and the *Electra*, *Philoctetes* and *Oedipus at Colonus* as definitely late, with the *Oedipus Tyrannus* in the middle between the two groups, and the *Antigone* as a transition to the *Oedipus Tyrannus*.

Moreover we should not lose sight of the fact that the evidence for 441 as the date of the *Antigone* is only the anecdote and not a notice in the *didascaliae*—and the anecdote cannot possibly be true if it is dated to 441, for the victor in that year was Euripides. 'So, unfortunately, we must admit that we do not have a firm date for the *Antigone*' (Wilamowitz, *Aristoteles und Athen*, ii, 1893, 298). The point of the anecdote is: Sophocles was elected *strategos* for being a poet; that is what the Athenians were like, they were so taken by the *Antigone*. Whoever told this story was, in any case, ignorant of Sophocles' political career, both of his office as *hellenotamias* in 443/2 and his other *strategiae*—that held during the Samian revolt was known from literature—not to mention his connections with Thucydides, who had already been ostracized in 443. To defend the anecdote by deriving the *propter hoc* from a *post hoc* (which would then, however, have to be an open-ended *post hoc* and thus go against the sense of the anecdote) would imply a chronological reliability on the part of its author which is hardly consistent with such ignorance. Another argument against too early a date for the *Antigone* rests upon the much-discussed borrowing from Herodotus, *Ant.* 904 ff. Borrowings from Herodotus only occur elsewhere in the later plays, *Oed. Tyr.* 981, *El.* 62, 421, *Phil.* 1207, *Oed. Col.* 337. Webster, 53, offers suggestions designed to avoid this difficulty. [The early dating is now accepted by most scholars; Paul Mazon and Alphonse Dain in the Budé edition of Sophocles think the *Trachiniae* the earliest extant play. On E. R. Schwinge's attempt to date it, see n. 19 below.—H. Ll.-J.]

2. The comparison with Medea is not conclusive, for Deianira's words might remind one just as much, or even more, of Aeschylus' *Agamemnon*: the long-awaited hero, coming home at last in victory—with a prisoner of war as his concubine, whom he expects his wife, the faithful mistress of the house (οἰκουρός), to receive, commending the foreign girl to her care. . . . The situation in the *Medea* of Euripides is by no means as close a parallel.

3. Pohlenz, 1930, 208 ff. [cf. 2nd ed. 203-4] seems to me to misjudge the style. 'Deianira is concerned with nothing but her personal life. . . . Then she suddenly realizes that she is an ageing woman, past her prime; then she dares the desperate struggle . . .' etc. Thus what in Sophocles is an objective fate is removed to the subjective sphere of the emotions; Pohlenz interprets as though Deianira were some sort of Eleanora Duse. When Deianira herself puts her fate into words the form should not be mistaken for an emotional modern monologue. 'How delicate and true to life it is, that it is only in the presence of the maidens whom she trusts that she pulls aside the veil that she had to throw over the most secret feelings of her heart in the presence of Lichas!' etc. In fact she does not 'pull aside' any 'veil from the most secret feelings of her heart'—anything of that kind would have had to be in a completely different dramatic form—but speaks of her *fear*; in doing so she speaks the truth, after having at first pretended not to be afraid, but to be welcoming everything that has happened with great joy.

Also, Tycho von Wilamowitz, 145, thinks 'that there is hardly another person in Sophocles who comes so near to being what we mean by a character. Here too we may surely detect the influence of Euripides.' But he goes on to state that this character, 'of which there is nothing in the saga', 'was not invented but borrowed from the character of Penelope in the *Niptra*, and in that play it was taken from the epic tradition'.

4. Thus for example F. Leo, *Der Monolog im Drama*, 1908, 14: 'But the execution is obviously influenced by Euripides' narrative prologues.' When he goes on to argue, 'It is not a monologue, because the old serving-woman is present and replies; it is not a dialogue, because it is not addressed to anyone . . .' etc., it goes without saying that the difference between monologue and dialogue is not to be determined by 'address', 'reply' and so forth, but by attitude and movement. Leo is completely off the track when he comments: 'She—Deianira—is in the habit of speaking to herself and lamenting and continually rummaging in her memories in their presence (i.e. that of her confidantes)': firstly, because this sets a piece of naturalistic psychological portrayal in place of what is daimonic and determined by fate, and secondly because in the whole of Sophocles there is no example of 'talking to oneself', which would imply (if anything) a distinction between two parts of oneself, one communicating its reflec-

252

253

tions to the other. A monologue, as opposed to a group scene, of the type that we find in modern drama, does not occur in Attic drama, as we need hardly say.

An opening in a monologue form, followed by the entrance of a second person, occurs in the satyr play *Ichneutae*, which is certainly early. Walter Nestle, *Die Struktur des Eingangs in der griechischen Tragödie, Tübinger Beiträge*, 1930, rightly argues that the manner of Euripides' prologues is a stylized form of an earlier practice.

5. The chorus beginning at 497 is unique in the whole of Sophocles, containing narrative in the manner of a ballad, heraldically stylized, almost, as W. Kranz remarks (*Stasimon*, 1933, 254 ff.), in the same style as the dithyrambs of Bacchylides. But this does not mean that it is an independent piece of music, an insertion, like the songs in the late tragedies of Euripides, for it amplifies what Deianira herself has already proclaimed, love's power over gods and mortals (443), so that the narration of the battle between Heracles and the Achelous becomes a mythical example of Deianira's *gnome*. At the same time it adds what could not be reported in the prologue (22, alluded to at 526). Moreover, at the same moment as it becomes clear that Deianira has lost Heracles' love, we are told how Heracles once won her, and this makes the chorus a link in the chain of doom. It seems more likely to belong with the earlier Aeschylean narratives in choral form than with the later works of Euripides. The sung narrative goes hand in hand with the numerous other narratives in the whole drama.

6. This line (25) has been athetized (most recently by Kranz, *Sokrates*, 1921, 32 [= *Studien zur antiken Literatur und ihrem Fortwirken*, 1967, 283]) because scholars have been unable to reconcile themselves to its form, that of a proverb; but this form is present from the beginning of the speech and is characteristic of the *Trachiniae* as a whole . Cf. 297 etc. Critics have been afraid that the 'pathos' would be misunderstood and destroyed here. But is that really so? It is a life-and-death battle. Deianira sits 'numb with fear' for her beloved: fear that Heracles will be defeated on her account, that is, on account of her 'beauty'. But the unique and particular is replaced by the universal gnomic figure, carrying a richer content of fate, and this hints at her suffering rather than expresses it. This conceals her love, and gives a better sense than if, as a result of the excision, which is apparently so attractive, we are left with: 'for I was not robust enough, being only a girl, to see such a thing.' Also the antithesis implied by τέλος δέ clearly gives the expectation of an unfortunate *issue* as the reason for her fear, which again is expressed only by the excised line.

7. This also explains why there is no conversation between three persons in the *Trachiniae*; there is none even in the scene of interrogation, since

254

Deianira stops talking (402) at the same moment as the two messengers confront each other, only to start again after Lichas has turned to her (436); but then it is as if the second messenger were no longer present.

8. Tycho von Wilamowitz, 145, interprets the scene from the point of view of its 'dramatic effect', and this is not really adequate.

9. Thus it is not a 'soliloquy' with a 'psychologically delicate transition', as Radermacher's commentary calls it.

10. The speech is again gnomic at first, taking examples of a general nature and applying them to her particular case; there is a similar linking of the particular and the gnomic in Anacreon, frr. 27 and 28 (Diehl). Ajax made similar use of Bias' *gnōmē* in his 'speech of deception' [cf. p. 24 above].

11. But this has nothing in common with 'intrigue' and the play of intrigue as a means towards dramatic complications: 'intrigue' arises from well-considered deliberation, not from pitiful delusion, does not direct itself destructively against its author, and does not involve a struggle with a fate which accomplishes itself even as the victim tries to escape it. Nor does μεμηχάνηται τοὔργον (586) refer in any way to this kind of play of intrigue, but to the love-potion, which is a motif supplied by the saga, and is therefore not part of the drama as 'intrigue' in the sense that 'cunning' is part of the *Electra* and the *Philoctetes*. This tells against F. Solmsen, *Philologus*, lxxxvii, 1932, 10 ff. [= *Kleine Schriften*, i, 150 ff.], who thinks that the 'intrigue' in the *Trachiniae* puts it among the Euripidean plays of intrigue, of the type that developed after the twenties.

12. Both themes are formulated at 534 ff., and again in the narrative at 554, in a manner which Sophocles abandoned in his later works. For *El.* 560, 565, 577 etc. should be seen in a different light; see below.

13. Pohlenz' explanation (1st ed., 205; [not in 2nd ed.]) involves a self-contradiction: 'Sophocles himself can hardly have been a man who took long to deliberate, and he imparts his own nature to his characters. Thus Deianira suddenly rejoins the maidens with a fully-fledged decision.' In that case, we would also have to argue that Sophocles was at the same time a man who deliberated very weightily, etc. etc.—The *Ajax* and the *Trachiniae* are unique among Sophocles' plays in two respects: they show as yet no knowledge of the ripening of decisions as a form of dramatic action, and all development of thought and all reversals in them take place off-stage. This phase in the history of tragic style is without any doubt earlier than the *Medea*.

14. This, too, is an archaic feature: thus, for example, in the *Persae*, Atossa's premonitory dream is followed immediately, in the same *epeisodion*, by its realization in the entry of the messenger and the news that he brings.

15. For line 940 is not relevant here, since it only denies that she desired the *results* of her action: Deianira is not the criminal that Hyllus took her to be. But that does not mean that her downfall is a result determined only by outward circumstances and independent of her state of mind.

16. The speech which Hyllus addresses to his mother follows the narrative which is reported to everybody after an awkward, obvious transition (807). To confirm that this is an archaic feature, compare the very different way in which the narrative of the *paidagogos* is addressed to the listeners in the later *Electra*: 688, 690, 761. In *Trach.* 806 we have: '*You* (pl.) will see him', not '*You* (sing.) will', for the narrative is addressed to the audience. This feature was still preserved later in the traditional rôle of the *exangelos* (the messenger from within).

17. Cf. 92 and 124. Deianira's silent exit is, it is true, an admission of guilt in that she acknowledges her 'daimon', but it is a misinterpretation to take it as an admission of guilt in quite another sense, as a confession of criminal intent. The silent exit is a necessary link in the chain of the tragic action, Hyllus' mistake is repeated in heightened form in Heracles' mistake. Eurydice's silent exit in the *Antigone* does not have the same significance. The action and tragedy of that drama would be no different if Eurydice were to leave the stage screaming accusations instead of in silence. Indeed, although she is silent about the charges against Creon, she is silent about them on the stage only in order to bring down her curses on the guilty man all the more terribly afterwards, as the narrative makes clear. The curse of a dying person has more power, is a more potent accusation. The meaning of her silence is limited to this contrast: first dark threats, then public suicide, both arising from despair and intended to bring down a curse. Should we infer from this that in the earlier tragedy, the *Antigone*, the poet merely 'touched on' a motif, which was to be 'fully sounded' only later, in the *Trachiniae*? That is the opinion of Johanna Heinz, *Hermes*, lxxii, 1937, 278. Are we to regard Eurydice's tragedy as the seed from which the full flower of Deianira's tragedy grows?

Moreover: Deianira's silence stems from her innermost being. This is not the only place where she is silent—cf. 22, 490; she is the quiet woman, who keeps to herself; Eurydice is rather the opposite. Was such a silence, stemming from a character's nature, first invented for Eurydice, a secondary character? Is this a motif which develops until it reaches its peak in the *Trachiniae*?

Thirdly: Jocasta's silent exit in the *Oedipus Tyrannus* is also followed by a misunderstanding, as in the *Trachiniae*. But even that does not create a developing series: Eurydice, Deianira, Jocasta. Eurydice's rôle is much too slight for any misunderstanding, for that would mean somehow showing her as mistaken, hopeful, guilty, participating in the tragic event. Here again her rôle is not the first sketch, the nucleus, from which the tragedy of Jocasta could develop.

18. It seems that we must assume that she goes across the courtyard, in which the servants have gathered, to 'hide' in the house. With the deletion of 901–3 (Tycho von Wilamowitz, 160, Pohlenz, *Erläuterungen*, 60 [cf. 2nd ed., 88]) μόνη in line 900 is left unexplained.—Whether the bier on which Heracles is carried in is the same as the one which Hyllus prepared for him, is a question which may be decided by those who are interested in such things. In spite of these lines, it is still possible that Hyllus comes from the house to meet his father.

[R. P. Winnington-Ingram, *Bulletin of the Institute of Classical Studies*, xvi, 1969, 44 ff. suggests that Hyllus is preparing a litter to go and meet his father when he hears of his mother's death, and abandons his intention. The action of Hyllus (901–3) may, he thinks, be imagined as suggesting to Deianira her own action (915 ff.). In any case Hyllus must be in the palace, but out of Deianira's way, when the Nurse goes to fetch him (927 ff.).—H. Ll.-J.]

19. It is generally believed that Sophocles took Euripides' *Alcestis* (performed 438) as his model: thus, *inter alios*, Leo Weber, *Euripides Alkestis*, 1930, 108, and most recently J. Heinz, *Hermes*, lxxii, 1937, 299 ff. But in the *Alcestis* the farewell to the bed is by no means the end, and that is not the only difference.

To seek internal contradictions in the nurse's speech (*Trach.* 900 ff.) which can be explained by borrowing of the same motif from the *Alcestis* (J. Heinz, 299) is to misunderstand the sense of the whole. In so far as one can speak of a contradiction here at all, it arises from the tragic situation; in a similar situation, King Oedipus behaves even more 'contradictorily'. The last steps of the poor woman, driven by her daimon, lead her through three stages which build up to a climax: 1. she hides and laments before the house-altar and household objects; 2. she wanders through the house and weeps at the sight of her close friends among her retinue; 3. in lines 912 ff., after a sharp break, she says farewell to her bed. Here she wishes to be alone and believes herself to be so. To demand that she sees no other face on her way there (Heinz, 299) is to tell the author what to do. It is all straightforward and unambiguous. There is no stronger proof of her forlorn condition than her farewell to the bed. Indeed, if the nurse had not followed her secretly, Deianira's death might even have appeared to be an admission of her guilt. So little interest does she have even now in justifying herself. Her silent exit and her death are of a piece.

Such a straight line is precisely what is conspicuously absent in Alcestis' farewell. The sudden change at which everything is altered begins at line 175. Until then she had been in control of herself, had been *sophrosynē* in person, had made all the preparations, decked the altars. . . But as she rushes to the bed, she is overwhelmed: ἐνταῦθα δή. . . Then she wanders through the house and returns again to the bed, though it now becomes her sickbed and the scene of her tearful farewell to her children and her servants. It is only here that we see what a struggle has been going on under the cover of her *sophrosynē*. Thus Euripides sets the farewell to the bed within a psychological contrast of which there is no trace in Sophocles. The richer and more evocative the details become in Euripides, the stranger it appears that the husband seems not to be present. The explanation that this is because the farewell to her husband is being saved up for the action on stage does not hold water, since she repeats her farewell to the children on the stage. But it would be impossible to put this moving farewell to her bed and an equally moving farewell to her husband side by side in the same passage. Thus in the *Trachiniae*, too, Deianira's farewell to her bed stands in the place of a farewell to her husband himself. But whereas this is natural and necessary in Sophocles, it is almost artificial and far-fetched in the other case. Of course a writer always makes a virtue of necessity. So too here. The chorus (199): 'and how is Admetus taking it?' 'Oh yes, Admetus . . .' Admetus is a different matter.

I am no more convinced by A. Lesky, *Philologische Wochenschrift*, lv,1935, 484 ff., than by Johanna Heinz. [E. R. Schwinge, *Die Stellung der Trachinierinnen im Werk des Sophokles*, *Hypomnemata*, Heft i, 1962, argues that *Alc.* 156 ff. shows the influence of *Trach.* 900 ff. This is no more certain than the view of Weber and Heinz that the relationship was the other way round. Both scenes belong to what was in all likelihood a standard type, of which the innumerable lost tragedies may have contained numerous examples.—H. Ll.-J.]

20. According to Tycho von Wilamowitz (92), sleep after an attack of madness is natural, sleep during such suffering as that of the dying Heracles is unnatural. Perhaps one ought to consult the medical profession about this—if Nessus' poison did not lie outside their province.—Pohlenz, *Erläuterungen*, 57 ff. [cf. 2nd ed., 86], pointed out the technical difficulty of bringing in Heracles screaming and raving from the start, instead of asleep.

21. According to A. Dieterich (*Kleine Schriften*, 1911, 48 ff.) and Ulrich and Tycho von Wilamowitz, the opposite assumption is still the usual one. Pohlenz is right. The following may serve as an example of the 'methodic' approach. T. von Wilamowitz (95) had argued that ποῖ γᾶς ἥκω; (984) in Sophocles arises less naturally out of the situation than ποῦ ποτ' ὢν ἀμηχανῶ; (1105) in Euripides, since in Euripides Heracles falsely imagines that he has arrived in the underworld. But *Odyssey* xiii 200 already existed as a model for Sophocles; Sophocles' Heracles is simply using the opening words which are standard for a character who wakes up in a strange place.

If Sophocles had simply taken over the scene from the *Heracles*, as these scholars believed ('borrowed as a stage-effect', 'not really woven into the context of the action, still identifiable as a separable, alien body', according to T. von Wilamowitz), then in spite of all the similarities he should certainly have left out precisely the horrible, fantastic element from his imitation with a detectable consistency. But there is not a single feature which points to such an omission. Euripides, on the other hand, is fond of depicting agitation raised to the point of hallucination, as in the *Alcestis*, the *Hippolytus* (Phaedra), the *Bacchae* (Agave and Pentheus), the *Trojan Women* (Cassandra) etc. Thus we may still say that it is more probable that Euripides wove one of his scenes of mental confusion out of Sophocles' ποῖ γᾶς ἥκω than that, conversely, Sophocles' ποῖ γᾶς ἥκω survives as a faint trace of the lengthy hallucination scene in the *Heracles*. (Cf. also E. Kroeker, *Der Herakles des Euripides*, Diss. Leipzig, 1938, 78.)

It should also be mentioned that the close similarity between Eur. *Heracles* 1353 ἀτὰρ πόνων δὴ μυρίων ἐγευσάμην and *Trach.* 1101: ἄλλων τε μόχθων μυρίων ἐγευσάμην has played a special part in this controversy. The context in Euripides is: 'I will put up with living. I will come to your city, as I am grateful to you for countless gifts: for I have known innumerable labours and never yet wept a tear, but now Tyche demands her tribute.' In Sophocles the same line completes the enumeration of individual labours: 'and I have known other, innumerable labours, but nobody has yet erected a monument for a victory against me; yet now blind disaster has conquered me.' It should not be imagined that there is anything wrong here, that the antithesis between μυρίων and οὐδείς is out of place. In Euripides, on the other hand, the antithesis between μυρίων δώρων and πόνων μυρίων is slightly forced: for here not only is μυρίων opposed to οὐδένα but δώρων is also opposed to πόνων, whereas δῶρα are by no means the reward for πόνοι nor are πόνοι the opposite of δῶρα. See Radermacher's commentary, 36. For a different view, see Tycho von Wilamowitz, 91.

22. Literally: 'No man will be able to say that I ever did this before.'

23. Wilamowitz, *Griechische Tragödien*, iv, 357: 'But again how distressing it is that we are then shown a Heracles who cares nothing for Deianira, who truly did not deserve her, and consequently does not deserve to be raised to Olympus either.'

24. 'The bombastic speeches of the mortally sick Heracles were to the taste of the later period (of Cicero and Seneca), dominated as it was by rhetoric. The poet makes no attempt to satisfy our desire that the hero who strides forth to his own pyre should show himself worthy of deification: we ought not to be reminded at all of Euripides' Heracles, who remains mortal.' Wilamowitz, *Griechische Tragödien*, iv, 354.

25. The form in which the solution of the riddle is given, τοῖς γὰρ θανοῦσι

μόχθος οὐ προσγίγνεται (1173), is a borrowing from Aeschylus' *Philoctetes* fr. 255 Nauck² [= fr. 399 Mette]: ἄλγος δ' οὐδὲν ἅπτεται νεκροῦ. *Oed. Col.* 955 is even closer to Aeschylus; but there in the mouth of Creon it is extremely ingenious: Creon already quotes the saying in the same form as in the fragment of Aeschylus in the collection of *gnomai*. It is surely no coincidence that such discrepancies between meaning and application do not occur in the early plays, the *Ajax* and the *Trachiniae*.

26. On the two oracles see W. Kranz, *Sokrates*, 1921, 35 ff. [= *Studien zur antiken Literatur und ihrem Fortwirken*, 1967, 285 ff.] In the oracle related in Apollodorus ii 4.12, promising immortality after twelve years' servitude, there is nothing of the sense given to it by Sophocles (on this I disagree with Tycho von Wilamowitz, 128). The first oracle, that Heracles would be overcome by no living person, only by a dead one, is suited both to his character and to his end. [The problem of the various references to the oracle has been treated by M. D. Reeve, *Greek, Roman & Byzantine Studies*, xi, 1970, 283 ff. The deletions he recommends would restore consistency; but I agree with Kranz that it is likelier that Sophocles allowed himself some freedom in the matter of the oracle's content. The *Philoctetes* furnishes an even more striking example.—H. Ll.-J.]

27. *Philoctetes* 728; Apollodorus ii 7. 14; Diodorus iv 38. 4.

NOTES to CHAPTER III (ANTIGONE)

261 1. In this, however, Hegel's breadth of vision still puts him well ahead of his followers: 'More interesting (than Aeschylus' *Eumenides*), though here it is completely transferred to the feelings and actions of human beings, is the occurrence of the same contrast in the *Antigone*, one of the most sublime works of art of all times, and one of the most magnificent in all respects. Everything in this tragedy is consistent: the public law of the state and the private love of family. . . The family interest is bound up with the pathos of the woman, Antigone, the welfare of the community with the pathos of Creon, the man. Polynices, fighting against his own native city, had fallen before the gates of Thebes, and Creon, the ruler, by a public proclamation threatens death to anyone who honours the city's enemy by burial. But Antigone takes no notice of this command, which is only concerned with the public welfare of the state, and carries out the sacred duty of burial as a sister should, from pious love for her brother. In so doing she appeals to the law of the gods; but the gods whom she honours are the gods of the underworld, of Hades (451), the private gods of feeling, love and kinship, not the daylight gods of free, self-conscious public and

civic life.' (*Ästhetik* ii, section 2, chap. 1) Similarly in *Die Philosophie der Religion* xvi, 133.

2. I, too, certainly believe that classical German drama and Sophoclean drama are related, but not in such a superficial manner. Cf. *Vom Schicksal des deutschen Geistes*, ed. W. Frommel, 1934, 61 ff.; *Jahrbuch fur die geistige Überlieferung*, ed. E. Grassi, ii, 1941.

3. On the relationship of the two parts Wilamowitz (*Griechische Tragödien*, iv, 344) says: 'However, it has to be admitted that Sophocles has dealt with the second part at such length that we lose sight of Antigone. It may be that he has been too gruesome; but he who truly appreciates the glory of the martyrs delights in the *mortes persecutorum*.' Thus he explains the offending aspects of the structure by attributing to the tragedian the delight in cruelty that characterizes his own religion.

P. Friedländer (311 [= *Studien zur antiken Literatur und Kunst*, 147]) explains the second part as 'repercussion': 'But in this drama the opposing force is also visibly personified, and the fact that it has to be struck by the rebound in the tragic collision is a law of which so-called "poetic justice" is probably no more than a moralizing constricted version. When the hero falls he will pull his enemy down with him.' It is true that this interpretation dispenses with moral atonement, but in its place it sets up a 'law' of tragic events of which there is no other example. Nor does this theory explain properly that Creon's fate has a curve and *peripeteia* of its own, Creon's own 'recognition of himself'.

4. It is possible to trace the early development of the notion of the gods making sport with men. In epic the best example is provided by the διάπειρα of Agamemnon in the second book of the *Iliad*. For a passage comparable with Sophocles we may adduce Theognis 139 ff.:

οὐδέ τῳ ἀνθρώπων παραγίνεται, ὅσσ' ἐθέλῃσι.
ἴσχει γὰρ χαλεπῆς πείρατ' ἀμηχανίης·
ἄνθρωποι δὲ μάταια νομίζομεν εἰδότες οὐδέν·
θεοὶ δὲ κατὰ σφέτερον πάντα τελοῦσι νόον.

The 'limits' (πείρατα) of his cruel lack of ways and means (χαλεπῆς ἀμηχανίης) 'confine' (ἴσχει) a man, all his acts are futile and blind, the gods cause everything to happen as they please.

5. It is usual to present Creon as the embodiment of a characteristic; he is reduced to the abstraction 'autocrat' (Wilamowitz), 'obstinacy' (translating αὐθαδία, 1028), 'vanity' etc. That is all very well, but it does not tell us what form these characteristics take in the case of Creon. There are fifteen kinds of obstinacy, but what is the significance of obstinacy in the case of Creon? He is a 'typical tyrant' (Pohlenz); but there are fifteen types of

tyranny. . . This throws no light on the essential. We are not interested in typical tyrants.

263   6. The relationship between reality and illusion is fundamental for Creon; it is expressed too by the chorus (620 ff.). For earlier forms of this contrast see Solon, Theognis etc.

7. No traces of an epic source for Sophocles have survived, it is true, but the downfall of the two daughters of Oedipus, following the downfall of the sons, would fit very well into epic form. In whatever way this may have been narrated, whether one sister or both were buried with the body which they had wanted to recover, or whatever happened—according to Ion [fr. 36 Blumenthal], who linked the offence against men with the offence against the gods, both sisters were burnt in the temple of Hera—in any case the story would have been one of the gruesome sequels comparable with the sequels to the destruction of Troy, such as the sacrifice of Polyxena, etc.

8. One can only come to view him as the representative of the idea of the *polis* and of the *koinon* against the *idion* if one pays attention solely to the content of his speeches and not to their manner. For the opposite view see W. Schadewaldt, *Neue Wege zur Antike*, viii, 1929, 59 ff.

9. For κέρδος in connection with political divisions and conspiracies, see e.g. Theognis 46 and 50, Aristophanes *Thesm.* 360 etc., Thuc. vii, 57. 9–10. If κέρδος is not taken in this political sense, but only as referring to the passive corruption of an agent, then not only does the whole of the speech become incomprehensible, but one cannot understand the reason for Creon's outburst before the assembled elders, still less his great denunciation of κέρδος (295 ff.). 'Ridiculous pathos', 'a compulsion to display his cheap wisdom', is the judgment of Bruhn, *Commentary* 21. But if that were all that his character amounted to he could not have a fate worth taking so seriously.

10. Tycho von Wilamowitz (34), has observed that there is a repetition for the sake of 'effect'. Pohlenz says (189 [= 2nd ed. 186]): 'We are intended to share her triumph to the full. That is why the poet invents a second visit to the corpse.' But that is too superficial. And what does 'effect' mean, if we are not told on what basis it rests? [On the double burial, see A. T. von S. Bradshaw, *Classical Quarterly* xii. 1962, 200 ff., and cf. Lloyd-Jones, ib., xxii, 1972, 220.—H. Ll-J.]

264   11. There is a comparable contrast between the speaker and what is spoken in Mephistopheles' lyrical description of Gretchen's love-pangs in the 'Wald und Höhle' scene of Goethe's *Faust*.

12. Pohlenz, 230 [cf. 2nd ed. 224].

13. 458, τούτων . . . ἐν θεοῖσι τὴν δίκην δώσειν in contrast with ἐν ἀνθρώποις. Bruhn explains: 'Before the gods who punish the wicked in the

underworld.' But this interpretation has already read too definite a content into the words. Δίκη ἐν θεοῖσι here has the quite general meaning of that justice which prevails above and beyond the δίκη ἐν θνητοῖσι.

14. Of course, if we follow Bruhn, who takes Zeus to mean Zeus Kata-chthonios, there would be no polarity here. But Zeus Katachthonios is only found as the complement of Zeus Ouranios. And since Dikē is here not called πάρεδρος Διός as usual, but is set over against Zeus as σύνοικος τῶν κάτω θεῶν, there can be no doubt of the polarity. Again, the antitheses between the divine and the mortal which follow show Antigone as bound not only to the chthonic gods but to the gods in general.

15. The hereafter seen from the standpoint of a mere mortal affects even the language; 'Who knows?' implies not doubt but affirmation of the other world.

16. If we do not extend the meaning to include the two different realms, we find ourselves explaining, like Bruhn, 'Thus I share Jocasta's love for Polynices, not Eteocles' hate for him.'

17. Wilamowitz (iv, 342) sees Antigone too in a Christian light: 'She dies as a martyr, sacrifices herself to what she considers her duty, resembling the martyrs in this also, that this life is nothing to her, but the life beyond is everything' etc.

18. Wilamowitz, i, 9: 'To enhance the favourable effect made by his heroine, Sophocles was able to invent the fact that she had paid her parents the last honours.' We are obviously not meant to remember that her 'dear mother' is the suicide Jocasta, and her father Oedipus who had cursed his children. But a glance at Attic gravestones should be enough to tell us why her father and mother have to be mentioned here.

19. See G. A. Megas, Hermes, lxviii, 1933, 425 n.3. On 'bride of Hades' see A. von Salis, Rheinisches Museum, lxxiii, 1920, 211.

20. The recent study by E. Buschor, Grabmal eines attischen Mädchens, published by F. Bruckmann, 1939 [revised edition Piper Verlag, Munich, 1959], is also particularly relevant here.

21. In my opinion, the conflict in these strophes, as well as in the last dialogue, is not a question of law but rather a clash between the sphere of the lofty, unlimited, doomed to death, and that of the self-preserving and limited. I cannot follow Schadewaldt (Neue Wege zur Antike, viii, 1929, 94), who is essentially trying to revive Hegel's thesis, though on the sounder historical basis of a more precise insight into the ethical idea of the polis. ἔσχατον θράσος (854) expresses that unfettered state, that ultimate precipitousness; she took so great a stride forward that she was bound to stumble. The stumbling-block is called dikē: her downfall is part of the order of things. But that is only true of Antigone's nature and fate as it runs its own course (and here it is even derived from her family). Her fate is at

one and the same time glorious and great in the eyes of the onlookers, and pious in the eyes of herself, Haemon and the people, and yet it leads to destruction in accordance with the order of things. The *dikē* against which she stumbles is not a different *principle* beyond her own, not state justice, of which Creon would be the justified but in human terms questionable representative—on the contrary it is part of her own being, immanent in her daimon. It is true that her own being drives her to transgress the prohibition, but this prohibition is not said to represent a different norm, independent of her own. Not a single word addressed to her insists on the validity, necessity or whatever of the other standard of judgment. There is only (873):

κράτος δ' ὅτῳ κράτος μέλει
παραβατὸν οὐδαμᾷ πέλει.

The command of 'might' should 'not be transgressed', not because it is inviolable, not because it is a norm, not because it is *koinon* or anything of that sort, but because it destroys the transgressor. And the τις (in σέβειν μὲν εὐσέβειά τις) does not limit the nature of this *eusebeia* by implying that there is some other kind of *eusebeia* besides, but indicates the sphere within which it is effective.

Nor is it possible to derive a conflict of spheres of justice from line 924. The context is: What an injustice towards the gods I would have committed! To think that I am so forsaken by gods and men that my piety seems a crime to them! If the phrase τὴν δυσσέβειαν εὐσεβοῦσ' ἐκτησάμην were an objective judgment of the necessary involvement of her *eusebeia* with *dyssebeia*, then it could not refer to the accusing questions which precede it. Finally, ὅσια πανουργήσασα (74): again, 'my πανούργημα is ὅσιον' cannot be converted dialectically into 'my ὅσιον is πανούργημα', for this is made clear not by logic but by the tone of the phrase.

The rôle of the chorus varies according to the nature of the action: it has to serve at one moment as contrast, at another as echo. Thus in the first half of the play it is more inclined to express horror at Antigone's boldness; in the second it is more inclined to admire her. As so often happens with unusual events.

22. Schadewaldt, *Neue Wege zur Antike*, viii, 85 ff., who interprets the *Antigone* in terms of ethical antinomies, ends up by making Antigone herself distinguish between the bearer of the *polis*-principle or *koinon*, who could be godless in his own person, and the *polis*-principle in itself, which as such could be holy. But the alternative (925 ff.) belongs to the type of sentence in which the second part has so much more weight than the first that the first only serves to strengthen the second.

23. It is the anecdote about the wife of Intaphernes, Herodotus iii, 119. Secondary literature is listed in the introduction to Bruhn's commentary. Further parallels: F. Dornseiff, *Philologus*, xciii, 1938, 407. [J. T. Kakridis, *Homeric Researches* (1949), 152 ff.] W. Schmid, *Geschichte der griechischen Literatur*, ii, 1934, 355, remains convinced that the passage should be excised, but this view is rarely held nowadays.

24. When Creon refers to the voice of the 'city' and the *nomoi*, 656 ff., he does it *in the drama*, i.e. for the sake of *reversal*: i.e. so that he may immediately set himself *against* the city in the ensuing *stichomythia*, 734, in order to enhance his own position; his self-enhancement is part of his nature and is already potentially active in the first half of the scene. To use his first words to show that he is a representative of the opinion of the *polis* or of the state is arbitrarily to take a passage in isolation and to disregard the sense of the whole. Now it is admittedly possible that Creon could still, in his own person, act as an imperfect medium for the idea, but in that case this would surely find expression in some kind of dissonance or break. But it is wrong, unless there is definite confirmation to the contrary, to take out of context any part of a speech that does not correspond with the speaker's character, because carried to its logical conclusion this would lead to the disintegration of the drama.

25. Similarly in the following passage: 1047, Creon: τοῦ κέρδους χάριν; then Tiresias, 1050: κράτιστον κτημάτων εὐβουλία; 1055, Creon's insult: φιλάργυρον; then that of Tiresias: αἰσχροκέρδειαν φιλεῖ; 1061, Creon: ἐπὶ κέρδεσιν; 1062, Tiresias: . . . τὸ σὸν μέρος. One is referring to salvation, the other to money. This is quite different from Euripides' handling of dialogue. Similarly in the *Oedipus Tyrannus*. Later Sophocles ceases to use this device.

26. Bruhn refers in his commentary to Euripides' *Heracles* 1232. The enlightened author of 'On the Sacred Disease', Hippocrates, ed. Littré, vi, 358 ff. [= Hippocrates, ed. W. H. S. Jones, Loeb Classical Library, ii, 127 ff.] takes a very similar line.

27. Compare the exits in the *Ajax* at lines 1159 ff. and in the *Antigone* at lines 1087 ff. In the *Ajax* the exit does not in itself constitute an action arising from the dialogue, but is a special act explained and accompanied by two lines from each person. Almost ceremonial, certainly formal and archaic. In the *Antigone* the exit itself is the last and deadliest 'arrow' fired by the seer. The words are no longer an explanation which accompanies the action; speech and action are one. Compare the exit of Haemon, etc.

28. Some scholars, it is true, have imagined that a change of tone and sense is also perceptible in the middle of Ajax's speech, at line 684, but they are certainly wrong.

29. οἴμ' ὡς ἔοικας ὀψὲ τὴν δίκην ἰδεῖν (1270), etc.

30. It is usual to supply the imprisoned Antigone as object [as this English translation does], but probably nothing needs to be supplied; cf. also *Antigone* 40.

31. Already in antiquity critics were of the opinion that the second part was inferior to the first: the scholion on line 1123 says that the poet wished to prolong the play beyond Antigone's death and by so doing dissipated the tragic pathos.

32. μάταιος (1339): the meaning is made clear by the relative clause which follows. Cf. also 1068 ff.

268

NOTES to CHAPTER IV (OEDIPUS TYRANNUS)

1. On the usual dating to the mid-twenties (*Oed. Tyr.* 629 = *Acharn.* 27) cf. Pohlenz, *Erläuterungen* 63 [cf. 2nd ed. 93]. [See p. xxii. The words ὦ πόλις πόλις might have occurred in several tragedies.—H. Ll.-J.]

2. For a different view of the opening scene see W. Ax, *Hermes*, lxvii, 1932, 425 ff.

3. As, for example, Volkelt, *Ästhetik des Tragischen*, 1906, 417: 'It is above all in the *Oedipus Tyrannus* that Fate obtrudes, setting traps which lead to capture in spite of all attempts at evasion, and with crafty forethought bringing together circumstances which lead those whom the divinity has marked out to an inevitable destruction.' This is to consider only the outward state of affairs; no notice is taken of the whole inward struggle in the first part of the play.

4. Almost the only critic to object to the assumption that the *Oedipus* is a 'tragedy of fate' is Wilamowitz, in the introduction to his translation of the play, 11 ff., although the distinctions that he draws are different.

5. 'Fate' as opposed to 'man's moral freedom' in e.g. A. W. Schlegel, *Vorlesungen über dramatische Kunst*, i, Heidelberg 1809, 178, 204 etc.

6. *Lettre III sur Oedipe*; cf. Bruhn in his commentary, 25.

7. See Bruhn in his commentary, 33 ff., on the similarity between the two scenes, although his deductions about the chronology are not correct.

7a. [In fr. ii Allen (Homer, Oxford Classical Text v, p. 113) Oedipus says that his sons shall divide their inheritance in battle, in fr. iii he says that they shall perish at each other's hands.—H. Ll.-J.]

8. In the translation by Wilamowitz, the sentence where the anacoluthon is evidence of the inner movement is divided into two parts, by making the νῦν δέ of line 263 refer to the νῦν δέ of line 258, and inserting a full stop after ἡ τύχη in line 263.

9. In his *Ödipus und die Sphinx*, Hofmannsthal composed entire scenes

269 (and good ones at that) out of the way in which the wanderer entered unawares into his inheritance and the legacy of his blood. In Sophocles this is effected by the sound and pace of the speeches.

10. Tycho von Wilamowitz, 86, thinks otherwise: 'It has been shown that the blinding of Oedipus has always been essential to the action' etc. Similarly Howald, 111.

11. The interpretation of this scene by Tycho von Wilamowitz is logical (75): 'But the behaviour of Tiresias is completely incomprehensible from beginning to end, if one stops to think about it.' It is only that his logic has gone astray.

12. Wilamowitz finds 'undue deference' here (*Hermes*, xxxiv, 1899, 60): 'He even calls him ἄναξ, but he has no relationship with him such as Creon has in the *Antigone*.'

13. The translation by Wilamowitz—'Never as long as the throne of truth shall stand.' 'It does stand; it is you, only you, who remains far from it'—is adventitious ornament to a certain extent. Similarly he translates 'light' as 'light of the sun': 'You can do nothing to me or to anyone who sees the light of the sun'; here 'light of the sun' is weaker than 'light'.

14. Cf. Bruhn's commentary on lines 288 and 378: 'As soon as Tiresias utters Apollo's name, Oedipus believes that he has discovered in Creon the man behind the seer. For it was Creon who had been sent to Delphi, and Creon who (288) had advised calling in the seer.' But that is only a matter of the external, practical motivation, whereas there must also be an inner state of preparedness.

15. The cry is an angry reproach and protest: that such things can happen in this city! Aristophanes *Acharn.* 27 and 75. Other critics offer other explanations, e.g. Bruhn believes that Oedipus is appealing to the judgement of the city which raised him to the kingship, 383 f. But that seems far-fetched, and does not lend itself to any gestures.

16. There is another type of interpretation, which does not perceive any of this: Wilamowitz, *Hermes*, xxxiv, 1899, 61: 'Yes, he (Creon) has had the seer brought, and when the oracle has been pronounced he preserves his belief in it (557), so that Oedipus is quite right in saying (658–9) that the

270 pardoning of Creon necessitates his own punishment as murderer.' However, in line 557 Creon knows nothing at all, so there is no question of his preserving his belief in the oracle. And in line 574: 'You know yourself whether that is what he says' means more or less: 'But I will not concern myself with that, you will have to sort that out with the seer.'

17. Modern psychology might give this another name, but I will dispense with it. Instead I would like to draw attention to the way in which Hölderlin expressed the content of this scene—thereby at the same time showing how limited my own interpretation is: 'Hence suspicion is

aroused afterwards in the scene with Creon, because the unruly mind, laden with sad secrets, becomes unsure of itself, and the faithful spirit suffers in an excess of anger, which, in its delight in ruin, simply follows Time that drags it to destruction.'

18. The great restraint of Sophocles is brought out clearly if one compares it with the emphasis on the blood relationship in Hofmannsthal's *Ödipus und die Sphinx*.

19. This has the following consequences: just as it was far from being Sophocles' intention to present Creon in the *Antigone* as a 'man of the enlightenment', it was equally far from being his intention to present Jocasta as an 'enlightened woman'. His concern is with what is eternally human and divine, not with the tendencies of his time. Even the unique chorus 897 ff. which condemns the impiety of the time proves nothing. Pohlenz says (225 [cf. 2nd ed. 219]) 'that in portraying Jocasta he had in mind women of Aspasia's type of mind and attitude, and he believed that they had a malevolent influence'. Moreover, doubt of the truth of oracles is as old as stories about oracles.

20. *Vorlesungen über dramatische Kunst und Literatur*, 1809, i, 180: 'The arrogant levity with which Jocasta mocks the oracle because it has not been borne out by events, but then soon after pays the penalty for it with her own death, has not, it is true, been passed on to him (Oedipus) . . .' Schlegel's interpretation is so moralistic that he even says: 'On the other hand it is another feature of her levity that she has not taken sufficient note of his likeness to her husband, which should have led her to recognize him as her son.' Similar views among modern critics are Bruhn's 'a completely superficial character'; and Wilamowitz's 'Jocasta's frivolity is clear as day' (*Hermes*, xxxiv, 1899, 59), etc.

271   21. On this Wilamowitz writes in the apparatus criticus of his edition: 'sed multo gravius haec esse corrupta docet tautologia v. 1. 2 et repetitum κέλευθος.' But whatever corruptions there may be here, there is still clearly a tautology, for there is bound to be one if someone takes three whole lines simply to give the name of a place. So it must be an indication of the 'pathos' of the passage. Nor does Sophocles seek to avoid tautology in the passage of the *Oedipus* beginning at line 1398, where it is carried along by the emotion of the blinded man. The three lines in Aeschylus fall into two parallel phrases, of which the first mentions only a meeting of three ways without a specific location, while the second adds the fateful Ποτνιάδων to this general description. Because of the interplay of question and answer in Sophocles, the crossroads and its position are mentioned separately, whereas in Aeschylus they come one after the other in a pair of parallel phrases, with a progression from the general to the particular, though it is not embodied in dialogue form.

We have no room here to go into the complicated question of the reconstruction of the Aeschylean tragedy.

22. Tycho von Wilamowitz, 79: 'The whole action of the *Oedipus Tyrannus* rests, one might say, on the poet's conscious use of an ambiguous and incorrect plural instead of the singular.'

23. Her argument is more difficult than appears at fist sight. C. Robert, *Ödipus*, 1915, 301 ff., has even developed from it a whole bouquet of 'extremely delicate psychological contradictions'. But 'nuances' which have to be 'expressed by the actor by means of a long pause' scarcely carry any conviction. Her argument remains obscure. The oracle about Laius has by no means come true as far as she is concerned, for her son died as a child. It follows that she cannot reason along these lines either that Tiresias is right, or that Apollo is. And yet she says: even if the witness retracts his statement, he will still never be able to speak the truth, since his evidence contradicts Apollo's oracle. But his evidence contradicts the oracle just as much if he sticks to his earlier utterance, the one which she wishes to be true. Now she suddenly supposes that a change is impossible because it would contradict Apollo's oracle—the very oracle which has been shown to be worthless as far as she is concerned! Thus Apollo is taken as a yardstick in the same sentence in which he is rejected as such. This line of reasoning springs from obvious anxiety, which searches for reasons where it can, without being aware that their premises cancel each other out.

24. *Ant.* 384 ff.: cf. 71 above.

25. A. W. Schlegel, *op. cit.* (in n. 20), 177, says that the first Oedipus drama compels admiration primarily 'because of the artful complication by which the fearful catastrophe—which even excites one's curiosity (an event rare enough in Greek tragedy)—is brought on inevitably by a chain of inter-linked causes'.

26. Bruhn observes that the use of καλῶς is plebeian.

27. To show what kind of expressions Sophocles avoids here, I quote the last two lines as translated by Wilamowitz: 'Ich kenne mich: verfehmt vor der Geburt, / Im Leben ein Blutschänder, Vatermörder.' ['I know who I am, proscribed before I was born, incestuous in life, my father's murderer.']

28. The best-known example of a *griphos* is that of Clearchus in the scholia to Plato's *Republic* 479 e: affirmation and negation of one and the same predicate and subject in the same sentence.—The explanation '1273 and 1274 should perhaps be thought of as spoken when he has already destroyed his sight but is still stabbing' (Wilamowitz, quoted by Bruhn) is surely too naturalistic.—Jebb points out that the imperfects remain imperfects even when changed into *oratio recta*. For this reason, then, ἔχρῃζεν cannot refer to those whom he loves and soon begins to love exclusively, his daughters (as Wilamowitz assumes).

29. Masqueray in his edition (Budé, Paris 1929) observes: 'Ce n'est là, au fond, qu'un prétexte qui justifie l'entrée en scène de l'aveugle.' ['Basically this is only a pretext to justify the blind man's entrance.'] A pretext!—tragic delight in monstrous self-revelation! In that case, is there anything that could not be called pretext? One would have yet further 'raison de souligner l'adresse du poète' [reason to admire the poet's skill].

30. There is scarcely anything so indicative of the difference between the source of the tragic in Sophocles and Euripides as the way in which Euripides' Oedipus, after the discovery that he has committed murder, does not blind himself but is blinded at Creon's command. (See Bruhn's commentary on Sophocles' *Oedipus Tyrannus*, p. 54.) Thus Euripides loses the tragic immanence of Sophocles' drama and replaces it with the protestations of a tragic dualism, such as, for example, the dualism between responsibility and higher powers, passion and rationality, innocence and meanness, nobility and brutality, righteousness and base materialism, the ego and the way of the world, etc.

31. I quote the lines, so that the reader may see from the actual words that there is a correspondence: *Ajax* 1003: ἴθ' ἐκκάλυψον, ὡς ἴδω τὸ πᾶν κακόν. *Trach.* 1078: δείξω γὰρ τάδ' ἐκ καλυμμάτων. *Oed. Tyr.* 1426: τοιόνδ' ἄγος ἀκάλυπτον οὕτω δεικνύναι.

32. Here Herwerden and others delete 1380, on the grounds that τραφείς would imply that Oedipus had been brought up in Thebes; but tragic consistency and pragmatic consistency are two different things.

33. Wilamowitz translates: 'Lass mir den Glauben, dass es so richtig war.' ['Leave me the belief that it was right thus.'] This diminishes the starkness of the tragedy: the dead are used as an excuse which Oedipus would like to be left to him, instead of being a reality, here as in the *Antigone*.

34. ἄθεος, ἀνοσίων παῖς, ἀσεβής etc.

35. The main emphasis falls on the words 'Apollo' and 'I'; the deeds of each coincide with, match or condition those of the other. If we wish to construe the connection of the two sentences with exact logic, we may interpret it: 'it was planned and carried out by Apollo (as the spiritual author, so to speak) but it was executed by myself', although the position of the word τελῶν does not give it such compressed antithetical force. Besides, it comes to the same thing in the end: since in any case with the emphasis on 'I myself' the sense of the distinction could never be taken to excuse the agent, or to draw a line between human and divine planning and accomplishment in order that the man may be allocated his share of the guilt (as Wilamowitz's translation implies). It is all an answer to the question 'What sort of daimon drove you on?' There is no doubt that a god was at work in such deeds.

36. As Pohlenz takes it, when he regards the freedom of 'action' as being

preserved in spite of everything, 224: 'And even if to us the outward appearance of the blinded man seems horrible, yet in his free act, in the attitude he takes towards his fate, there lies a greatness which can elevate our spirits.' Here we see Schiller's influence. [But cf. 2nd ed., 217.]

NOTES to CHAPTER V (ELECTRA)

1. On the structure cf. Friedländer, 296 ff. and Howald, 113 ff.
2. The fact that in this play the deed is a just one is certainly the condition for the use of trickery, which is permitted and commanded. But it is the trickery, not its justness, which is developed and emphasized; the deed must be just if it is to be carried out according to Apollo's will. If Sophocles had wanted to do no more than justify the oracle, the god and the deed that he commands, along the lines of the pre-Aeschylean saga, it would not be at all clear why it was necessary for him to use the 'trickery' and its consequences, and indeed the whole 'intrigue' and the suffering which it causes. Pohlenz, 342 [cf. 2nd ed., 323] and others regard the basic idea of the *Electra* as being anti-Aeschylean, a justification of the divinity and its commandment.
3. Thus for example compare *Philoctetes* 55, λόγοισιν ἐκκλέψας . . . with *Electra* 37, δόλοισι κλέψαι, etc.
4. That is why Aristophanes says of Euripides in the *Thesmophoriazusae* (412 B.C.), 94: 'In intrigue we take the cake.'
    On the drama of intrigue as a genre and its rise, see Solmsen, *Philologus*, lxxxvii, 1932, 1 ff.
5. Critics have, in their time, excised these eight lines on account of this very lightheartedness, as unworthy of Orestes and of Sophocles. *Contra*, with philological and critical arguments, see J. Vahlen, 'Index lectionum aestivarum 1883' in *Opuscula academica* i, 1907, 208.
6. For example Bethe, *Geschichte der griechischen Dichtung*, 1924, 208: 'The monstrous woman, hardened by her violent obsession with revenge, her unutterable hatred and profound bitterness. . . He asked how a girl could become like this and he shows us how it happened.'
7. For other, not entirely satisfactory, explanations of this scene, see Wilamowitz, *Hermes*, xviii, 1883, 214 ff., Kaibel, 66 and 81, and T. von Wilamowitz, 168. It is true that, from a purely external point of view, two forms of prologue are combined here, one in dialogue-form (or apparently so) and the other monodic; it is true that they may both be called Euripidean; but that will not explain the particular form and the particular signifi-

cance of this combination. The sharp break, the 'almost', is not a result of the use of two different forms of prologue, but is itself the form which results in that 'use', if that is what we want to call it.

8. *Trach.* 154 ἐξερῶ, 534 τὰ μὲν φράσουσα, 554 τῇδ' ὑμῖν φράσω etc., to mention here only those examples which can be indicated briefly.

9. For a different view see Kaibel, *Commentary*, 125: 'Das ist die natürliche Rhetorik der Gerichtsrede . . .' ['This is the rhetoric natural to a legal speech . . .']

10. Because of the controversy which still surrounds the dating of the *Trachiniae*, I repeat that this kind of reversal or turning-point within a scene is not found in either the *Trachiniae* or the *Ajax*. The relationship of this phenomenon to Sophocles' whole way of constructing scenes, which also undergoes a change from the *Antigone* onwards, is shown on pp. 36 and 66.

11. Another means of achieving these contrasts is the rich use of figures of speech which penetrate through so as to involve the other person, which as it were 'demonstrate' Sophoclean 'rhetoric': σκέψαι γὰρ εἰ . . . (442); ἆρα μὴ δοκεῖς . . . (446); οὐκ ἔστιν . . . (448) etc. etc. In the *Trachiniae*, which critics have attempted to date to the same period, there is of course nothing at all of this kind, nor could there be.

12. The details of Sophocles' 'borrowing' and 'development' from Aeschylus' *Agam.* 1415 ff. [in *Electra* 530 ff.] are listed in Kaibel's commentary, 156 ff., but he fails to trace the individual changes back to the reason which underlies them all.

13. The harmony with which the first *epeisodion* comes to a close has already begun to change into dissonance at the end, 470, in preparation for the opening of the second *epeisodion*.

14. One need only observe the abundance in this passage of forms of speech which involve the other person: ὅρα (580), ἀλλ' εἰσόρα (584), εἰ γὰρ θέλεις (585) etc., to be reminded again above all of the *Philoctetes*.

15. Just as in the *Oedipus Tyrannus* the transition hardly conceals the inner defeat, so this passage in the *Electra* hardly conceals the failure of a false justice and an empty claim—a failure which Clytemnestra does not even admit to herself.

16. Kaibel interprets lines 630 ff. as follows: 'Electra, tired of futile wrangling, replies: ἐῶ . . . and declares that she will not say another word. It would be natural for Electra to leave the stage at this point, voluntarily or at Clytemnestra's command. But since she is needed in the next scene, she remains, and out of this dramatic necessity Sophocles creates a particular detail of characterization: the sinful Clytemnestra at prayer (638).' One will not get very far if one writes off anything unusual in a situation as 'dramatic necessity'.

17. Here again is something which lies outside the range of the *Ajax* and the *Trachiniae*.

18. Admittedly almost all the critics interpret the passage differently, even Kaibel, 53 and 174: in his opinion the poet is giving himself 'the opportunity of captivating his audience by the artful use of a gripping, vivid narrative, so that they accept what they know to be fiction as the truth: it is only by this means that they can participate with genuine sympathy in Electra's outbursts of pain, the cause of which is in fact fictitious'. Kaibel is followed by Tycho von Wilamowitz, 190 etc. But we should note how, for example, the deception and illusion in the lamentation of the chorus as they break in at 765 are shown to be transparent by ὡς ἔοικεν, a phrase as inappropriate to the normal form of lament (see Kaibel for examples) as it is to the normal outburst of emotion. There is nothing in the character of the speaker to explain the phrase; its function is simply to allow the audience to see through the poet's game. Now if the chorus hints unambiguously at the deception here at the end of the messenger's speech, then it is clear that the opening is to be taken in the same way (678 ff.): Clytemnestra: 'Tell me the *truth!*' Paedagogus: 'This I was sent to tell.' Sophocles clearly intends the audience to realize that he had really been sent with the opposite intention, to deceive. But if that is the case, we can no longer feel any uncertainty about the way in which the whole messenger's speech is to be taken.

19. Bruhn, like most commentators, maintains that Clytemnestra's maternal feeling is no more than a pretence; Kaibel disagrees (see his Introduction, 41 ff., and his commentary on 675 and 776). But Bruhn's assumption can be shown to be mistaken in various ways, especially by the construction of the scene. Maternal feeling is superseded, displaced, by a sense of safety, of final liberation from fear, and finally by a sense of satisfaction. It is because of this last emotion that Clytemnestra's thoughts move from Orestes to Electra. Anyone who sees no more than pretence in this has failed to perceive that this scene is a struggle between two types of emotion, which continues until one of them gained the upper hand; he has failed to perceive that Clytemnestra's speech vacillates and shifts its ground, that she begins with one thing and ends with its opposite, that at first the two sides of the scale balance, and then one tips over—in a word, he has failed to perceive its *dramatic* quality. There is no need for me to repeat once more that developments and inward reversals of this kind do not occur as early as the *Ajax* and *Trachiniae*.

20. The evidence for this lies in the third act of Goethe's *Iphigenie*. In preparation for his *Iphigenie* he had already read Sophocles' *Electra* in the original at Weimar and then taken it with him to Italy. See his letters to Herder of the end of August 1786 and of 14 October 1786. E. Maass, *Goethe*

und die Antike (Berlin 1912), 348. Cf. also Bruhn's commentary on Sophocles' *Electra*, pp. 43 and 45. [Cf. also E. Grumach, *Goethe und die Antike* (Berlin 1949) i, 254-5.—H. Ll.-J.]

21. Practically all the commentators think otherwise. Masqueray in his Budé edition writes (205): 'Mais là encore il emporte de ne pas réfléchir'—['But at that point' (i.e. at the point where Electra addresses her laments to the empty urn) 'we are required not to stop to think.'] 'Si l'on songe un instant que cet Oreste qui est vivant devant nous, et que l'on croit mort, ne vient en scène que pour provoquer les déchirants adieux de sa soeur, l'illusion est perdue . . .' etc. ['If we stop for one moment to consider that this Orestes who is alive before us, and who is believed dead, has come onto the stage only in order to call forth his sister's heartrending farewell, the illusion is broken . . .' etc.] However, 'rien de tout cela n'a lieu grace à l'adresse de Sophocle'! ['none of this happens, thanks to the skill of Sophocles'!] But there is one criticism that the poet does not escape: his Orestes 'risque une expression ambiguë, une seule, il est vrai, où il fait allusion à la situation, dans laquelle il se trouve . . . Nous voulons bien être trompés, nous ne demandons même qu'à l'être, mais nous ne tenons pas du tout à ce qu'on nous le fasse remarquer, et encore moins à ce qu'on en sourie devant nous.' ['risks one ambiguous expression, only one, it is true, when he alludes to the situation in which he finds himself . . . We would like to be deceived, that is just what we are asking for, but having our attention drawn to it is something that we do not like at all, and even less do we like being laughed at!'] Poor old Sophocles! How happy we would have been with his recipe if it were not for that one 'expression'; mais là encore il importe de ne pas réfléchir! But Kaibel, too, thinks that it is necessary to make excuses for Sophocles here: 'Für den Dichter rechfertigt sich das Wagnis nur durch die dramatische Zweckmässigkeit und durch den Erfolg' ['The risk taken by the poet is only justified by its dramatic propriety and by its success'] (*Commentary* on 1119)—i.e. not by any poetic quality! Other critics take a similar view.

22. One veiled expression is ἔνθα χρῄζομεν (1099): 'where we want to go'. For in one sense Orestes knows perfectly well where he wants to go: apparently to bring the news of the death of Orestes, in fact to kill Aegisthus; but in another sense there is the destination of which he is unaware, that his sister will be present and that he is going to recognize her. In 1104, ποθεινὴν . . . παρουσίαν is similarly veiled and ambiguous: there are two meanings, one conscious and the other unconscious. Also κοινόπουν: we can hear the sound of the footsteps of revenge in the heavy adjective. These touches are matched by an equal ambiguity in the replies of the chorus (1102): εὖ θ' ἱκάνεις and (1105): εἰ τὸν ἄγχιστόν γε—for

278

the chorus are aware that Electra is 'closest' as Clytemnestra's daughter, and unaware that she is the sister of the Orestes who is standing before her.

Thus, because of these ambiguities, we should interpret the entrance of Orestes above all by comparison with the ambiguities and veiled language of the *Oedipus Tyrannus*. It is true that once more the veiled language in the *Electra* is above all an ironic game, of the type which made 'fate' in the Oedipus into something transparent; but the simplest way to understand the form that it takes in the *Electra* is again by comparison with the interplay of illusion and reality which we find in the *Oedipus*. An independent, exclusively psychological explanation, however, is untenable: that would be going too far. Such an interpretation has indeed been attempted by Kaibel, who explains what he finds strange in the entrance of Orestes as follows: 'Orestes is conscious of the unreal and unnatural, the precarious and dangerous nature of his rôle,' so that his language becomes 'constrained, stiff, formal and affected'; 'in order to conceal his true character he exaggerates almost to the point of παρατραγῳδεῖν'. 'In no other tragedy does a stranger introduce himself with as much formality as Orestes does here.' But suffering beneath a falsehood, stilted formulas intended to overcome inner insecurity, a mind divided between its true nature and the rôle that it is playing, all this hardly suits the figure of Orestes at this point, and this interpretation replaces clear-cut contrasts with the flicker of psychic—not even psychological—nuances.

279

Tycho von Wilamowitz, 203 f., says that the entrance in this scene is the result of practical requirements, 'from the audience's point of view', 'in order to bring about Electra's participation in the conversation'. But no poetic form can ever be explained by such considerations.

23. The 'spectator', seeing the urn of ashes, is certainly not intended to 'forget' that Orestes is standing alive in front of Electra, any more than previously during the speech of the *paedagogus* the spectator is intended to 'forget' that Orestes is really alive and well; for the later situation, considered solely as a situation, is no more than an intensification of the former.

24. Kaibel (242) interprets the scene differently: he believes that Orestes recognized Electra at the beginning, as soon as he saw her. This would turn the passionate outburst at 1177, which he has been holding back with such difficulty, into an exclamation of amazement: 'Die Frage muss in möglichster Unbefangenheit gesprochen werden, mehr Verwunderung als Mitleid verratend' ['The question must be spoken as naturally as possible, betraying amazement rather than sympathy.'] That this interpretation is incompatible with the force of the secretive, restrained pathos of this scene is absolutely clear. Kaibel has fallen victim to his own method of

psychological interpretation. But if Orestes has not succeeded in recognizing his sister by lines 1124–5 ('she asks as if she were one of his friends, perhaps, or of his blood'), then line 1177 cannot be explained from the outward, psychological situation either, but only from the inner situation, as a transparent insight into the poet's ironic game. Furthermore, Orestes must first break through to the real Electra; he is still a long way from her, but his words at 1124–5 are, as it were, indications of a nearness which is still concealed from him. We may compare this technique with the transparent insights which occur in the *Oedipus Tyrannus*, which are similar (even if in that play they are not concerned with the mind but with the *daimon* and fate).

Tycho von Wilamowitz, 203 f., argues correctly against Kaibel, at least in destroying his arguments. Cf. also W. Schadewaldt, *Monolog und Selbstgespräch*, 1926, 60.

25. In Aeschylus' *Choeph.* 219 ff. it is Orestes who reveals his own identity. He is the only active partner in the *anagnōrismos*. Electra is hesitant, still vacillating. For Electra to break through the deception of another and her own blindness to recognize her brother is an innovation of Sophocles, the point to which his whole play leads. This is so essential for his *Electra* that it is only at this break-through that the special identity which Sophocles gives to his heroine is brought to perfection, and her fate brought to its culmination. This clearly implies that Sophocles' *Electra* was written before that of Euripides. For in Euripides Electra likewise recognizes Orestes by herself, not however by breaking through to him, but by external means: she is put on to the right track by a third person, while Orestes stands by in a quite unbelievably passive manner. Euripides has missed the actual point of the innovation: the tension between the innermost being of two persons, a tension which is the reverse of that in Aeschylus. The act of recognition is not essential to the character of Electra in Euripides, but none the less it is Electra who does the recognizing. And, as in Sophocles, it is she who speaks the first half of the lines, while Orestes simply echoes her. Clearly after Sophocles it was unthinkable to present the scene in any other way.

It looked as if the controversy about the two *Electras* had died down, but the priority of Euripides' version has recently been championed again by Pohlenz, *Erläuterungen*, 93 [= 2nd ed., 131–3.]

26. On the secondary importance of the recognition token Tycho von Wilamowitz, 210, writes: 'it is only at line 1217 that Electra is at last led to the truth; then come three ἀντιλαβαί, and she has recognized him before he can speak. This is splendid, and the use of any object as a token of identity becomes superfluous; Electra is certain in herself, and as a result of the whole scene. The ring which Orestes then displays is of purely secondary

importance; to some degree it does no more than fulfil a formal require-
ment.'

27. Cf., for example, Kaibel on 1344: 'The subject of τελουμένων is omitted with the same sensitivity with which the fearful deed is always spoken
of in Sophocles', etc.

28. Kaibel, however (in his note on line 1464), argues that this is not so:
'This clumsy machinery was probably no great delight to the Athenian
audience, who were quite capable of accepting dramatic illusion; and to
understand the action it was not necessary for them to see anything that
they could not see just as easily through the opened door as on a wooden
trestle.' But modern taste is not a reliable indication of ancient taste, and
when this stage apparatus is brought into action in the *Ajax* (344) the verb
used for 'opening the tent' is identical with that used here for 'opening the
doors' (1458). The use of no more than the space inside the doorway of the
palace, which Kaibel envisages, would allow too little room for the
hesitations, revelations and self-deception of Aegisthus in his prolonged
mime. Strangely enough, Kaibel takes line 1464 to mean that Electra had
been going meanwhile to open the door. But τἀπ' ἐμοῦ can only be
understood if she is claiming to have played her part in obeying what
Aegisthus had commanded all the Mycenaeans to do. In 1459 ἄνδρα τόνδε
νεκρόν should be supplied as the object of ὁρᾶν. In 1458, σιγᾶν ἄνωγα is a
gesture of announcement to the assembled people.

On the *ekklyklema* see also Tycho von Wilamowitz, 225 f.

29. Pohlenz 334, 338 and 343 [cf. 2nd ed. 316, 320, 324], believes that
Sophocles' *Electra* was made possible only by Euripides' *Seelendrama*, and
that it owes its 'inner form' to the influence of the younger poet. But we
should not overlook the fact that the word *Seele* is highly ambiguous: in
the case of Sophocles it means lively movement, *élan*, tone, the voice of the
heart, whereas in the case of Euripides it is the battlefield of the passions
and reason, λογισμοί and πάθη. Sophocles' *Electra* is not a 'drama of the
soul' like the *Medea*, for it lacks the psychology of Euripides; and the *Medea*
is not a 'drama of the soul' like the *Electra*, for it lacks the sustaining tone of
Sophocles.

NOTES to CHAPTER VI (PHILOCTETES)

1. This is now almost universally accepted. [Not nowadays: see Introduction, p. xxii. The extensive recent literature about this play is listed by J.–U.
Schmidt, *Sophokles Philoktet: eine Strukturanalyse*, 1973, 254 ff.—H. Ll.-J.]
2. In Euripides both the basis and the significance of the intrigue had been

different: 'That is what man is like, ambition never lets him rest'—οὐδὲν γάρ οὕτω γαῦρον ὡς ἀνὴρ ἔφυ, said Odysseus meditatively in Euripides' *Philoctetes*. That is characteristic of the period and manner of the *Medea*.

3. By translating this line 'denn der Dienst verlangt Gehorsam' ('for service demands obedience'), Wilamowitz introduces here and elsewhere something of a Prussian attitude which is alien to the text. 'The opening of the play shows us the general with the lieutenant who has been allotted to him', and so on. But ὑπηρέτης in this line refers to service for a particular purpose; it does not mean 'service' as a permanent moral relationship.

4. In Wilamowitz's translation this takes on a different tone:

'Entsetzlich, sprich nicht weiter. Erst noch muss ich
Gewissheit haben. Ist dein Vater tot?'

['Horrible, say no more. First I must be certain. Is your father dead?'] This tells us nothing of the inner situation. It is 'tragedy' but it is not Sophocles. For Philoctetes is not asking because he is in doubt and would like to be certain, but because he is so shattered that he cannot pass this over as quickly as Neoptolemus is eager to. That is also why the great name must be retained—'son of Peleus' is what the text says, not 'your father'. The fact that Germans do not normally use the patronymic is irrelevant.

5. Grammatically ἦλθόν με νηΐ . . . (343) is the direct continuation of ἐπεὶ γὰρ ἔσχε . . . (331) With this sentence the false note on which the narrative began is picked up again. The dialogue in between has an altogether different tone; it is quite distinct. Thus there are two superimposed levels of tone. This too is something unknown in the earlier plays.

6. Every time that Sophocles introduces imitative play-acting in the *Philoctetes*, as for example the play here with the traditional gnomic formula at the end of a speech, Wilamowitz falls into an attitude of amazement and reproach (iv, 19): 'The end of his speech, 385 ff., with its attack on the leaders, who are made responsible for all the failures of the people, may seem odd. It is really out of place, but not only do poets like to end with a generalizing *gnome*, they also like to point a moral which goes beyond the context of the play.' He is interpreting late Sophocles as if it were Schiller. Since the meaning of the *gnome* and the purpose which it serves in the play do not harmonize, he sees it as a fault, without considering the possibility that the dramatist himself might have been attracted by this very dissonance.

7. That is, 'you are my witness then as now'. Elsewhere the precedent is usually introduced by εἴ ποτε καί . . . For examples see E. Norden, *Agnostos Theos*, 1913, and W. Ax, *Hermes*, lxvii, 1932, 415.

8. Wilamowitz can only express astonishment at this game: 'The prayer to the Asiatic mother of the gods, with which the chorus (391) supports the

lies of Pyrrhus [= Neoptolemus] which it is now hearing for the first time, is deeply offensive to us. The chorus joins in the deception too skilfully and too emphatically. Sophocles wished to enliven the long scene with some lyric, and therefore the utterance of the chorus seems unnaturally emphatic to us. This justifies the general effect, but nothing justifies the content of the strophe.' Similarly Tycho von Wilamowitz, 279: 'We may suspect even as early as this that the poet was hardly reckoning with an audience which kept the actual situation fully in mind.'

9. The song of the chorus in the rôle of adviser (507 ff.): 'If you hate the Atridae (in your place) I would set their ill treatment of him to his gain and would carry him to his home and so escape the nemesis of the gods,' is the continuation of the deception in 453 ff.: 'From now on I shall take precautions. I shall look at Troy and the Atridae both from very far off . . . where the worse man has more power than the better . . .'. If Sophocles had intended the actual situation to be forgotten, he could easily have made the chorus sing of departure, sorrows, the journey home, or any other subject, but in fact he again brings forward the enmity of the Atridae, in other words, something that the chorus knows very well to be a falsehood. Thus the opening words of the chorus: 'Have pity on him, prince . . .' are not a true outburst of pain either, but part of the game of illusion. When Tycho von Wilamowitz says (281): 'An unsophisticated listener will take Neoptolemus' sincere words of farewell, the selfless plea from the chorus and their commander's hesitating consent as seriously as he takes Philoctetes' pleas', then he has underestimated not only the pleasure that Sophocles takes in the unpleasant development of the deceit, but also the way in which the dramatist plays with the contrasts between truth and falsehood, between the pretence and the reality of suffering, between genuine and dissembling hearts. Moreover, the two strophes of the chorus have the same attitude: 'and so escape the nemesis of the gods' is the same misuse of religious matters as in the corresponding strophe at 391. One interlocks with the other.

In this instance we do not get very far by asking what the chorus should, could or might have said in order to satisfy its 'intention' or 'the action'; the question is rather what it *does* express. The fact that other matters need to be expressed in the choruses between the acts is not incompatible with this.

10. Cf. 1243 ff.

11. In a metaphorical sense as well; cf. *Oed. Col.* 663.

12. There are many different interpretations of the significance and purpose of the merchant scene, but all of them are apparently limited to a consideration of its practical features: 'The information that the merchant brings is primarily calculated to make Pyrrhus [= Neoptolemus] leave quickly; Odysseus was tired of waiting' etc. (Wilamowitz). Likewise

Tycho von Wilamowitz (283): 'For the moment, the effect of the merchant scene is that Philoctetes' joy at leaving is worked up to a pitch of extreme impatience; otherwise the action remains precisely at the point which it had reached before the arrival of the merchant', etc. Weinstock, *Sophocles*, 75, rightly interprets it as a preparation for what is to come in 769 ff.

13. The anthologists have preserved fragments of the *Philoctetes* of Aeschylus which contain outbursts of pain which demonstrate the same difference: fr. 255 Nauck² [= fr. 399 Mette]:

'Ω θάνατε παιάν, μή μ' ἀτιμάσῃς μολεῖν·
μόνος γὰρ εἶ σὺ τῶν ἀνηκέστων κακῶν
ἰατρός, ἄλγος δ' οὐδὲν ἅπτεται νεκροῦ.

Here the lament takes the form of a monologue; even though the chorus is present and listening, one has no sense of any tension between outburst and restraint, between inner feelings and outward appearance, speaker and listener, mind and situation.

14. Thus Jebb, Radermacher, and Wilamowitz (translation, 25, note). But how is a member of the audience, who has been listening to Neoptolemus, that is to say, to what he hears, supposed to notice that he is on the wrong track?

15. Radermacher on 974: 'The silence of Neoptolemus . . . is more meaningful than any speech.'

16. There is nothing of all this in Wilamowitz; he would take the scene to mean: 'His (Odysseus') brutal authority has power over Pyrrhus [= Neoptolemus] again.' Therefore he sees in Odysseus only 'an unscrupulous attitude', 'examples of shameful cowardice': 'At this point we might well believe that his father is the arch-trickster Sisyphus.'

17. The closest correspondence between the scenes is between *Phil.* 954 ff. ἀλλ' αὐανοῦμαι . . . and *El.* 819 ff. αὐανῶ βίον . . . Cf. above pp. 154 f.

18. Neoptolemus may be compared with Antigone at the corresponding passage in the *Oed. Col.*, 1192; on the latter see Wilamowitz in Tycho von Wilamowitz, 358.

19. Since the dramatist is concerned with 'free will' (ἑκών), the same concept is required in the god's pronouncement, 1332. On the earlier development of the problem, see W. Jaeger, 'Solons Eunomie', *Sitzungsberichte der Berliner Akademie*, 1926, 69–85. [= *Scripta Minora*, i, 1960, 315 ff.]

20. The end of the *Philoctetes* is called an 'inartistic, violent scene' by Wilamowitz, iv, 277.

21. Wilamowitz translates: ' . . . deine Fahrt zu anderm Ziel zu lenken'

('. . . to guide your journey to another destination'). But this does not bring out the implication that Philoctetes' path is the wrong path, the one the god prevents him from taking. Wilamowitz passes over the significance of this *deus ex machina* as rapidly as he would like the play to pass over it: 'Then Heracles appears; he sets everything in order with a few dignified words; the end comes quickly. With a conclusion of this sort, it is wise to speed up the tempo of the action as much as possible.'

NOTES to CHAPTER VII (OEDIPUS AT COLONUS)

1. Thomas Mann of Goethe.
2. Wilamowitz in Tycho von Wilamowitz, 332 and 352. For arguments against this see: Pohlenz, 365 [= 2nd ed. 343], and F. Altheim, *Neue Jahrbücher für Wissenschaft und Jugendbildung*, i, 1925, 184 ff.
3. One should not confuse these with the numerous scenes, especially at the beginning of a play, in which suppliants stand round an altar, as in the *Oedipus Tyrannus* or the *Heracles*. In such scenes it is not a matter of reception, of strangers and homeland, but of rescue from some kind of distress. All too often comparisons are made between features that are purely external, and the conclusion drawn that one was borrowed from the other.
4. On the political tendencies of Euripides' *Heraclidae* and *Suppliant Women*, see Pohlenz, 376 and 381 ff. [= 2nd ed. 353 ff. and 360 ff.], with the notes. [See also G. Zuntz, *The political plays of Euripides*, 1955.]
5. It is possible that the *Eleusinians* also served as a model in so far as it glorified Eleusis, the deme of Aeschylus, just as the *Oedipus at Colonus* glorifies the deme of Sophocles. But this remains no more than a possibility.

In general the *Oedipus at Colonus* is regarded as inspired by the *Phoenissae* of Euripides, but they are similar only in subject-matter; see Wilamowitz in Tycho von Wilamowitz, 335.
6. Tycho von Wilamowitz, 313 and 335, put forward in his notes the idea that the literary model for the central part of the *Oedipus at Colonus* was Euripides' *Philoctetes*. His father took over this idea and developed it independently, but without any greater success. It is true that in both plays someone is fetched; but fetched for what, for what purpose?—the sense is quite different in the two cases. Again, in Sophocles there are not two parties fighting for Oedipus, nor does Oedipus make any *decision*; they only turn into parties if they are abstracted from the events on the stage. Rather, the motif of fetching home is repeated and intensified: first by

286

cunning and force, then by honesty and honourable *peithō*, first by his deceitful brother-in-law, then by his wretched son. . . Creon does not enter first, as Odysseus does in Euripides, nor does he wonder how Oedipus is to be fetched, and so forth. The essentials have been left out of consideration; this comparison shows how comparisons should not be used.

7. Cf. above 39 f.

8. For a generally cautious discussion see Walter Nestle, *Die Struktur des Eingangs in der attischen Tragödie, Tübinger Beiträge*, x, 1930. On the opening of the *Oedipus at Colonus*, ibid., 67, 81 and 121. But the categories postulated by Nestle do not lead far in this case; 'extreme realism' hardly expresses the essential nature of this *parodos*.

9. Cf. above 186 ff. Note the finale in this play also.

10. Indeed, here too, Wilamowitz, historian that he is, has reconstructed the course of events correctly enough (in Tycho von Wilamowitz, 343 f.): 'In order to hear of the wanderers, Theseus must have set out before he learnt the name of Oedipus. . . Dramatically it was necessary to avoid another scene of questioning, and to avoid Oedipus' introducing himself again: therefore Theseus had to know him already; only if he knew him would his hasty journey from Athens be credible. This explains the preparatory lines in both scenes. One may criticize the way it is done: it is clear that the lines correspond with each other; it is also clear that Sophocles is to blame for it.' This hardly touches the actual drama.

11. In order to show that this scene, together with the whole central portion, is unconnected with the framework of the play, Wilamowitz (in Tycho von Wilamowitz, 334) bases his argument on line 385: 'Is it then possible that he can say in 385: "Can you expect that the gods take me into account at all ὥστε σωθῆναί ποτε?" This σωτηρία can only refer to his return to Thebes.' Similarly Pohlenz, *Erläuterungen*, note to p. 364 [= 2nd ed., note to p. 342]. To which the answer is: Certainty and doubt *have to* alternate, and not only here; without this alternation there would be no drama. In the same way, Oedipus' feeling that he belongs to Colonus alternates with the considerations that bind him to Thebes. Without this alternation there would be no renunciation, no curse upon Thebes, in other words, again, no drama. When faced with alternations such as these, Wilamowitz continually finds different presuppositions and different types of writing; but that is a way of explaining a drama which demands that it should not be a drama. . . Colonus is the symbolic *negation* of Thebes; there could be no 'Thebes' without 'Colonus'. . . As it happens, this play is one of the most thoroughly unified of all.

12. Cf. in particular *Phil.* 827; see above 181 ff.

13. Wilamowitz (in Tycho von Wilamowitz, 349 f.) is of the opinion that Sophocles has to use this chorus to purify Oedipus of moral guilt before he can be heroized. But there is nothing about a purification anywhere else in the play.

14. According to Theseus' words in line 632, an ancient guest-friendship exists between him and the family of Oedipus. Wilamowitz (in Tycho von Wilamowitz, 350 f.) rightly remarks that this does not tally with these earlier lines. But the meaning is obvious. First, ancient rights of friendship and kinship such as these are appropriate to the genre of the suppliant play (cf. Aesch. *Suppl.* 272, Eur. *Heracl.* 205 ff.); secondly, Sophocles requires the ancient friendship between Thebes and Athens so that the prophecy of their future quarrel will not hang in a vacuum.

15. A line from an oracle to that effect was unearthed by the learned Istros at a later date, according to the scholion on line 57 [V. de Marco, *Scholia in Sophoclis Oed. Col.*, 1952, p.9].—On the historical aspect see Wilamowitz in Tycho von Wilamowitz, 324. Wilamowitz (ibid., 322 f.) offers, *inter alia*, strangely materialistic notions about the 'secret'.

16. *Oed. Col.* Chorus: ἰὼ γᾶς πρόμοι = *Suppl.* ἰὼ πόλεως ἄγοι πρόμοι . . .; *Oed. Col.* Theseus: τί τοὔργον . . . = *Suppl.* Danaus: οὗτος, τί ποιεῖς . . . etc. In each case this is preceded by a violent, almost successful attempt to remove the suppliant from asylum. Theseus and Danaus are 'helpers' in the ancient sense of βοηθεῖν, 'those who hasten to the cry'; cf. Latte, *Hermes*, xxxvi, 1931, 39 [= *Kleine Schriften*, 1968, 259].

17. It is true that here for once the gods are mentioned: 'So it pleased the gods' (964); but how weak this is in comparison with the vehemence with which the responsibility of the gods was invoked in the earlier plays! Here it only serves to emphasize that it was 'not I, as a conscious and voluntary agent'.

18. There is no evidence for any political situation in which this could have been intended as a compliment to Thebes; such a situation would have to be postulated for the sake of this speech. Wilamowitz has ventured to do so (in Tycho von Wilamowitz, 368 f.): 'We must infer from the evidence of Sophocles that the party of Ismenias was opposed to the subordination of Thebes to the Spartans as early as the last few years of the war, and that there were some people in Athens who put their hope in this party.' His speculation would mean that Athens made use of the tragedy of an 89-year-old to speak for a minority in an enemy state during wartime. And Wilamowitz saw nothing wrong with that. Contrast Aristophanes' *Frogs* 1496 ff.!

Pohlenz does not go as far as Wilamowitz (*Erläuterungen*, note to p. 368) [= 2nd. ed., note to p. 347], but he perceives an 'extra-literary intention to whitewash Thebes', and to support his view he regards whole passages as added for the posthumous performance of 404. To my mind this is too arbitrary.

If only Theseus were not the person he is shown to be elsewhere in the play, then all of this might fit. But as it is . . . !

19. Lines such as 925, 'No matter how immaculate my claims', clearly belong to the sphere of law, not politics. At the corresponding point in Euripides' *Heraclidae* there is a discussion about the right to kill prisoners of war (961 ff.). The question was a matter of current concern.

20. Similarly at lines 1148 ff. Sophocles dispenses with the conventional messenger's narrative, which should have come next if he had followed the example of Euripides' *Heraclidae* (799 ff.) and *Suppliant Women* (650 ff.) (cf. Radermacher's commentary on the *Oed. Col.*). The way in which Sophocles does this shows to what extent he, while realizing his dependence on the traditional form, is nevertheless able to rise above it. I know of nothing comparable in other tragedies.

21. On the 'technique' see Wilamowitz in Tycho von Wilamowitz, 356 f.; but he does not progress beyond a distinction between the 'natural' and the 'effective' (in the sense of the 'unnatural').

22. Creon had pleaded his right to 'retaliation' in the aftermath of Oedipus' passion, on the grounds that the *thymos* (the seat of all the emotions) does not grow old except in death (954).

23. Of Antigone Wilamowitz remarks (Tycho von Wilamowitz, 358): 'But could and should Antigone speak in this way?—that daughter, the girl from whom her father did not even expect an adequate account of her rescue, speaking to *this* father?' On the *Philoctetes* see above 189.

24. Pohlenz holds a somewhat different view (365 [= 2nd. ed., 343 f.]): 'The *Electra* was an attempt to understand and justify the matricide commanded by the gods; the *Oedipus at Colonus* is an attempt to do the same for the paternal curse.' 'He does not approve of the curse of Oedipus . . . but that does not exonerate his sons.' His view that Polynices 'deserved his punishment' suggests that Sophocles intended to make an example of him. But then the Polynices scene would certainly no longer be relevant.

25. Neither does Oedipus make any discovery at 1354, for his son has himself repented and acknowledged his offence (1265); on the contrary, here too his fate is being decided; once something has been left undone, it is not possible to make amends for it.

26. Achilles in the *Phrygians*: see Nauck² p. 50.

27. Wilamowitz (359) is surprised that there is no longer any trace here of the shattering emotion of the first speech; he says that Sophocles has 'separated the different emotions . . .; he is a long way from having achieved a psychological balance in his composition.' The views of

Pohlenz are very similar (*Erläuterungen*, 100 [= 2nd ed., 139]): he regards Polynices as 'a superficial but sympathetic character'.

28. This also explains, for example, the Sophoclean modification of the saga observed by Jebb, Introduction, 24: that the quarrel between the sons is no longer the result of the father's curse, and other such changes.

29. The end of this scene was completely misunderstood by Wilamowitz (in Tycho von Wilamowitz, 362): 'Certain death is before his eyes, but he rises to impressive greatness. . . The whole future lies spread so clearly before his eyes; but he will not be diverted from what he believes to be the duty of a general.' This fails to take into account line 1423, which speaks not of the duty of a general but of wounded honour, revenge and satisfaction. . . And it may be doubted whether false optimism is the true duty of a general (1430). Certainly he is by no means evil, as Creon is evil; he is even a hero, and yet . . .

30. Erwin Rohde, *Psyche*, ii, 1898, 244 [= Eng. trs., 1925, 456]: 'The poet is not one to gloss over the harsh realities of life with trite phrases of vapid consolation, and he has clearly perceived that the usual effect of unhappiness and misery upon men is not to illuminate but to enfeeble and vulgarize them.' This is a psychological interpretation of the scene, not a symbolic one. That it is false can be seen from the obvious lack of psychological development and motivation in any of the characters.

Wilamowitz gives up completely (in Tycho von Wilamowitz, 362): Sophocles and his audience, he says, would have the saga, and Aeschylus' *Seven*, in mind . . . 'But there is no excuse for the last speech . . . It is not easy to determine how far the poet's conscious intention is at work here . . . The tragedy was not composed in a single sweep, nor in a single mood . . .' To others the poet appears to justify the curse, e.g. Weinstock, *Sophocles*, 197; Pohlenz, 365 [= 2nd ed., 343–4]. Jebb, Introduction, 23, writes very aptly: 'Throughout the scene of Polyneices there is a malign sublimity in the anger of the aged Oedipus . . .' etc. (and he compares Oedipus with King Lear).

31. Jebb, Introduction, 24: 'The total impression made by the play as a work of art depends essentially on the manner in which the scene of sacred peace at Colonus is brought into relief against the dark fortunes of Polyneices and Eteocles.' This is correct from the point of view of aesthetics, but we must grasp its significance for the meaning as well.

32. Anyone who is not satisfied with this account can search the text for the cue for the thunder. Incidentally, as for my views on this point, I thunder with Wilamowitz (in Tycho von Wilamowitz, 333), as against Pohlenz, *Erläuterungen*, 100 [= 2nd ed. 140]; in other words, I thunder right at the beginning, before line 1447. A heavy colon should be placed before the word ἔκτυπε in line 1456. The usual formula for the fulfilment of

a divine command, 'whether it be now or later', appears here in reverse, that is, the fulfilment comes immediately, and is not postponed: 'Your thunder, O Zeus, is witness to that!' This interpretation means that from the beginning the whole strophe leads up to the last line. Pohlenz, it is true, believes that the chorus is 'making comparatively calm remarks' at the beginning, but where else does a chorus do so in resolved dochmiacs?
33. Radermacher, Introduction, 6, suggests a secret family tradition, a family cult at Colonus. Wilamowitz (in Tycho von Wilamowitz, 323) argues against the explanation by analogy with the cult of Dirce on the grounds that this would imply the existence of a known grave.
34. It is again a lengthy, very emotional song, and even requires two singers in addition to the chorus. Its metre corresponds with its inner movement. Wilamowitz analysed this chorus, but none of the others, in *Griechische Verskunst*, 1921, 521.

NOTES to CHAPTER VIII (FRAGMENTS)

1. After Nauck [2nd ed., 1889] the fragments were re-edited by A. C. Pearson, Cambridge 1917. See also R. Pfeiffer, *Philologus*, lxxxviii, 1933, 1–15 [= *Ausgewählte Schriften*, 1970, 85–97]; Carl Ernst Fritsch, *Neue Fragmente des Aischylos und Sophokles*, Diss. Hamburg, 1936; A. Körte, *Archiv für Papyrusforschung*, xiv, 1941, 116–17; [D. L. Page, *Select Papyri III: Literary Papyri*, Loeb Classical Library, 1941, 12–53. The fragments preserved on papyrus (except for the *Ichneutae*) have now been edited with commentary by Richard Carden, *The Papyrus Fragments of Sophocles*, Berlin 1974.—H. Ll.-J.]
2. Wilamowitz, *Neue Jahrbücher für das klassische Altertum*, xxix, 1912, 449–76 [= *Kleine Schriften*, i, 1935, 347–83]. Ernst Siegmann, *Untersuchungen zu Sophokles Ichneutai*, Diss. Hamburg, 1941 = *Hamburger Arbeiten zur Altertumswissenschaft* iii, provides valuable new readings and suggestions. [For the text, Pearson, *op. cit.*, 224 ff. and Page, *op. cit.*, 26 ff.—H. Ll.-J.]

INDEX NOMINUM ET RERUM

INDEX LOCORUM